Hugh O'Shaughnessy writes regularly for the *Observer* and the *Financial Times* on Latin American affairs and is a regular contributor to the BBC.

He was one of a small group of journalists who managed to land on Grenada just before the United States invasion and one of the only two to witness the occupation of the island's capital, St George's.

GRENADA:
An Eyewitness Account
of the U.S. Invasion
and the Caribbean History
That Provoked It

Other books by Hugh O'Shaughnessy

OIL IN LATIN AMERICA
CHILE, TRAGEDIA AMERICANA

GRENADA:

An Eyewitness Account
of the U.S. Invasion
and the Caribbean History
That Provoked It

by

Hugh O'Shaughnessy

Dodd, Mead & Company, New York

First published in Great Britain by
Hamish Hamilton Ltd., 1984.

Copyright © 1984 by Hugh O'Shaughnessy
Published by Dodd, Mead & Company, Inc.
79 Madison Avenue, New York, N.Y. 10016
Manufactured in the United States of America

First Edition

Library of Congress Cataloging in Publication Data

O'Shaughnessy, Hugh.
    Grenada: an eyewitness account of the U.S. invasion
and the Caribbean history that provoked it.

    Originally published: Grenada: revolution, invasion,
and aftermath.   London: H. Hamilton and The Observer,
1984.
    Bibliography: p.
    Includes index.
    1. Grenada—History—American invasion, 1983.
2. Grenada—Politics and government—1974-
I. Title.
F2056.8.084   1985   972.98'45   84-21092
ISBN 0-396-08524-5

2251665

Contents

Exchange Rates

£1.00 = US$1.50
£1.00 = Eastern Caribbean $3.90

List of Illustrations

Illustrations appear after page 102.

To Georgie, Frances, Thomas, Matthew and Luke, with love.

Preface

My thanks go to Donald Trelford and my colleagues on the *Observer* who helped me to write this book and to Geoffrey Owen, editor of the *Financial Times*, who gave me time to write it.

Some of those who gave me assistance would not want to be named. The others include Ricardo Alarcón, Tanya Benedictus, Thompson Cadore, Boysie Charles, Tony Cozier, Reggie Dale, William Demas, Karen de Young, Séan Doggett, Marcelo Elissetche, Major Douglas Frey, Leslie Gardner, David Haslam, Darcus Howe, Harold Hoyte, Alister Hughes, David Jessup, John Kelly, Vaughan Lewis, Jenny Lo, Einstein Louison, Randolph Mark, David Montgomery, Pearl Paterson, Jenny Pearce and all my colleagues at the Latin America Bureau, Leslie Pierre, Hon. George Price, Peter Pringle, Kendrick Radix, Randolph Rawlins, Gilberto Rizzo, Noll Scott, Lieutenant-Colonel Ray Smith USMC, Edwin Stiell, Jean Stubbs, David Thomas, Tillman Thomas and Hubert Williams. To all, named and unnamed, I give my thanks.

My special thanks go to my son Luke O'Shaughnessy who helped prepare the index, and to my editors.

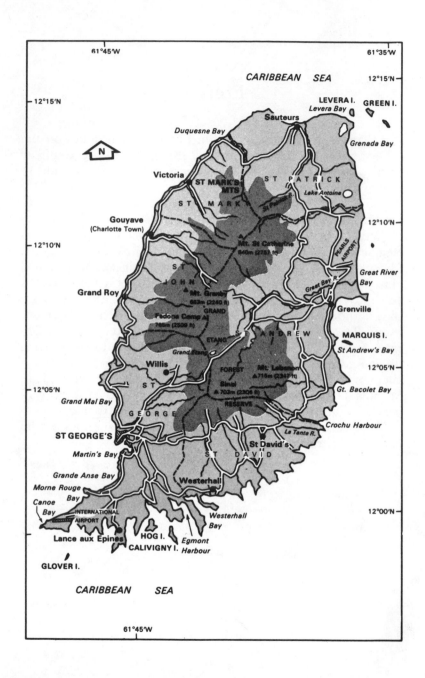

CHAPTER ONE

The Battle

'We got a lot more resistance than we expected.'
General John Vessey,
Chairman of the US Joint Chiefs of Staff

At 6.40 in the morning on Thursday 27 October 1983 a platoon of US Marines edged nervously past the main branch of Barclays Bank in St George's, the capital of Grenada, towards Fort Rupert. They need not have worried. No resistance awaited them there. Two days before, a US jet had blown a hole clean through the roof of the citadel, scattering the defenders and leaving one officer in the Grenadian People's Revolutionary Army dead near the gateway of the redoubt. Those who had been manning the two Soviet anti-aircraft guns, set on the battlements beside the eighteenth-century British cannon and mortar, fled leaving the place deserted. At the PRA medical centre a few yards away at the main entrance to the fort the doors blew in the wind.

Though few of them may have realised it, the marines' occupation of the fort was loaded with symbolism. What was now Fort Rupert had first been laid out in 1705 by the French and named Fort Royal. In 1763 Grenada became British and the stronghold was renamed Fort George after George III. The name was kept when, in 1974, Grenada ceased to be ruled from London and became one of the crop of independent ministates which were springing up in the Caribbean as Britain wound up its colonial empire. The most recent change of name had come in 1979 when left-wing revolutionaries led by Maurice

1

Bishop overthrew the corrupt and often brutal administration of Sir Eric Gairy, the man who brought Grenada to independence and who became the island's first Prime Minister. Bishop rechristened Fort George after his own father, Rupert, who lost his life in 1974 in a demonstration against Gairy.

Shortly after the marines nervously but peacefully took possession of Fort Royal/Fort George/Fort Rupert the Stars and Stripes was raised. The United States set its stamp on a fortress where two successive colonial régimes and a left-wing government had ruled. Republicans from Washington had followed French and British monarchs and a revolutionary to become masters of the island.

The proximate cause of the marines' presence on Grenada was also well symbolized by their capture of Fort Rupert. As they entered the fort they passed the spot where, eight days previously, troops loyal to a bitterly doctrinaire faction of the revolutionary government and under the orders of General of the Armed Forces Hudson Austin had fired into an enthusiastic crowd of several thousands of Grenadians demonstrating in favour of the popular and more easygoing leader of the revolution, Maurice Bishop. The crowd had just freed him from the house arrest into which his ideological rivals had consigned him and were impatient to hear him address them once again. That was not to be.

Volleys from automatic weapons and from three armoured cars dispersed the crowd, killing several score of them. Bishop was arrested once again and, within half an hour, shortly after 1 p.m. on 19 October, the revolutionary Prime Minister and his closest supporters were executed in cold blood within the walls of Fort Rupert. Revolutionary had killed revolutionary.

With that action the Grenadian revolution had aborted itself. The presence of the US Marines a week later was the demonstration that the administration of President Ronald Reagan was willing, even eager, to inter the evil smelling foetus left behind after the bloody affair of 19 October.

Acting in the name of the US President, the marines had swept out of power the doctrinaire group which had ruled Grenada in the week following Bishop's death. In doing so the

2

US troops demonstrated that the US administration was willing and able to use force for the first time in history to impose its will on that part of the former British Empire now known as the Commonwealth Caribbean.

The operation the marines and their army colleagues were engaged upon, though in a military sense piffling, was one of very great importance for the Caribbean and for the relations of the US with the rest of the world.

It had been nursed in secret at the State Department and the Pentagon in Washington where, for four and a half years, officials had been seeking ways of putting an end to the left-wing government of Grenada.

Bishop's desire for independence and for his countrymen to follow him in support of policies which were not favoured by the US government had enraged Washington. In the view of British officials that rage reached paranoiac proportions when Grenada started close co-operation with Cuba and the USSR. Grenada's action challenged the hegemony that Washington was expecting to extend throughout the Caribbean after the withdrawal of the British who had dominated it for two centuries.

Washington's hostility had, in its turn, strengthened the increasingly close links between Bishop, constantly preoccupied by the threat of a violent ouster, and the Cubans and Soviets. During the Reagan administration, when Washington took a more and more muscular attitude towards Moscow, the Soviet government welcomed the opportunity the Bishop Government gave it of creating embarrassments for the US similar to those being caused by the US for the USSR in countries such as Poland and Afghanistan. The Cubans, for their part, rejoiced that a revolutionary government had at last come to power in the Commonwealth Caribbean which was disposed to share with them a hostility to the US and join with them in adopting the Russian interpretation of Marx's ideals known as Marxism-Leninism.

Washington's opportunity had come after the events of 19 October when Bishop and his companions were murdered by a faction within the ruling New Jewel Movement who were fanatically committed to a Leninist canon.

The Reagan administration seized the chance of ending the left-wing reign in Grenada, demonstrating the military superiority of the US in the region and frightening groups in the Caribbean and Central America who were in the process of challenging US hegemony or who were considering it.

It was fortunate enough to be able to do this in collaboration with the governments of seven small states who were at the time ruled by parliamentary governments of conservative leanings.

From the point of view of domestic Grenadian politics and of the state of government in the Commonwealth Caribbean things could hardly have been more favourable to Washington's strategies. Tens of thousands of people in Grenada were welcoming the invasion and it was receiving support in many corners of the Caribbean.

On the larger world stage, however, it was to be condemned decisively at the United Nations, and by Mr Reagan's closest allies. By acting illegally and by doing a job that would sooner or later have been done by the Grenadian people themselves Ronald Reagan was weakening respect for international law and building up a store of resentment in the region against the US. The echoes of the Grenadian invasion were destined to reverberate not only round the Caribbean but round the globe.

From their position the marines could look out over the little city. St George's lay quietly in the warm early morning sun. Around the tiny landlocked harbour the buildings rose on rocky tiers covered in a profusion of vegetation like the set of some beautiful, extravagant Italian opera. The stores and warehouses of the island's merchant companies stood locked and silent along the Carenage or quay. Not a soul was to be seen in the tiny streets which ran up the hills from the water's edge past the towers of the Catholic cathedral, the Anglican church and the Presbyterian kirk, through the tin roofs of shops and offices, to the smarter houses on the higher ground.

In the harbour the vessels lay still – a collection of rowing boats, launches and small schooners, the four broad-bottomed fishing boats that the Cuban government had given Maurice

Bishop to help the island start a fishing industry, a shabby inter-island steamer, the *Cato*, registered for some good business reason at the Danish port of Nörrsundby, its dirty red and white ensign drooping at its mast.

Round the corner at the deep water quay a more modern, Greek ocean-going freighter, the *Kronaos*, lay immobile like the rest, halted in the midst of delivering the cornflakes and motor bikes, the paperback books and lampshades and other staples of modern living which allowed the 110,000 Grenadians to keep roughly within reach of the patterns of consumption of their Caribbean neighbours.

Less than a mile away, past Government House, the residence of Sir Paul Scoon, the Governor-General, stood Fort Frederick. Flying an indistinguishable flag Fort Frederick, flanked by the former Fort Matthew, now the mental hospital, and a former barracks, now Richmond Hill Prison, peered over St George's as it had done for two centuries.

Looking out of the calm sea the marines could see the aircraft carrier *Independence* and its escorts, some away on the horizon, some within a few hundred yards of the shore. Across the harbour mouth lay the ruins of Butler House, the former hotel which had been taken over as Bishop's Prime Ministerial office. On Tuesday afternoon and evening Butler House, named after Tubal Uriah 'Buzz' Butler, one of the founding fathers of the Caribbean labour movement, had been strafed and strafed again from the air. Twice the firemen with their modern East German fire engines had gone to try and put the flames out, only to be turned back by continuing attacks from the jets. The blaze was eventually to consume the building and burn itself out.

Within the walls of Fort Rupert the platoon, soon to be reinforced, took up defensive positions against an enemy which had melted away. Below them, in the General Hospital, doctors, surgeons and nurses were still busy trying to save the lives or mend the bodies of two lots of casualties. The first were the survivors of the massacre of 19 October, men, women and children who had been caught up in the demonstration

5

in favour of Maurice Bishop and who had been shot, trampled or who had fallen down rocks and over walls in their effort to get out of the line of fire of General Austin's troops.

The second batch, numbering, like the first, several score, had been General Austin's troops themselves, members of the 1,000 strong regular PRA or keen revolutionaries and ordinary Grenadians who opposed the invasion and who were willing to put the sketchy part-time training they had received in the militia to the test in the battle with the US troops.

The regular staff of the General Hospital had been augmented by volunteers, including one Cuban-American, Dr Raúl Jiménez, who had been teaching the aspiring US medical students at St George's University Medical School. Without x-rays, with only emergency power and with faltering supplies of blood and oxygen the doctors and nurses saw more than a few patients die on their hands. As the marines took up their positions a few yards above them in the fort, the hospital staff did their best for some unexpected charges. During Tuesday's raid the US aircraft had mistaken the former Fort Matthew for Fort Frederick and demolished the mental hospital. They killed at least thirty inmates and scattered scores of demented people throughout the town until some good people rounded them up and shepherded them down past the entrance to Fort Rupert and on to the General Hospital. It was not until a week after the raid that the work of digging the corpses out of what Grenadians had familiarly called the Crazy House was over.

Under the marines' gaze lay a terrified St George's, without electric light or power, with irregular supplies of water, with no telephone or telex connection with the outside world, a city in which some of the poorer people who had not been able to lay in stocks of food were beginning to go hungry. A few scattered skirmishes were to continue during that Thursday but the marines' entry to Fort Rupert put the seal on US control of Grenada.

The outcome of the battle for Grenada had never been in doubt. A week before the invasion, a US Navy task force of nine vessels had been steaming across the Atlantic bound for the Eastern Mediterranean with orders to relieve the US forces who were being increasingly enmeshed in the murderous and intricate politics of the Lebanon. The force was commanded by Rear-Admiral Joseph Metcalf III who flew his flag in the USS *Guam*. Commissioned in 1965, the *Guam* displaced 18,300 tons, had a complement of 609 men and could carry up to twenty helicopters, seven of which could be dispatched from its flight deck simultaneously. With her was a much bigger and more modern vessel, the USS *Saipan*. Commissioned in 1977, she displaced 39,300 tons and could carry more than 1,700 troops apart from the ship's company of 902 officers and men. For her amphibious assault duties she could carry up to twenty-six helicopters.

Off Grenada Admiral Metcalf's force was to rendezvous with six more vessels, the chief of which was the USS *Independence*, a veritable floating air base. Commissioned in 1959, the *Independence* displaced 79,300 tons and had capacity for up to seventy aircraft. The ship and her aircraft were serviced by 4,940 men.

The fleet had on board the 22nd Marine Amphibious Unit, more than 400 marines equipped with helicopters and assault ships capable of landing five M-60 tanks, thirteen amphibious armoured vehicles and jeeps mounting anti-aircraft missiles. The 22nd MAU, commanded by Lieutenant-Colonel Ray Smith of Shidler, Oklahoma, was trained and equipped to be capable of securing a bridgehead against all but the most overwhelmingly superior opposition. The Unit's task in Grenada was to capture the civil airport at Pearls on the eastern coast of the island and then secure St George's, the capital, sited near the southwestern tip. To back up the aerial bombardment that the fleet could mount, C-130 Hercules were poised at Grantley Adams International airport in Barbados less than an hour's flying time away. They were equipped with rapid-fire Gatling machine guns – macabrely named Puff the Magic Dragon – which were able to pour fire onto an area the size of a football field from a height of several thousand feet with a noise which, from a distance, resembled nothing so much as the rumblings of some giant's intestines.

The capture of the Cuban-built, but still uncompleted, airfield at Point Salines at the southeastern extremity of Grenada was entrusted to 500 airbourne Rangers who would be reinforced after the assault by men of the 82nd Airborne Division brought in directly from Fort Bragg, North Carolina, by A-141 Galaxies and C-130 Hercules transports.

Logistical support was provided by Galaxies and Hercules of Military Airlift Command which installed itself at the airport in Barbados and which rapidly transformed the old, disused passenger terminal there into an operations centre. Within two or three days Admiral Metcalf was estimated to have had 15,000 men under his command.

War material was stockpiled in Barbados – not just men and their personal weapons, ammunition and warplanes but small artillery pieces, jeep-mounted missiles, tanks and armoured personnel carriers (amtracks) with advanced communications equipment, bulldozers, fork-lift trucks and excavators, prefabricated offices, photocopiers and thousands of other pieces of equipment which rapidly gave the impression that the US forces had been in Barbados for months. When Pearls and Point Salines were taken, all this material poured into Grenada. At the height of the build-up, lines of troops half a mile long could be seen trampling beside the runway at Point Salines while the low hills at the eastern end of the airport looked like so many anthills covered with soldiers.

The US task force was augmented by a politically important, but militarily irrelevant, group of soldiers and policemen from six other countries. Antigua and Barbuda, St Lucia, Dominica and St Vincent (members with Grenada, St Kitts-Nevis and Montserrat of the Organization of Eastern Caribbean States) provided the policemen. Some of these men had been trained for nothing more arduous than traffic duty and were photographed in Barbados in their white jackets and navy blue trousers with a smart red stripe.

Others, such as the police from Dominica, which had suffered threats of intervention and invasion from buccaneering mercenary groups, had been trained in the use of automatic weapons, wore battledress and were clearly to all intents and purposes soldiers. They were, however, the merest token force fielded by four mini-states whose combined population came to scarcely more than 400,000 people and whose total area was less than 2,800 square kilometres.

More expert were the men of the Jamaica Defence Force and the Barbados Defence Force, the successors of regiments raised locally during British rule which had fought spasmodically in two world wars and whose officers continued to be trained at the Royal Military Academy, Sandhurst.

The dispatch of a detachment of police from the newly independent St Kitts-Nevis was marked by chaos. Dr Simmonds, the Prime Minister, owed his position to a deal between his People's Action Movement and the Nevis Reformation Party based in the smaller of the two islands. The Nevisians formed a coalition with Simmonds to oust the state's largest party, the St Kitts Labour Party.

Simmonds had abolished a full-time Defence force, maintaining only a police force. Five Kittitian policemen were sent by Simmonds to Barbados but, they claim, were not told of their ultimate destination. On arrival, and when they learnt of the real reason for their dispatch, two of them refused to go to Grenada and the Kittitian participation in the invasion was delayed.

None of the five policemen was a Nevisian, which led to jokes being made in Basseterre about how a government controlled by Nevisians made sure that no Nevisian would be expected to put his life in danger on the far shores of Grenada.

None of the Caribbean troops and policemen, a total of some 300, took part in any fighting. Their role, the US authorities determined, should be that of guarding Grenadian prisoners and the Cuban internees and accompanying US troops on patrols of St George's once all resistance had been crushed. In neither of these roles did they suffer any casualties, a fact that the six governments must have welcomed with relief.

Against such a heterogenous force from the world's most powerful nation and from some of the smallest independent countries on earth was set the People's Revolutionary Army, the Grenadian militia and the Cubans.

The PRA consisted of about 1,000 men whose officers had, a week before the invasion, taken over the government of the country through a sixteen-man Revolutionary Military Council. The RMC was headed by General of the Armed Forces Austin, a former prison warder, who had helped Maurice Bishop to seize power from the Government of Sir Eric Gairy in March 1979 but whose men, for reasons we will seek to analyse later, had been responsible for the murder of Bishop on 19 October.

Since its formation in 1979, after Bishop's *coup d'état* against Gairy, the PRA had been established as the mailed fist of the Grenadian revolution. Training and overseeing were provided principally by Cuba, which maintained a military mission of about forty instructors permanently on Grenada. Other military input was provided by smaller groups of East German, North Korean, Libyan and Soviet personnel but the principal model for the PRA was unequivocally the Fuerzas Armadas Rebeldes (FAR) – the Cuban armed forces. Equipment was provided mainly by the Soviet Union and Eastern European states and consisted of AK-47 and AK-47 Special automatic rifles, 80 mm. light anti-aircraft weapons, rocket launchers and some half a dozen 8-wheel armoured personnel carriers of Soviet manufacture, steel helmets and IKA military trucks of East German manufacture and minor pieces of equipment from Cuba itself.

In store too were the relics of the British military presence such as a number of SMLE bolt-action .303 rifles of the sort which the British used in the Second World War.

More important perhaps than the weapons in the hands of the PRA were their political attitudes and their morale. The former can best be illustrated from the pages of an exercise book which belonged to some anonymous PRA soldier and which was left lying in Fort Rupert after the US rocket attack. Amid notes on his weapons and observations about tactics, ambushes and other minor manoeuvres, the soldier had re-

10

corded in an unsteady hand the following, learnt, it will be observed, within a year of the establishment of the PRA.

Camp Fedon   Topic 25   Feb 17th 80
The need for Political concousness
In our New Revolutionary Army or high level of Political and revolutionary Awareness is a defnite Measure of the Readiness of the soldier to defend the homeland and the Rev the soldiers Who is concous of the Arms of the Revolution who is july aware that his is upholding the Power of the Working People that he and others defending a cause whose victory means a better way of high for this Justice generation is the soldier who will give his life to the homeland, in the firm believe that he as made the most contribution of the Revo imperilist foreign donation of our enemy and explatation of Rasoway, e.g. cocoa, nutmeg, banana
Revolutionary Army Remember that you are champions of the intreast of the Workers and Peasesentry a defender of the Peoples some of the great Revolution Worker and Pleassent it is your duty to set a fine example of the Revolutioni concouness you should be the first to engage the enemy and the last to rest similarly you should set an example of the Revolutionary and this is to courage And Discipline it is you sacred duty to maintain a spirit of comradeship cohesion and solidary in the Ranks of the PRA
We must see our selves Army as soldiers
Ready to die in the defence of the homeland and of socialism

Four years of political and military training of the sort exemplified in the exercise book had turned out a force which considered itself an elite and which was highly motivated. It had not been without its problems in the preceding weeks however. The confinement of Bishop to his house by his political enemies in mid-October had caused nationwide protests and demonstrations. The killing of Bishop in cold blood on 19 October and the subsequent curfews had sent great shock waves through the population and there were many occasions between the Wednesday when Bishop died and the Tuesday

11

when the US forces invaded when ordinary Grenadians took the opportunity to express their repugnance towards the actions of the PRA even to the extent of spitting on soldiers publicly in the street.

Around the professional, full-time, Cuban-trained PRA the Bishop government had been building a militia much on the lines of the Cuban model. This was raised as a part-time force recruited from among the staunchest supporters of the revolution and government workers and, pulling in more or less voluntarily, those who were keen, or felt obliged for one reason or the other, to demonstrate their loyalty to the government. As Iván Martínez, the Cuban Ambassador to Barbados explained at a press conference outside Bridgetown on 29 October, Bishop had always been fearful of an invasion and had wanted to do all he could to arm the people. The militia was the first step towards arming the people to resist an assault from the United States.

A report on the state of mobilization prepared for the government on 28 March 1983 listed the members of the militia enrolled at the various principal government departments, e.g. fifteen at Butler House, the Prime Minister's office, nine at the Government Printery, thirty-six at the Ministry of Education, ten at the Customs Office, nine at the Ministry of Foreign Affairs.

Beside each name was an indication of the member's interest, e.g. combat, combat/security, combat/information, medic/childcare, security, driving. Of the twenty-four names listed as mobilized at the government-controlled Radio Free Grenada, twenty-one were listed as 'infantry (combative)' and the remaining three were designated 'medic'. Of the twenty-one listed as ready for combat duty, nine appear to have been women.

A report on the mobilisation of the militia, carried out on 30 March 1983 and prepared for the government, showed that, in the seven principal towns and villages on the west coast of Grenada, 134 comrades turned out. At Grand Roy it was reported, 'Two (2) hours discussion on the role of the Militia in this period and the importance of high levels of discipline –

20 comrades present'. At Victoria, a few miles to the north, the report read, 'Cultural activity. Recording of calypso about the Militia on the tape – 30 comrades present', at Dequesne, 'No weapon in Militia but 10 comrades turned out for the discussion on Mobilisation for the route March'.

Reviewing the experience in the Parish of St David's on 30 March the report commented that in the villages of Bellevue and Petitespiance '4 persons do not believe the threat [of a US invasion] 3 persons said that prayers can stop Reagan from coming.' In the Ruquin area the report commented, '1 person said that prayers is a necessity now.' Six months before the US invasion it was clear that the doctrine of the efficacy of prayer expounded by the Catholic church to which two-thirds of Grenadians were said to owe their allegiance was still widely accepted. Surveying the village of Apres Tout, however, the report commented, 'The people in that area take the threat serious.'

General comments recorded in the report included:

'I will pray harder; ah afraid the gun.'

'We want uniforms and boots.'

'I don't think he is so mad to Invade our Country.'

'Well Lord, what we go do? What little Grenada do Reagan?'

'We must fight to defend our Homeland.'

At Birch Grove the mood was reported to be 'Low to Fair, but more to Low'. The response to visits to five schools was said to be 'Fair, among teachers 50 – 50'.

The picture emerges therefore of a militia of a few thousand people who had had a rudimentary training in the handling of arms, many of whom were keen to do their bit in the repulse of any US invasion but with those in their ranks who clearly relied more on supernatural assistance than their own limited military prowess to throw back the enemy.

The morale of the militia, as of the PRA, had been affected by the circumstances surrounding the murder of Maurice Bishop. Less highly motivated and professional than the PRA, the militia had been devastated by Bishop's death at the hands of Grenadians who called themselves revolutionaries. Questioned shortly after the announcement of the US invasion on 25 October about how many would respond to the call for a mobilisation of the militia a taxi driver on Carriacou, Grenada's sister island, laughed bitterly and said, 'No one aint goin'. We not goin' for de men dat killed Maurice.' Besides killing Bishop, General Austin and the RMC had already demonstrated their distrust of the militia and their fear that it might mobilise against the RMC and had ordered the disarming of those militiamen who were carrying weapons.

Those Grenadians who did fight could count on a large quantity of arms, some of which were deposited in caches round the island. Military pacts between the government and Cuba, the Soviet Union and North Korea involved the supply of weapons, ammunition and training.

The first arms the PRA received from abroad came the month after the revolutionaries seized power. In April 1979 3,400 Soviet and US rifles were received from Havana and 3 million rounds of ammunition, together with machine guns, pistols, rocket launchers, cannon and anti-aircraft guns. By the time of the invasion stocks had been increased substantially as Bishop, forever fearing an invasion, built up enough supplies of weapons to achieve his long-term objective of having enough to arm the whole population.

Under the military pacts he was in the process of receiving 10,000 more rifles and a large assortment of other weapons, armoured vehicles and patrol boats.

Countries with Marxist-Leninist governments were not the only ones keen on equipping him. Despite a refusal by Britain of his request in 1979 for a small number of British armoured cars, offers of NATO arms were made to him in 1983.

A letter dated 7 April and received on 20 April came from A. Bergmans, writing on behalf of ASE Europe N.V., a Belgian arms exporter, and read as follows:

We would be very pleased to receive your enquiries and will do our utmost to reply you [sic] within the shortest delay and at the most attractive conditions.

The list included Browning pistols, FAL rifles, 105 mm. recoilless guns, 81 mm. and 120 mm. mortars, 155 mm. towed howitzers, ammunition for everything from NATO rifles to field artillery, grenades, mines and bulletproof vests.

The letter could hardly have been dispatched had ASE Europe not had confidence that they could have obtained permission to ship arms and ammunition to the Grenadian government. The offer of brand new NATO arms from Belgium, interesting in itself, becomes all the more important in the light of the US criticism that the PRA had too many arms for a small country.

The Cuban personnel on Grenada numbered 784. Of these the vast majority were engaged on the most important development project in Grenada, the building of Point Salines airport. According to official Cuban statements, which were later accepted as correct by the US government, no more than forty-three were military personnel. Their position was a delicate one. The previous Friday, 21 October, two days after the killing of Bishop, the Cuban government had issued a statement condemning his murder, declaring three days public mourning and demanding exemplary punishment if it could be established – and the statement left no doubt that the Cubans thought it could be established – that a crime had been committed.

It was clear, therefore, that it would have been awkward for the Cuban personnel in Grenada to have gone into battle for the sake of a Revolutionary Military Council whose actions the Havana government had just condemned. According to Iván Martínez, the Cuban contingent had been given orders not to attack any invader but to limit themselves to defending themselves if attacked. Martinez revealed however that Colonel Pedro Tortoló Comas of the FAR happened to arrive in Grenada the day before the invasion and was, therefore, on hand to co-ordinate the Cuban operations.

Tortoló had arrived in Grenada direct from Havana in civilian clothes. His mission, he was to say in a press conference back in Havana later, was to instruct the Cuban community in what they had to do if the US forces really attacked. Then his orders were to return to Havana on the Tuesday.

15

A powerfully built negro with a forceful, not to say slightly arrogant, personality, Tortoló was born on 28 June 1945 to a Havana washerwoman. His official biography states he was registered by his mother in her name and was brought up by her alone. He does not appear to have known his father. He chose an army career and was destined to go far. From 1966 to 1970 he attended the Frunze military academy in the USSR and three years later went back to the Voroshilov staff college. Until mid-1983 he had commanded the Cuban military mission in Grenada. At the time of the Grenada crisis he was holding an important job as Chief of Staff of the Army of the Centre in Cuba, helping to command troops who were on twenty-four hour alert for a possible US invasion, a possibility that had become all the more immediate in Cuban minds as the Reagan presidency got under way.

His job was to tell his compatriots in Grenada under what specific circumstances they should fight and how they should do it. In the event, he was to command them as they fought. The raw material he had at his disposal was not the most promising. Among the 784 Cubans, forty-four of whom were women, there were 636 construction workers.

Many of these men were first-class experts at their job and, like virtually every Cuban, had been taught to use a rifle. That did not make them first-class military material. Many of them were in their forties and fifties. Though their lifestyle and their profession clearly made them more active than office workers they were far from being in peak physical condition. There were, too, the forty-three military personnel, including a score of officers, who had been training the PRA and supervising the militia. The eighteen Cuban diplomats stationed in the small compound on the ridge not far from Fort Frederick, and thus several miles away from the main body of Cubans at Point Salines, were to take no active part in the fighting apart from trying with decreasing success to relay messages between the Cubans in combat and Havana after the former had destroyed their communications equipment. There were twelve personnel from Cubana Airlines, seventeen public health workers, twelve doctors, dentists and nurses, including three who had been brought back from Carriacou the previous Saturday, twelve teachers, and the rest were made up of agriculture and fishery workers and Cubans from the Ministry of the Interior whose jobs were not specified.

Tortoló did what he could with this bunch. In his account he claims that he himself was sleeping when the US attack was launched. At one point, he says, US troops came at him from two sides behind the cover of two dozen unarmed Cubans whom they had captured.

Other Cubans, caught without sufficient supplies of ammunition despite the vast stocks on hand, gave themselves up. The death toll in the two days of fighting came to twenty-four, the most senior army man killed being Captain Sergio Grandales Nolasco, a 49-year-old expert in armoured vehicles and transport.

The *Viet Nam Heroico*, the Cuban passenger cargo ship which was ordered out of St George's harbour by the US troops, took no part in the fighting apart from helping, like the Cuban embassy, in relaying messages between Cuba and Grenada.

Not surprisingly, accounts differ about whether the incoming troops of the US 22nd Airborne opened fire first on the quarters the Cubans occupied adjacent to the eastern end of Point Salines airport or whether the Cubans started the fight by firing at the US paratroops as they descended. US commentators favour the latter version, the Cubans the former. Whatever the truth a battle raged for hours around Point Salines between US forces and the Cubans.

The fact that the Cubans listed as construction workers were able to use weapons on the US troops was taken as proof by many in the US that the Cuban contingent was in fact made up of soldiers out of uniform. This was denied by Martinez at his press conference who added with some bravura that all Cubans knew how to fight and could and would do so when the occasion demanded. The truth lies somewhere between the Cuban myth and the US contention and consists in the fact that the large majority, if not all, of the Cubans working on the island would have gone through the sort of civilian militia training which the Grenadians themselves were so anx-

17

emulate. It seems unlikely that any Cuban technician would have been sent to the exposed outpost of revolutionary Grenada, constantly menaced since 1979 by US hostility, without having been given basic weapon training. The statement made by Major James Holt of the 82nd Airborne of the Cubans that 'They were professionals' must, therefore, be treated with some scepticism.

Vastly outnumbered, equipped with hardly a fraction of the weapons and accoutrements available to the US forces and their Caribbean auxiliaries and with their morale seriously impaired by the murder of Bishop, the Grenadian forces and their Cuban allies were nevertheless ready when the US troops landed to put up a fiercer fight than Washington or any outside observer foresaw.

The first US troops ashore were a small detachment of Seals, marine special forces, who, early on Tuesday morning, landed on the west coast of the island just north of St George's and who moved swiftly to Government House to secure the person of Sir Paul Scoon, the Governor-General. Scoon, nominated by Gairy, had been appointed by the Queen to his post in 1978. He was knighted a few days before Bishop overthrew Gairy on 13 March 1979. A quiet black teacher and administrator, he had risen to become Gairy's private secretary. As Governor-General he carried out on behalf of the Queen of Grenada, Elizabeth II, those symbolic duties expected of the monarch in a country which remained, in constitutional theory at least, a monarchy. Under Gairy, as later under Bishop and then under the short-lived régime of Hudson Austin, he remained acting head of state and the ultimate repository of legality. The political importance Scoon could have in justifying, prospectively or retrospectively, the invasion of Grenada made it imperative that he be the first objective of the US forces. The Seals secured Scoon in his grand, airy residence at Government House with its royal portraits and daguerrotypes of Queen Victoria, its neat lawns and the court on which Scoon had often played tennis with Bishop. Having secured

18

him, however, the US troops were kept pinned down by Grenadian fire and it was not until 7.45 a.m. the following morning that they were able to rush him away to the helicopter which ferried him from the Queen's Park stadium to the USS *Guam* for urgent discussions with Metcalf and his political advisers.

The main force of the 22nd MAU left the *Guam* by the helicopter shortly after 6 a.m. on Tuesday and after a brief fight with the anti-aircraft guns of the Grenadian garrison took Pearls airport on the western coast of the island. In the action the troops lost one of their helicopters.

As the 22nd MAU hit Pearls, 500 Rangers dropped from 10 Hercules onto the airport of Point Salines whose runway the Cuban workers had all but completed. There, resistance was stiffer than at Pearls as men of the PRA joined with youngsters of the militia and with the Cubans under Colonel Tortoló.

In a speech delivered at a mass meeting called in Havana on 14 November, to pay tribute to the Cubans killed in the invasion, Castro was to give his version of the first encounter between the US and the Cubans:

The assertion that the Cubans initiated the acts of hostility is equally false and cynical. The irrefutable truth is that the Cubans were sleeping and their weapons were stored at the time of the airdrop on the runway and around the camps. They had not been distributed. There weren't enough to go round, and they weren't distributed until the landing was already underway. And that is when the Cuban personnel went to the places assigned to them for that emergency. Even so, our personnel, now organized and armed, had time to see the US paratroopers regrouping on the runway and the first planes landing. That was the invader's weakest moment. If the Cubans had fired first, they would have killed or wounded dozens – perhaps hundreds – of US soldiers in those early hours. What is strictly historical and strictly true is that the fighting began when the US troops advanced towards the Cubans in a belligerent way. It is also true that

19

when a group of unarmed co-operation personnel was captured, they were used as hostages and forced to lead the way in front of the US soldiers.

The start of the US attack on the Cubans was put by Castro at 7 a.m.

The fighting between the US troops and the Cubans began despite contacts between the US and Cuban governments.

At 9 p.m. on Saturday 22 October Cuba had sent a message to the Cuban Interests Section of the Swiss embassy in Havana (in the absence of diplomatic relations between Washington and Havana contacts were maintained in the Cuban capital through a group of US diplomats who were formally, through a traditional diplomatic fiction, assigned to the embassy of Switzerland).

According to a statement issued on the day of the invasion in Havana the US diplomats were informed:

That we are aware of their concern about the numerous US residents there. That we are also concerned about the hundreds of Cuban co-operation personnel working there in different fields and about the news that US naval forces are approaching Grenada.

That according to the reports we have, no US or foreign national, nor our personnel has had any problems. It is convenient to keep in touch on this matter, so as to contribute to solve favourably any difficulty that may arise or action that may be taken relating to the security of these individuals, without violence or intervention in the country.

According to the Cuban statement, the reply to this communication was received from Washington only three days later at 8.30 a.m. Cuban time, an hour and a half after fighting had broken out between the Cubans and the US troops.

The US reply said:

The United States Government is aware that military and civilian personnel of the Republic of Cuba are present in

Grenada. It has taken into full account the message on this subject which was delivered on the night of 22 October from the Ministry of Foreign Relations to the Acting Chief of the United States Interests Section in Havana. It wishes to assure the Government of the Republic of Cuba that all efforts are being and will continue to be made to ensure the safety of these persons while an order will be granted for their safe passage from Grenada as soon as circumstances permit. The Government of the United States agrees to the Cuban proposal of 22 October to maintain contact concerning the safety of the personnel of each side. The appropriate civilian representatives with the United States Armed Forces presently in Grenada have been instructed to be in contact with the Cuban Ambassador in Grenada to ensure that every consideration is given to the safety of Cuban personnel on the Island and to facilitate the necessary steps by Grenadian authorities for their prompt evacuation. The United States Armed Forces will be prepared to assure this evacuation at the earliest possible moment on ships of third countries. Alternatively, should there be a vessel of the Cuban merchant marine – not a warship – in Grenadian waters at present that vessel may be authorized to conduct the evacuation of Cuban personnel.

In addition, any Cuban views communicated to the Department of State through the Cuban Interests Section in Washington or through the United States Interests Section in Havana will be given immediate attention.

Whatever the real intentions behind these diplomatic notes and whatever the timing of their delivery and reception, the US troops were now in battle with the Grenadian defenders and with the Cubans under Colonel Tortoló.

As soon as Point Salines was sufficiently under the control of the Rangers, hundreds more men were brought in from the 82nd Airborne Division who had been flown to the area from their base at Fort Bragg, North Carolina.

The principal objective of the strike at Point Salines, apart from knocking out the Cubans, was the securing of the True

Blue campus of the St George's University Medical School. The school, a privately owned institution, was one of a number of such study centres set up on Caribbean islands in order to give preliminary coaching in medicine to US students unable to secure places in medical schools in the US itself. The True Blue campus, at the eastern end of the runway, was at the time of the landing occupied by only a few dozen students. The bulk of those who had not been flown out in the charter flights of the previous day from Pearls were billeted at a dormitory block a mile or two to the northeast on the road to St George's. Despite the heavy clashes round Point Salines none of the students was injured.

With the two airports secured the US forces built up their presence on and around the island with astonishing rapidity.

Throughout Tuesday US aircraft and helicopters made strike after strike at and around St George's and Point Salines.

Before noon jets attacked Fort Rupert scattering the crews of the anti-aircraft guns and leaving one PRA officer dead with his pistol in his hand in the courtyard of the citadel.

Throughout Tuesday the regular PRA and members of the militia, sometimes boys and girls in their early teens, kept up a resistance. Every time US aircraft flew low enough to be within range of Grenadian weapons, and many times when they did not, the Grenadians opened up with anti-aircraft and automatic fire, as I witnessed from a vantage point at the fire station on the Carenage. PRA soldiers wearing East German helmets, some with Cuban army leather belts, screeched round the city in Land Rovers and in the little Japanese pickups of the Central Water Commission and other government bodies. Their combination of coolness and dedication was remarked on by many who watched them. As night fell, the city, darkened for lack of power, was lit up by the blaze at Butler House. The water supply became spasmodic and the automatic domestic telephone system was the only public utility that appeared to be functioning normally. In the middle of Tanteen Field, a few hundred yards from the Carenage, lay the remains of a wrecked US helicopter brought down by Grenadian fire in the middle of the afternoon.

22

A PRA corporal devoted more than an hour on Tuesday night to helping six fellow journalists and myself who had arrived in St George's by boat from the neighbouring island of Carriacou just after midday that day. We were trying to get to a telephone, telex or radio to get dispatches out to our newspapers. As the US jets rumbled overhead we careered round town trying to find the manager of the Cable and Wireless office and get the telex service operating again. Antoinette, a telephone operator, was brought from her house by Land Rover to try and get the main switchboard operating once more. The corporal recounted with great pride, though not total accuracy, that the PRA and the Cubans had succeeded in recapturing part of Point Salines airport and that, with the city of St George's still in Grenadian hands, the invaders were confined to Pearls airport and the adjacent town of Grenville.

For a moment that afternoon it seemed that the fighting might stop as suddenly as it had started. At 6 p.m. Grenadian time John Ferch, the senior US representative in Havana, handed the Cuban Deputy Foreign Minister, Ricardo Alarcón, a note in which on behalf of his government he expressed regret for the armed clashes and put them down to 'confusion and accidents'.

The visit from Ferch coincided with a lull in the fighting and to the Cubans it seemed that an effort was being made by the US to bring about a ceasefire from which all sides could emerge with honour. Three and a half hours later the Cubans replied that they accepted that an honourable way could be found to end the battle. In Havana it was widely believed that hostilities had ceased de facto. Sighs of relief were beginning to be breathed by the Cubans who, for all their often bellicose language, did not relish the prospect of heavy casualties among personnel who had had for the most part only the most rudimentary military training.

As the late hours of Tuesday passed US aircraft circled in the skies over St George's and the Cuban positions but aerial attacks were not carried out.

The US troops were however closing in on St George's. At around 4 a.m. from the window of my bedroom in St George's

I saw marines of the US 22nd MAU landing at Grand Mal Bay, a few hundred yards north of the city limits, by helicopter, having flown round the island from their bridgehead at Pearls.

Not long afterwards, the Cubans claimed, heavy attacks were renewed by the US forces on their positions around Point Salines.

The ephemeral truce which had been put into effect and which both sides had given every sign of having accepted was no more. There were to be many more dead and injured on the Wednesday that was dawning.

Under Colonel Smith the MAU took up their positions at Queen's Park, the city's cricket ground and general purpose stadium, beside the sea. Three M-60 tanks blocked the road to the north of St George's, cutting the city off from the rest of the island. The marines established themselves without great difficulty and at 7.45 p.m. took delivery of Sir Paul Scoon.

Lounging at the gate of his amtrack command vehicle from which he could keep contact with Admiral Metcalf on the *Guam*, with the aircraft in the air and with the 82nd Airborne on the southern tip of the island, Colonel Smith tried to get a clear picture of the amount of resistance which still awaited him in the city.

He directed the delicate task of taking St George's with the minimum of civilian casualties, for the principal objective of the operation had been originally announced by President Reagan as the saving of the lives of US and other citizens.

The arrival of several hundred marines with their amtracks and tanks at the gates of the city, the aerial bombardment of the previous day and the sorties which the US jets had kept up throughout the night seemed enough to convince the bulk of the PRA and militia in the capital that there was little point in resisting further.

Those who had been fighting throughout the previous day and night started to throw away their uniforms and do their best to melt into the civilian population in what clothes they could find. On Wednesday there was little more resistance to the invasion within the city. Early in the afternoon Colonel

Smith sent a detachment of his marines to take Fort Frederick on its eminence overlooking the city. This was achieved rapidly with only a few desultory shots being reported from the ruins of the Crazy House, destroyed from the air the previous afternoon. On the steep road up to Fort Frederick two Grenadian armoured vehicles stood abandoned, one on fire near Government House, the other ticking ominously within sight of the fort.

Under the brow of Morne Jaloux, the ridge on which Fort Frederick and the Crazy House stood, several hundred prisoners at the Richmond Hill Prison were beginning to break out of their cells. Their guards had gone early that morning, leaving one prisoner dead of bullet wounds he received as he tried prematurely to free himself. In the courtyard of the prison, which had once been the barracks for British regiments garrisoning the island, several hundred prisoners, common criminals and political detainees, milled about trying to free fellow inmates still confined in their cells. Among them were Alister Hughes, Grenada's most prominent journalist, as fierce an opponent of the New Jewel Movement as he had been of Sir Eric Gairy's government. Hughes had been confined for five days and many inside and outside Grenada, including his wife Cynthia waiting for him in their little house in the middle of St George's below, had virtually given him up for dead. With him were Leslie Pierre, another opponent of Bishop who had unsuccessfully tried with Hughes to launch an opposition newspaper during the Bishop era, Winston Whyte, a former supporter of Gairy who broke with him but who was nevertheless arrested by Bishop almost as soon as he took power in 1979 and Lloyd Noel, a longstanding member of the NJM who was confined in 1981 after he resigned his post of Attorney General in protest against the autocratic direction the revolution was taking. Convinced by a US journalist and a French photographer and me that it was safe to leave Richmond Hill, the small band hurried out with their bags of belongings and were ferried down the hill by car to freedom. As they left, they waved to the marines in Fort Frederick across the small ravine a few hundred yards above them. Climbing over the trees felled by the previous day's aerial bombardment they did not notice a demented woman inmate of the Crazy House, walking about moaning, her baggy dress hanging open to her navel.

The last major engagement of the invasion took place between Point Salines and St George's. Shortly before dusk on Wednesday the US forces seized the Grand Anse campus of the St George's University Medical School where the bulk of the US students had been beleaguered since the invasion had got under way a day and a half before. After an aerial bombardment by helicopter gunships and Hercules, men of the 82nd Airborne took the premises and stood guard over the students while the last resistance was crushed at Radio Free Grenada. The students were helicoptered out to Point Salines as the battle ebbed between the US paratroops and the Grenadian and Cuban defenders.

Tortoló himself, with a dozen Cubans, was surrounded with the main party at Point Salines but managed to break out unseen along a gully, according to his account. As they left they were undecided whether to take to the hills for a guerrilla battle. They decided to make first for the Cuban embassy which, by this time, was surrounded by US forces. After about six hours wandering round they finally took shelter in the Soviet embassy. Tortoló's war was to make him the butt of some unkind jokes in Havana, such as how he was going to replace Juantorena, Cuba's sprinting champion, in the Cuban team for the next Olympics, and how the Tortoló brand of tennis shoes made you run faster on the court.

Later that day a few remaining defenders were rounded up at Calivigny barracks. By Thursday 500 Rangers, 500 marines and 5,000 paratroopers together with 300 Caribbean auxiliaries were in control of Grenada.

The mood on the island was one of relief and loudly expressed joy at the invasion.

'This is the greatest day in the history of Grenada,' one young clerk exclaimed.

'God Bless America' was a slogan chalked up widely on the walls of the city. At the checkpoints set up by the US troops in and around the town many Grenadians were eagerly chatting to the marines and paratroopers whom they clearly regarded as their saviours from the régime of Hudson Austin. The expressions of relief were the preserve of no particular class or age group though the older and better off Grenadians were more emphatic in their statements than other sections of society.

With the US troops in control of Grenada and the immediate future unclear it would have taken a foolhardy or deeply committed Grenadian to voice condemnation of the US action. But beside the genuine and generalised welcome for the invading troops there obviously co-existed reservations and doubts about the effects of the invasion.

The men and women, girls and boys who two days previously had been playing their part in a hopeless attempt to stave off the invading troops could not all have died or fled the island. Those who had worked for the triumph of Maurice Bishop and his New Jewel Movement from its founding in 1973 and for the revolution he initiated when he seized power in 1979 were silent but not absent.

The majority view nevertheless seemed to be that of Alister Hughes, the journalist, restored to his home after some unpleasant days in Richmond Hill Prison. 'Don't call it an invasion,' he said. 'It was a rescue mission.'

CHAPTER TWO

The Island

'Just south of paradise, just north of frustration.'
Anonymous

There is no more beautiful place in the Caribbean than Grenada.

From a plane, flying at 20,000 feet, Grenada can be taken in at a glance. It sits in a sea which can be azure, silver or crimson, depending on the sun. From that height the shallows and shoals off the eastern or Atlantic coast show up as a streak of yellow. At the far southern point there is visible the tiny black slash that is the new airport of Point Salines. The mountainous centre of an island which is only twenty-one miles long by twelve miles wide appears foreshortened and reduced.

On the ground, the traveller realises that he is in a country which could have served as a model for some early nineteenth-century Romantic poet's view of the Garden of Eden. The peaks which, from the air, looked squat and negligible rise up majestically, their flanks swathed in jungle. Down their sides tumble and drip streams and torrents fed by clouds which drop more than twelve feet of rain a year on their summits.

A country road, potholed to be sure, is arched over by massive bamboos, thirty feet or more high. By the roadside cocoa trees grow, their trunks comically sprouting crimson pods in season full of purple cocoa beans surrounded by delicious lemon flavoured cream. The flat places along the road grow sugar cane, tall, thick and green like the lawn of some giant's bowling green but with razor sharp fronds capable of cutting deep into the reaper's skin.

Not for nothing is Grenada called the Spice Island. In 1843 the Hon. Frank Gurney brought nutmeg from the island of Banda in the Dutch East Indies and, over the past 140 years, the tree has flourished till today Grenada grows one third of the world's supply. A large tree can reach up to 60 feet in height. Anyone who inherits a mature tree which has lived a decade or two beyond its first unproductive eight years may sit in its shade and collect 3,000 or 4,000 nuts a year, enough to keep him from starvation.

But there are also cloves, black pepper, allspice, ginger roots, turmeric, with which to make curry and colour rice, and the incomparable bark of the cinnamon tree.

There are bananas, eggplants, cassava, pumpkins, tomatoes and yams. There are guavas, grapefruit, custard apples, cashew nuts, lemons, limes, paw-paw, soursops, tangerines and tamarinds. The flora of Grenada make the vegetation of the temperate zones of the planet look niggardly indeed.

In the island's forests lurk monkeys and mockingbirds, tree snakes and piping frogs, fish-eating bats and armadillos which, when cooked, taste like pork, and mongooses.

Over the seas, full of red snapper and flying fish and dolphins, fly frigate birds, pelicans and laughing gulls.

No work of man was ever likely to rival in grandeur the hand of nature in Granada but the towns and villages that successive generations of Grenadians have constructed blend in well with the terrain and the vegetation. St George's rides a promentory and the russet roofs of the houses make the island's capital look like some tropical Amalfi. Drama is provided by the eighteenth-century forts which dominate the highest ring of hills round the little city.

There are no great plantation houses such as are to be found in Barbados and Jamaica, rather a network of little towns and villages which bear witness to the island's French past – Sauteurs, Grand Roy, Lance aux Epines: or to its English conquerors – Grenville, Victoria, Westerhall.

Christopher Columbus first sighted Grenada on his third voyage of discovery in 1498 and gave it the name of Concepción. But, for some unknown reason, it became Granada or

Grenada from the second quarter of the sixteenth century. For a hundred years or so the island was left in the hands of its fierce Carib occupants while the Spaniards set their minds to digging out the gold and silver that their continental empire was to yield to them.

The first European settlement came when in 1609, 203 Englishmen tried to colonize the island and were killed or driven off by the Caribs.

It was not until 1650 that a permanent European settlement was established when a certain wealthy Frenchman from Martinique, Monsieur du Parquet, set out to tame or conquer the island. This he eventually achieved four years later when he forced the Carib defenders to the northern tip of the island. There they resolved to jump off a cliff into the sea rather than be captured by the French. The cliff was called La Morne de Sauteurs, Leapers' Cliff, and the village in its shadow is today still called Sauteurs. After a quarter of a century of exploitation by French private enterprise, Grenada became a possession of the French crown in 1674. In 1700 a census showed that the population consisted of 257 whites, 53 free coloureds and 525 slaves. In 1763 sovereignty over Grenada passed to England under the Peace of Paris which confirmed *de jure* the *de facto* capture of the island the previous year by a British fleet. In this heyday of the sugar trade the island was an immensely valuable acquisition for Britain. In 1763 Grenada had 82 sugar estates functioning and was nearly as prized a possession of England as Haïti, then called St-Domingue, was for France. The incoming British planters doubled Grenadian sugar exports in a little over a decade and Grenada's foreign trade boomed.

Dr Eric Williams, in his book *Capitalism and Slavery*, quotes figures showing that Britain's imports from New York in the years between 1714 and 1773 totalled £1,910,796 while imports from Grenada between 1763 and 1773 came to £3,620,504. In ten years Grenada sold to Britain nearly twice as much as New York had sold in sixty.

By 1778 the island was back in French hands. Britain and France were again at war on the issue of American independence. In an operation which seems a grim foreshadowing of the US invasion of 1983 a huge French fleet under the Comte d'Estaing appeared off St George's and 10,000 men pounded the British garrison of 540 till they surrendered at Fort George. Under the Treaty of Versailles, however, the island went back to British rule in 1783 and the British took revenge for the travails they had suffered under French rule.

The French revolution of 1789 set off earthquake repercussions in the slave economies of the Caribbean. Within two years a revolt of slaves in St-Domingue established the first free republic in Latin America and the first modern free black state. European planters throughout the region trembled when they learnt how the black republicans had overthrown colonial rule and used the same atrocities on the whites as the whites had used on them for more than a century.

They cannot have been reassured when they learnt that one of the first of the Haïtian leaders, Henri Christophe, later King Henri I, had been born in Grenada on 6 October 1767 and had lived the first ten years of his life there.

The political tremors from the slave revolt in Haïti were felt in Grenada in 1795 when Julien Fedon, the son of a slave mother and a French father, led the most serious challenge ever to colonial rule in Grenada. For fifteen months, with the moral support of the revolutionary government in Paris and the active collaboration of those Frenchmen remaining on the island, he fought the British garrison, reinforcements sent in from the other British islands and a contingent of 4O Spanish soldiers sent from Trinidad, which at the time was still part of the Spanish empire. By the end of the year Fedon controlled virtually the whole of the island with the exception of St George's.

Fedon's fate was sealed, however, with the arrival of General Sir Ralph Abercromby, an intelligent and experienced Scottish soldier who had studied the campaigns of Frederick the Great of Prussia. He surrounded and attacked Fedon's camps, avenging Governor Ninian Home. Home and fifty other British prisoners had been put to death by Fedon after a British attack on his camp in which his brother had been killed. Fedon himself was never captured. He escaped the British encirclement perhaps to die of exposure in the forests or be drowned in a bid to escape to Trinidad. The Fedon legend was to become a powerful tool and example to the NJM and its army nearly two centuries later.

The Emancipation Act of 1833 relieved the simmering discontent that pervaded Grenada after the crushing of Fedon but created demands for new sources of labour. These were satisfied with the importation of indentured labourers from Malta, Madeira and India, thus completing the present racial mix in Grenada.

The introduction of nutmeg and the expansion of cocoa plantations revolutionized the economy of the island and the extensive cultivation of sugar gave way to a multiplicity of small-holders who cultivated their 'gardens' or small plots in the shadow of the great estates of the powerful white planters.

In the second half of the nineteenth century the imperial government in London started to revise its ideas of how best to administer the West Indies. In many islands, including Grenada, the local assemblies were abolished in favour of the system of Crown Colonies, or of direct rule from London through a Governor with plenary powers. The local assemblies, some of which could trace their history back to the first British settlements in the seventeenth century, were hardly democratic organizations in that they recognised the right to vote only of those handfuls of planters and merchants who could pass strict property qualifications. The tiny middle classes were not represented, nor, of course, the mass of the population of slaves, indentured labourers or poor whites. The introduction of direct rule from London was aimed at blowing some fresh air through the politics of the region while at the same time doing nothing to present an immediate threat to the social structures of the islands. The local assemblies were replaced with councils nominated by the Governor. He was free to accept or reject whatever advice these councils gave him and there were no effective trammels on his powers.

Grenada's accession to Crown Colony status, however empty of real reforming content, was the beginning of a process which was to lead firstly to the timidest of moves for effective social

33

reform and much later to the revolution and revolutionary ideas of the NJM.

If Fedon was the father of revolution and revolt in Grenada, the founder of reformism was an Irish-Negro, William Galway Donovan who, in the last decade of the nineteenth century, founded in St George's *The Federalist and Grenada People*. Its motto, 'A Naked Freeman is Nobler than a Gilded Slave', summed up its political attitudes.

Donovan took under his wing a young reporter, Theophilus Albert Marryshow, who was destined to become the most important political figure in Grenada for much of the twentieth century. In his newspaper, *The West Indian*, Marryshow called time and time again for the reform of the Crown Colony system and the federation of the whole of the West Indies in one nation which sooner or later would rule itself within the British Empire in the way that Canada, Australia, New Zealand and the other dominions were already ruling themselves.

Marryshow never accepted the doctrine of class warfare and continually called for a national consensus to raise the status of the poorest in society. In 1917 he founded the Representative Government Association which lobbied for greater local influence in government. In 1933 he organized a massive protest in St George's against increased taxation. But he was never able or willing to found a strong trade union movement.

In his classic history, *The Growth of the Modern West Indies*, Gordon K. Lewis sums up the man cruelly but perhaps not inaccurately.

> But, for all his noble gifts Marryshow, at the most, was a West Indian Fabian, a Royalist-Loyalist whose staunch Whig constitutionalism never permitted him to fight the colonial power except on its own polite terms.

Trade unionism was, however, to be the key to change in Grenada. One of the greatest figures of West Indian trades unionism was born in Grenada, though he claimed his most famous victories in Trinidad, the island to the south whose bigger and more prosperous economy was always to attract

Grenadian immigrants. 'Buzz' Butler went as a boy to work in the oilfields in Trinidad and, in 1937 as a leader of the Oilfield Workers Trade Union, he led a massive protest at Fyzabad in the southeast of Trinidad in favour of better working conditions and self-government. Trinidadian politics were never the same again. He subsequently founded his own political party, the Butler Party, which had little more to offer than a commitment to the trade union struggle and a opportunity to express personal loyalty to the person of Butler.

Lewis remarks, with characteristic tartness, 'Butler's contribution to Trinidadian political thought was his promise in the 1950 election that if returned to power he would abolish dog licences.'

Marryshow told Butler on one of the latter's visits to his birthplace that Grenada was not yet ready for the politics of trade unionism but that did not stop Butler's career setting an example to Grenadians.

The most important figure to follow it was Eric Matthew Gairy, the shadow of whose personality was to fall over the island for more than three decades.

As a young man Gairy, like Butler, left Grenada to work in the oilfields. Going to the Dutch island of Aruba off the coast of Venezuela he got his first political experience organising the workers in the large Standard Oil refinery there.

In 1950, before he was thirty, Gairy was back in his native Grenada where he registered his Grenada Manual and Mental Workers Union, which was to be the springboard for his political career. Within six months of its founding Gairy was using the GMMWU to organise the first general strike the island had ever known.

Inebriated by his oratory, encouraged by his total disrespect for the white establishment and the Governor and delighted by his womanizing cockiness, the workers of Grenada, urban and rural fell for handsome, dashing Gairy. As the strike pursued its course the Governor had Gairy and his right hand man Gascoigne Blaize arrested on 22 February 1951 and put on a boat for Carriacou. The violence redoubled as the crowds blocked the roads and rioted, demanding the release of the two men. The Governor had to call for help from the Royal Navy and extra police were called in from Trinidad, St Lucia, Barbados and Jamaica. Several people were killed and others wounded. In the end, after eleven days, the Governor had to give in and release them both. Gairy came back from Carriacou a hero and an idol. He remains a hero and an idol to many, especially to the rural workers who had never before felt they had a champion.

Moving quickly to transform his trade union backing into political strength, Gairy organized a Grenada People's Party for the October 1951 elections. The GPP won 71 per cent of the vote, crushing the opposition led by Marryshow and taking six of the eight seats on the Governor's Legislative Council or 'parliament' and gaining places on the Executive Council or 'cabinet'.

Within little more than a year Gairy had achieved what no Grenadian leader had achieved before, the creation of a potent and effective trade union organization which united town and country workers and the transformation of trade union power into political power. No less important, he demonstrated to humble black Grenadians that their domination by a white élite of planters and traders need not go on for ever. A new Grenada took shape as the irreverent Gairy crushed the reverent Marryshow at the polls, and earned his place in the history books of the Caribbean.

In the years of power that now stretched in front of him Gairy demonstrated that he was more interested in the cult of his own personality – and in the undoubted political benefits that that brought him from a large proportion of the Grenadian voters – than in the transformation of society and the overthrow of a colonial economic system.

In November 1953 Gairy called a second general strike in support of pay demands but this time it did not achieve the success of the earlier stoppage.

He kept up his image of irreverence however. Within a month of joining the Executive Council, Gairy was fined £8 for using obscene language. A year later he was suspended from the Legislative Council for abusing fellow members and in

March 1954 he forfeited his seat on the Executive Council for being absent without leave.

In elections in September 1954 his Grenada People's Party, now reorganized as the Grenada United Labour Party, or GULP, carried seven of the eight seats in the Legislative Council though Gairy's supporters' share of the votes fell to 46 per cent.

When the ministerial system was introduced in March 1956 Gairy became Minister of Trade and Production and there began that series of imputations and condemnations of his financial irresponsibility some of which by the standards of today appear of a minor order and which have accompanied him to this day. In November 1956 a commission cleared him of abusing his government position in order to make money out of a land deal but, three months later, his colleagues on the Legislative Council censured him for 'wanton waste of public funds'.

In the September 1957 elections Gairy suffered a temporary setback at the hands of the Grenada National Party and its leader Herbert Blaize. Blaize was a more moderate and conventional leader than Gairy and had a strong following in the island of Carriacou.

Gairy's GULP won nearly 52 per cent of the votes but, under the first-past-the-post constituency system, won only two of the eight Legislative Council seats. Blaize, supported by a coalition, took office. During the election campaign Gairy kept his reputation for irreverence and insubordination bright. He earned himself the penalty of five years' disenfranchisement for marching a steel band through an opponent's meeting.

GULP was back again in 1961 and Gairy, his period of disenfranchisement over, returned to politics, becoming Chief Minister in August 1961 and commanding a majority of eight of the ten seats in the Legislative Council. His wife Cynthia he appointed Minister of Social Services.

As he took office once more the allegations flourished. A Commission of Enquiry appointed in June by the Jamaican born Administrator James Lloyd found Gairy guilty of 'squandermania' which included having spent £4,000 on furnishings at the Chief Minister's residence. A piano had cost £700 and a radiogram £300 and civil servants had been bullied into agreeing to the expenditure. Humble Grenadians loved him for it. He turned the issue to his advantage representing the Commission of Enquiry as a collection of men who did not want blacks to have radiograms, pianos or decent housing. He talked to the Communist Premier Cheddi Jagan in what was then British Guiana and warned that Grenada might have to consider Communism as an option, a move which earned him a rebuke from the Catholic church.

In the aftermath Britain suspended the Grenadian constitution and dissolved the Legislative and Executive Councils and Gairy was out of office. In the elections which followed, Blaize's GNP ran a successful campaign on the issue that Grenada should throw in its lot with Trinidad and Tobago and form a unitary state with the neighbouring islands with which Grenada had always had strong connections. But, though the Grenadian electorate expressed enthusiasm for a merger with the oil producing islands to the south, the Trinidadians were in no hurry to take on responsibility for providing jobs and rudimentary social services for their poorer neighbours. Blaize's plan collapsed in ruins and in the 1967 elections Gairy and GULP were back again.

In this period of office Gairy began to show his worst side. Power was centralised in his hands and he started that expansion of his business interest which was to make him a very rich man in Grenadian terms. At the same time he pushed ahead with the pseudo-mystic interests. Grenadian workers, particularly country people, continued to see him as 'Uncle Gairy' who had given them attention and importance for the first time. And there was for a time no political alternative to him other than GNP which was seen as the party of the planters and the richer middle class.

Gairy was not to lose an election again. He won in 1972 and started the process which was to make Grenada an independent country. The British after the war had made efforts to weld its Caribbean colonies into a federation. These efforts bore fruit briefly in the Federation of the West Indies which lasted from 1958 to 1962. The rationale behind the idea was that the region contained small political units which would never be viable politically or economically, territories such as the Turks and Caicos Islands with less than 7,500 people, the British Virgin Islands with 10,000 inhabitants, the Cayman Islands with a little over 15,000. The unviability of such small units militated against the British strategy, pursued under Labour and Conservative administrations, of ridding Britain of colonial appendages whose retention made Britain subject to criticism in the United Nations and other international forums. Moreover the colonies which for several centuries had been a source of wealth to the metropolis looked increasingly as though they would become a drain on British funds as their populations, newly awakened politically, began to demand higher living standards.

Whitehall's strategy was supported by many West Indians such as Marryshow in Grenada who believed in the concept of a pan-West Indian identity within which Jamaicans and Trinidadians, Grenadians and Barbadians could co-exist politically. The Federation came into being on 3 January 1958 when Princess Margaret inaugurated the legislature in Port of Spain, the Trinidadian capital, which was also chosen as the seat of the Federation.

In the lower House of Representatives 47 members were chosen to represent the 10 member territories, 17 from Jamaica, 10 from Trinidad and Tobago, 5 from Barbados, 2 each from Antigua, St Kitts-Nevis-Anguilla, St Lucia, Grenada, St Vincent and Dominica and one from Montserrat. A 19-member Senate included two senators from each territory with the exception of Montserrat which had one. It was expected that a successful Federation would sooner or later take the smaller territories off Britain's hands.

The Federation was doomed to failure. Despite the similarities of race, language and political culture among the territories of the region the tradition of separatism, even parochialism, persisted and still persists. The elementary fact that the average voter in Grenada was unlikely to know much about politicians or events in, say, Jamaica and that a typical Trinidadian was unconcerned about the problems of, say, St

39

Kitts was compounded by the jealousies and rivalries of established politicians, only one of whom could become Prime Minister of the Federation. In 1961 Jamaica and Trinidad signalled their intention of quitting the Federation and each opting for independence on its own. With the departure of the two biggest political units the Federation quietly expired the next year.

Britain was not to be put off so easily from the objective of relinquishing responsibility for those potentially troublesome islands whose viability as independent states was open to question. As Jamaica, Trinidad and finally Barbados quit the Federation, Britain tried to put together a minor federation of the small islands of the Eastern Caribbean. In this process London looked towards Grenada which was the most prosperous of them. Whitehall recognised that, if Gairy did not have in his hand the key to the success of a federation of the Eastern Caribbean, the enterprise was unlikely to succeed without the active participation of the wiliest of the island leaders. Gairy was, however, unwilling to play, perhaps because the opposition of the Treasury in London prevented the colonial strategist from offering enough financial aid to make the deal attractive. In any event Britain was forced to put forward the idea of Associated Statehood, a scheme under which the little islands were deemed to be in free and voluntary association with Britain which looked after their external defence and relations with the outside world. In 1967 Grenada became an Associated State though Gairy made it plain that his goal was the complete political independence of his country.

The arrival of Associated Statehood and full internal self-government for Grenada in 1967 and GULP's victory in the elections of that year made Gairy virtually untouchable. The former colonial masters, Gairy knew, would tolerate virtually any domestic upset in the island without interfering. Interference by Whitehall would only suck Britain back into a colonial entanglement from which both major parties in London were keen to be free. The days of supervision from London, censures and the suspension of constitutions was over. The Governor who, when Gairy had started his political career, had been an awesome figure whom Gairy had to ridicule was now reduced to a figurehead, the representative of a distant monarch in London who reigned but who did not rule.

In such circumstances and backed by the votes of poorer Grenadians Gairy came into his own. He attended to his business interests in hotels and night clubs, he made life difficult for his adversaries and favoured his supporters. This led to allegation and counter allegation.

To back up his rule he had at his disposal the Grenadian Defence Force, known locally by its opponents as the Green Beasts, the police, and an irregular force of thugs called the Mongoose Gang after the weasel-like animal which inhabits Grenada's forests.

Gairy came to need them in the 1970s. At the end of the 1960s the Caribbean appeared to shudder violently. In 1969 the normally peaceful Dutch island of Curaçao, traditionally given over to refining oil and extracting the maximum amount of money from visiting tourists, was in chaos as rioters burnt down the centre of Willemstad, the capital.

More immediate and ominous for Gairy were the events in Trinidad in 1970 where part of the army mutinied and were within an ace of ousting Prime Minister Eric Williams. The parliamentary politics which had got Trinidad independence and which carried on Westminster traditions sedately on the island appeared for a moment likely to dissolve. There arose the spectre of a Black Power rebellion whose roots were to be found in the more violent political tradition of the United States.

A young lawyer, returning from his law studies at Gray's Inn in London, joined with others in a demonstration in favour of the protesters and Grenadians arrested in Trinidad and in condemnation of Gairy's way of government. Later he recalled, 'In those days demonstrations were something new to Grenada and many people thought we were crazy parading up and down with placards. In fact a demonstration then was big when you had six people involved'.

That was enough to mark the 26-year-old Maurice Bishop as an enemy of Gairy in the tiny society of St George's. He was constantly harassed by the police and Gairy railed against Bishop's colleagues as 'hot and sweaty youth'.

From now on it was war between Eric Matthew Gairy and Maurice Bishop.

Maurice Bishop was born on the island of Aruba in the Dutch Antilles off the coast of Venezuela on 29 May 1944 to Rupert and Alimenta, his wife. Rupert was a man who had started work at fourteen and had virtually educated himself. Like Marryshow and Gairy, Rupert Bishop decided he could advance himself better if he went to work in the oilfield than if he stayed at home. He and his wife emigrated to the Dutch island to work in the Standard Oil refinery there, one of the biggest in the Western Hemisphere. By 1951, however, he and his wife were back in Grenada with Maurice and his two sisters and the boy went to school for the first time.

His father started business in a small way as an import agent and made a reasonable, though not spectacular, living. Maurice was put to Wesley Hall Primary School and to the St George's Roman Catholic school before winning a scholarship to Presentation College, the best academic school in the island run by a group of Irish teaching brothers who had established themselves on the island in 1947 in a colonnaded mock palazzo on Cemetery Hill overlooking St George's. They ran their college on traditionalist and conservative lines which were to the taste of Rupert. Self-taught and self-reliant he was never disposed to spoil his son and constantly dinned into him the virtues of work, application and education. The story is told of how Maurice came back with an excellent mark of 95 per cent at the end of a term. 'Where are the other five marks,' Rupert cried, and gave Maurice five hefty slaps.

The young Maurice grew like a beanstalk which made him seem embarrassingly too tall to be going to school. His height was made all the more conspicious by the school uniform of white shirt and trousers which made Presentation boys look like a permanent cricket team. They were constantly being teased by the rival Grenada Boys Secondary School at the other end of town who used to call out to them, 'Whatsa score?' and 'You battin' next?'

At school the gangling Bishop distinguished himself as a debater and a social creature who, for instance, joined the College's Red Cross team. He became president of the students' council which the brothers encouraged their pupils to organise long before the revolution which made such councils mandatory in all schools. A churchgoer from a devoutly Catholic home, he became editor of the school magazine *Student Voice*.

At 19 he left the island to follow a legal career and qualify as a barrister at Gray's Inn, one of those bastions of British legal conservatism which were once described as 'the purest survival of medieval republican oligarchy to be found in Europe'. The year after he qualified, 1966, he married a Grenadian nurse, Angela Redhead, by whom he had two children, John and Nadi.

'Bish' as his London friends knew him had his first taste of London politics in the West Indian Students Society of which he became president, and in the legal aid clinic which he helped to set up in Notting Hill Gate, the depressed corner of Inner London which a decade earlier had broken out in violent racial riots.

Having qualified to practise law Bishop did not immediately return to Grenada but took a job in the British civil service where he was employed examining the accounts of surtax payers. His years in London were formative ones for him. Days devoted to study in a profession whose British members formed the backbone of the establishment were succeeded by nights in which he experienced the deprivation of the West Indian colony in a dreary part of the capital and the aspirations of his fellow Caribbean students who, as a group, were destined to become the future leaders of the West Indies. In the tax office he had a privileged view of how the rich lived and arranged their affairs.

Physically, Bishop, at 6 foot 3 inches, towered over his colleagues, psychologically his easy manner and self-confidence made him popular and a leader, a man who found it easy to communicate with people. He was an excellent public speaker.

Speaking with the benefit of hindsight at Grenada's National Education Conference in July 1982 Bishop said:

> The colonial masters recognized very early on that if you get a subject people to think like they, to forget their own history and their own culture, to develop a system of education that is going to have relevance to our outward needs and be almost entirely irrelevant to our internal needs, then they have already won the job of keeping us in perpetual domination and exploitation. Our educational process, therefore, was used mainly as a tool of the ruling élite.

Back in St George's in 1970 Bishop had the world at his feet. As a recently qualified London-trained lawyer with some knowledge of the civil service and tax affairs he was in great demand. At the same time his own mind was effervescing with practical ideas about how to help the failed revolutionaries in Trinidad and give legal aid to the Grenadians in their ranks who had been arrested after the army mutiny and attempt at general insurrection had collapsed.

He had not become, and never was to become, an admirer of the Soviet system of government. His political ideas as he settled back into Grenadian society were drawn from a number of sources. The black nationalistic movement that he had seen in action in Trinidad was one. A second was Julius Nyerere's African socialism and the Ujamaa village system in Tanzania. Another was the writings of the veteran Trinidadian Marxist C.L.R. James who, in a long career in the Caribbean, Britain and the US, had re-assessed Hegel, Marx, Lenin and Trotsky from a Third World point of view. James had been a member of the Independent Labour party in London and Chairman of its Finchley branch, leaving in 1936 to found, with other Trotskyists, the Revolutionary Socialist League. He had worked with future African leaders such as Jomo Kenyatta and Kwame Nkrumah and had written a history of the Haïtian Revolution, had studied the black movement in the US and had been

44

expelled from that country. A confirmed West Indian nationalist and no longer a Trotskyist, James had been Secretary of the Federal Labour Party which was the ruling group in the ephemeral West Indies Federation.

James' independent Marxism was to be a lasting influence on Bishop.

The beginnings of Bishop's adult political action came when he joined other young West Indian intellectuals at a meeting on Rat Island off the coast of St Lucia in 1970 to discuss Black Power and talk of the prospects for political change in the Eastern Caribbean. From the Rat Island meeting developed the Forum group, a loose grouping of reformers who agreed to keep in touch with one another as they pursued their political aims in their respective islands.

Forum groups were set up in St Lucia, St Vincent and Grenada. In Grenada Bishop organised Forum into holding protest marches through the streets in protest against Gairy's policies. They never attracted more than a handful of supporters and drew down on Maurice the criticism of his father who did not see this as the right outcome of the careful education his son had just completed in England.

By the end of the year, however, the politically heterogenous Forum groups were falling apart. With a group of friends Bishop started another small organisation, the Movement for the Advance of Community Effort (MACE) which, *inter alia*, was committed to the annual celebration of African Liberation Day.

In November 1970 Bishop's first big legal case took place. A group of nurses started a demonstration against the conditions in St George's General Hospital. Their demonstration was joined by schoolchildren, trade unionists and members of Blaize's GNP. Gairy's police weighed in with batons and tear gas and made a number of arrests including Bishop. When the time came to charge the demonstrators Bishop and another young lawyer, Kendrick Radix, who had recently finished his legal studies at University College, Dublin, undertook the defence of the 22 nurses who were to stand trial.

The case became a rallying point throughout the Caribbean

for those who wanted to express their disgust with Gairy. Bishop and Radix were joined in their task of defending the nurses by several lawyers from elsewhere in the West Indies and, after a seven-month trial, all the defendants were acquitted. Bishop's name was made. The trial also put Bishop in contact with like-minded Caribbean lawyers committed to human rights work. They were to collaborate more formally six years later when they founded the Caribbean Human Rights and Legal Aid Company which started to offer legal services for victims of human rights abuses wherever they were needed.

The 1970 trial helped to crystallise Bishop's political thoughts. Political disappointment was, however, waiting for him. The 1972 elections again threw up a victory for Gairy and GULP. The GNP and Herbert Blaize could not get over their image as the party of the planters and island oligarchs and Gairy was still working his magic over his followers, particularly in the countryside.

His image had been done no harm in 1970 when a Grenadian girl, Jennifer Hosten, won the title of Miss World at the annual beauty competition in London. Gairy had been a member of the jury. (Later, when Grenada became independent, Hosten was nominated by Gairy to be Grenadian High Commissioner in Ottawa.)

His victory at the polls allowed Gairy to bring in new laws to limit demonstrations and ban the use of loudspeakers without police permission. It also contributed to the establishment of two new political groups which, when they came together, would overthrow him.

In St George's, Bishop and Radix joined to start a tiny new political movement, the Movement for Assemblies of the People (MAP) which had something of an intellectual image. Meanwhile in the parish of St Andrew's and the village of St David's two groups were at work, one aimed at promoting political debate in the countryside, the other more concerned to rescue and develop Grenadian culture in song and dance. Grenada, after all, had been the birthplace of the Caribbean's greatest calypso singer, Mighty Sparrow, whose political lyrics, catchy tunes and attractive personality had made him an idol in Trinidad, where he had gone to live, and in the rest of the English-speaking West Indies.

It took the return of Unison Whiteman in 1970 from a course on government and economics at the black-run Howard University in Washington, DC, to bind these two small groups together in the Joint Endeavour for Welfare, Education and Liberation – JEWEL.

Very soon JEWEL won its first political victory. Lord Brownlow, a wealthy British landowner who had acted as *aide de camp* to the Duke of Windsor, created a good deal of discontent by closing a road through his estate at La Sagesse which gave access to a popular beach. JEWEL saw that public protests were getting nowhere so that started a 'People's Trial' of the offending peer whom they convicted *in absentia* of taking away the rights of the people. They then tore down the fence blocking the road and pushed their way through to the beach once again.

Not many months were to pass before MAP and JEWEL decided it would be more productive if the two organizations were to merge. At a joint congress held on 11 March 1973 the merger idea was approved by the small membership of both parties and the New Jewel Movement – NJM – was born.

Recalling James' and Marryshow's West Indian nationalism the NJM manifesto called for the economic integration of the islands 'under popular ownership and control'. It called for an independent Grenada to join the Non-Aligned Movement and demanded new policies to deal with Grenada's economic, social and political problems and called for popular mobilisation through the establishment of grassroots organizations. The NJM aim was 'developing a concrete programme to improve housing, apparel, education, public health, food and recreation for the people.' The party, tiny though it was, was on the road to presenting the radical, populist alternative to Gairy which the GNP had never managed to muster.

The NJM did not have long to wait before it was pushed into the centre of the stage. Hanging over Grenada that year was the question of the terms under which the Associated State of Grenada would move to full political independence and take over the residual powers of control over defence and foreign affairs which were still being run from London.

Britain was keen for the associated statehood scheme to be replaced by full independence for the small islands as quickly as possible. Contrary to the hopes of the civil servants in Whitehall, the United Nations Decolonization Committee did not accept that, as freely associated with Britain and empowered to seek full independence whenever they wanted it, the little islands could no longer be classed as colonies. The UN deemed them still to be colonies.

Moreover, all Britain's nightmares came true when intractable political problems combined with high farce in the Anguilla affair. The tiny island of Anguilla, the smallest partner in the three-island Associated State of St Kitts-Nevis-Anguilla revolted against rule from St Kitts. It declared itself an independent republic and adopted an eight-page constitution which was approved by a meeting of the islanders by a majority of 1,739 to 4. West Indian parochialism had surely reached its nadir when less than 2,000 electors launched their flat scrubby little island, 36 square miles in area with no natural resources, into the world as a sovereign state. Operation Calypso was launched and before dawn on 19 March 1969, 100 British paratroopers descended on the island to restore the status quo. They were followed by a contingent of British policemen and a platoon of Royal Marines. The situation was more reminiscent of Gilbert and Sullivan than of Realpolitik. It strengthened even further the resolve of the British government that its colonial presence should be wound down as quickly and as comprehensively as possible. The region was of scant commercial value to Britain, was of no strategic importance to London and seemed consciously or unconsciously to conspire to make faces red in Whitehall.

There was therefore delight in London when the Government of Grenada, the most prosperous and viable of the Eastern Caribbean islands, sought a firm timetable for the move to complete independence. In Grenada itself, however, feelings were more mixed. Independence and the removal of Britain's residual responsibilities were seen as opening the door to a full dictatorship by a man who had already shown tyrannical instincts.

Political ferment was increased in April 1973 by trade union ferment as power, telephone and water workers staged a strike at the beginning of the month. On 20 April Gairy's police shot a young protester, Jeremiah Richardson, in the head and killed him. His family went to the month-old NJM for help as a wave of protests which, *inter alia*, closed Pearls airport for several days.

There was no let up in the tension as Gairy and Blaize took off for London and a constitutional conference in which the details of the island's impending independence were to be thrashed out. At the beginning of June the NJM convened a mass conference on independence which was attended by thousands of Grenadians and during which the Gairy government and its plans for independence were condemned. Tempers were not eased when Gairy and Blaize returned to the island with the news that Grenada was indeed going to become a sovereign state in February of the following year.

Growing in confidence the NJM planned another of the mock trials which was proved so effective in the Brownlow case. On 4 November a People's Congress held at Seamoon in St Andrew's parish was attended by thousands of Grenadians. *In absentia* Gairy was convicted of twenty-seven 'crimes' which ranged from alleged brutality to incompetence. He was called upon to resign within a fortnight or face a general strike.

As tension rose in Grenada the government determined to cow the NJM into submission. The police and the Mongoose Gang caught up with six of the party leaders, Bishop, Whiteman, Selwyn Strachan, Hudson Austin, Kendrick Radix and Simon Daniel on Sunday 18 November. The day was set for the start of the strike, at Grenville, near Pearls airport where they were visiting businessmen in connection with the strike.

The six were beaten unmercifully and thrown into Grenville police station without medical attention. Bishop, who was badly lacerated about the head and eyes, was forced to go to St Joseph's Hospital in Barbados for surgery.

The day went down in Grenadian history as Bloody Sunday.

All Grenadians except the most confirmed supporters of GULP were horrified by the beatings. The same day a Committee of 22 was formed which promoted a petition calling for the disbandment of the Mongoose Gang, an end to arbitrary police procedure and punishment for those responsible for the outrage at Grenville. The committee included all the island's trade unions except Gairy's GMMWU, the churches, business groups and civic organizations.

In the face of the immediate reaction of all but his most hardened supporters Gairy agreed to disband the Mongoose Gang and to appoint a commission of enquiry under the Jamaican lawyer Sir Herbert Duffus. In the face of these concessions the Committee of 22 decided to call off the general strike. Many protesters wanted the events of Bloody Sunday to bring about the downfall of Gairy and, when he refused to resign, another island-wide strike was called for 1 January 1974. It was to last for months and blight the ceremonies of Grenada's achievement of independence.

Protest and police violence fed on each other in a vicious circle. On 21 January Bishop's father Rupert was shot and killed by police as he sought to block the doorway of a first-floor room at Otway House, headquarters of the Seamen and Waterfront Workers' Union in the Carenage of St George's.

When it was eventually reported, the Duffus Commission tabulated in detail the thuggery of the Gairy Government. Gairy was found to have been responsible for the setting up of the Mongoose Gang which was described as 'an unlawfully constituted body of men paid from public funds.'

The leaders of the Gang included Moslyn Bishop, 28 convictions for offences including larceny, assault on the police and wounding; Willie Bishop, 19 convictions; Raphael Brizan, 20 convictions; Alstan Hood, 8 convictions; Albert Clarke, 15 convictions; Norrel Balfon, 34 convictions; Redhead Hercules, 33 convictions and Crofton Fraser, 32 convictions.

Duffus itemised how the Gang tried to lynch an innocent man, Eric Campbell, whom Gairy had told them to bring in dead or alive, and how Gairy himself seized one Leonard Greenidge by the collar at Mount Royal in May 1973 while he was punched by a member of the Gang. He added that two magistrates, I.I. Duncan and Lloyd St Louis had failed to act with firmness and competence and that Nolan Jacobs, Gairy's Solicitor-General, had acted with gross impropriety during bail hearings. All three, he suggested, should be sacked.

Some of the harshest words were reserved for Assistant Superintendent Innocent Belmar who, Duffus said, should be sacked from the police force and precluded from holding office in the public service.

Shopkeepers and the owners of vehicles looted or damaged by the Gang should receive compensation and the police should be speedily reorganized. Gairy demonstrated his attitude towards the Duffus Commision criticisms by promoting Belmar.

The setbacks the NJM had suffered in 1972 and 1973 caused the leadership to rethink party strategy and organisation. Whether the party liked it or not the island was moving towards independence and the last trammels of control from London were about to be taken away. As Gairy's police became harsher, many members of the NJM who had joined with more enthusiasm for change than determination to make sacrifices in a political struggle fell by the wayside.

After the 1973 elections it was decided that the NJM should be recast in a mould much closer to the vanguard party theories espoused by Lenin, without, however, committing the party in any way to a full Marxist-Leninist outlook. The old mass membership made up of any Grenadian who was sympathetic and who could afford the money for a membership card was phased out and a new system adopted under which a central core of committed members, willing if necessary to suffer beatings, imprisonment or even death in the cause of the fight against Gairy, oversaw the work of sympathizers. The latter were organized in cells, a handful of members coming together to form a cell in each village and in each principal part of St George's.

Ideologically, the party had not crystallized into one uniform tendency. One principal founder of the JEWEL Movement, Teddy Victor, was suspicious of what he saw as the shift in the political centre of gravity of the party from the countryside

51

to the town of St George's and the subsequent undervaluing of the contribution of the country people. The movement, for him, was becoming too dependent on the intellectuals who, like Bishop, had come to the NJM through the MAP. In the years up to the revolution he also became increasingly unhappy at the influence of Cuban and Soviet models on NJM thought. He looked rather to models in which he felt the peasantry was given its rightful role and respect.

Such influences were hardly overwhelming in the mid 1970s. NJM members watched the Cuban leadership as it tried to give the Cuban Communist Party a more formal structure and separate the role of the party from that of the state. Physical contacts with the Cuban government were minimal, the Cuban leaders in Havana, preoccupied with events in Spanish speaking Central America and with the turbulent and quarrelsome leaders of the Nicaraguan revolutionaries in the Sandinista movement in particular, found little time for the minutiae of political life in the small islands of the Eastern Caribbean. The first official party-to-party contacts came when the NJM sent a small delegation to the World Youth Congress held in Cuba in 1979.

Soviet political thinking had penetrated the party but, as in the case of relations with Cuba, the party-to-party contacts were virtually non-existent.

CHAPTER THREE

Independence

'He who opposes me opposes God.'
Eric Gairy

As the hands of the clock touched midnight and marked the first seconds of 7 February 1974 a new monarchy was born in the Western Hemisphere. Amid the ceremonial that the British had perfected on dozens of other occasions when their colonies achieved independence, the Union Jack was lowered for the last time and the flag of the independent state of Grenada was hoisted for the first.

What had been planned as a glittering occasion turned out to be a miserable affair. The Queen was to have been represented by her cousin Prince Richard of Gloucester. In the event it was decided in London that he could not be catapulted into the mess in St George's. His place was taken by Major Leo de Gale, the Governor, who had been appointed only days previously after the hurried departure of Dame Hilda Bynoe, a medical doctor who, as Governor, had been formally representing the Queen on the island since 1968 Dame Hilda had resigned on the eve of independence, convinced she could not handle the political challenges that a deeply divided society presented. De Gale, one of Grenada's richer white citizens, had taken on the job at the last moment at Gairy's suggestion out of a generalised sense of patriotism. He was not the sort to see his island go into independence in a state of complete constitutional chaos. As Grenada moved from colonial status to independence de Gale was transformed from Governor to

53

Governor-General, from being the local representative of Elizabeth II, Queen of the United Kingdom of Great Britain and Northern Ireland, to the incarnation of Queen Elizabeth II, Queen of Grenada. The British government was represented at the lowest possible level of hierarchy by Peter Blaker, a Parliamentary Under-Secretary at the Foreign and Commonwealth Office, a young and promising Conservative back-bencher from the House of Commons who had just got his foot on the lowest rung of the ministerial ladder.

On an island where striking power workers had made the supply of power sporadic and which had been facing hunger as trade unionists in Trinidad and Barbados blocked supplies in solidarity with strikers in Grenada the ceremonies were a sad farce.

Bishop was arrested on the afternoon before independence and charged with attempted assassination. The police searched his house and reported they had found bombs, plans and telescopic sights for rifles. He was released on bail after two nights in detention.

The miserable day, which had been selected by Gairy because he regarded two and seven as his lucky numbers, was rounded off by a firework display from Fort George. Three tons of British fireworks, which had been smuggled past dockworkers in Barbados who were refusing to handle cargo for Grenada and which had cost the Grenadian treasury £3,000, were let off, generating some of the only light to be seen on an otherwise darkened island. Just before the celebrations started the management of the Holiday Inn decamped, leaving the keys and the responsibility for the independence banquet in the hands of the Danish pastry cook.

As the reins of power in Grenada began to fall out of the British hands which had held them for two centuries, the island began to attract attention from the government of the most powerful country in the region, the United States.

The United States had enunciated its desire for a controlling interest in the Western Hemisphere on 2 December 1823 when President James Monroe sent a message to Congress in Wash-

54

ington in which he declared that European powers had no right to extend their 'system' to the New World. At the time of its enunciation it was something of an empty statement in that the government in Washington, scarcely half a century old, had neither the military power nor the diplomatic leverage to enforce it. And indeed it was not enforced. The European powers continued to intervene, wherever and whenever they liked, in a hemisphere Monroe had, a trifle presumptuously, sought to arrogate to US influence. The French blockaded the Mexican port of Veracruz when the Mexicans could not pay their bills in 1838 and, in the 1860s, set up a puppet régime there under the Emperor Maximilian. Britain extended its influence in Nicaragua and in the Bay Islands off the coast of Honduras and consolidated its hold on British Honduras, now Belize. After a period of indecision it took control of the Falkland Islands in 1833. Spain mounted several expeditions to try and reconquer some of the American empire it had lost after the Napoleonic Wars. In 1861 it resumed sovereignty over the Dominican Republic adding it briefly to the rump of empire it still controlled in Cuba and Puerto Rico. Sweden maintained a hold over St Barthelemy and Denmark over three of the Virgin Islands. The Dutch controlled some of the Antilles and Dutch Guiana. The French had French Guiana and Guadeloupe and Martinique.

The US did nothing to prevent European manoeuvres in the Western Hemisphere because there was nothing it could do. As US power and influence increased, however, successive governments in Washington looked back to what had become known as the Monroe Doctrine as a justification of an increasingly active role in the Hemisphere in general and the Caribbean in particular.

Secretary of State Richard Olney reflected the growing self-assurance of the US when, in 1895, he reminded Britain of the Monroe Doctrine, commenting: 'Today the United States is practically sovereign in this continent, and its fiat is law upon the subjects to which it confines its superposition.'

In 1898 President McKinley threw his country into war with Spain which had been facing decades of guerilla warfare with nationalist guerrillas in Cuba. In a short, sharp action he won for Washington Cuba and Puerto Rico in the Caribbean and the Philippines and Guam in the Pacific, as if to demonstrate the correctness of Olney's boast.

Cuba was allowed formal independence but, under the Platt Amendment, the US reserved to itself the right to restrict Cuba's foreign borrowing and to intervene on the island when it felt 'orderly government' was being threatened.

The US conquest of Cuba was the first of thirty-three military interventions in the Hemisphere which were to take place before the invasion of Grenada. All were to take place in the Spanish- and French-speaking Caribbean region.

The expansive self-confidence of the age of McKinley and Theodore Roosevelt, tinged as it was with jealousy of the British Empire, was well exemplified in the work of one George W. Crichfield who, in his book *American Supremacy: The Rise and Progress of the Latin American Republics and Their Relations to the United States under the Monroe Doctrine*, wrote:

Now, what shall be said of Venezuela, Colombia, Ecuador, Bolivia, Santo Domingo, and Haiti, and the rest of Central America? . . .

It is a waste of time to argue in connection with these States about sovereign rights. The United States should take immediate possession of each and every one of them, without waiting for a pretext. It should govern them in precisely the same way as it governs other territory of the United States . . . With the United States in control of South America, I venture to predict that within ten years we could take a Pullman car at Maracaibo and go straight through to Buenos Ayres without change, and in ten years longer it might be that we could step into another car and go to New York. Under the present régime such conditions would not be brought about in ten thousand years . . .

If the United States were to take possession of the whole of the Western Hemisphere, from the Rio Grande to Cape Horn, the total area of its territory would be only about equal to that of the British Empire, and its population not more than one third as great.

What Englishmen can do Americans can do. The United States, with vastly greater territory and population, is as truly a breeding place of creative energy, of originating and productive enterprise, as England or any other country.

In such a political atmosphere Theodore Roosevelt came to the presidency in 1901 and, in 1904, pronounced his corollary to the Monroe Doctrine:

Chronic wrongdoing or an impotence which results in a general loosening of the ties of civilized society, may in America, as elsewhere, ultimately require intervention by some civilized nation, and in the Western Hemisphere the adherence of the United States to the Monroe Doctrine may force the United States, however reluctantly, in flagrant cases of such wrongdoing or impotence, to the exercise of an international police power.

The year before, Roosevelt had prepared the way for his country to take strategic control of the Caribbean by encouraging a group of separatists in the neglected Colombian province of Panama to set themselves up as an independent republic which was instantly recognized by Washington. By 1914 US engineers had completed the Panama Canal started by the Frenchman de Lesseps and the US controlled the waterway between the Atlantic and the Pacific and took under its control, effectively as a colony, a strip of land bordering it, the Panama Canal Zone.

Roosevelt's successor as President, William Howard Taft, set out US ambitions as follows in 1912:

The day is not far distant when three Stars and Stripes at three equidistant points will mark our territory: one at the North Pole, another at the Panama Canal and the third at the South Pole. The whole hemisphere will be ours in fact

57

as, by virtue of our superiority of race, it already is ours morally.

Five years later Washington bought from Denmark St Thomas, St John and St Croix in the Virgin Islands archipelago for 25 million gold dollars.

When Franklin Roosevelt was elected in 1933 the 'Big Stick' strategy enunciated by Theodore Roosevelt three decades before gave way to a 'Good Neighbour Policy' in which Washington sought to influence the countries of the Hemisphere politically rather than militarily. The Platt Amendment regulating Cuban life was abrogated and US Marines who had been occupying Haïti to collect debts owed to the US were withdrawn.

When the Second World War came the US was in an excellent position to demonstrate its physical control of the region. After the invasion of France in 1940 the Banque de France sent a large quantity of gold by warship to Martinique for safekeeping. The US Navy joined with the Royal Navy in a blockade of Martinique and Guadeloupe which were ruled by a French admiral answering to the Vichy Government. The two islands were brought to the edge of starvation.

Hitherto US influence had usually been confined to those parts of the Caribbean in which Britain did not have any interest but, in 1941, the US began to exert military control even in the British Caribbean. Under a deal worked out between Roosevelt and Winston Churchill, the US provided Britain with fifty badly needed destroyers for the Royal Navy in exchange for 99-year leases in eight British territories in the Western Hemisphere including Jamaica, Antigua, St Lucia and Trinidad.

In his message to Congress Roosevelt declared:

This is the most important action in the reinforcement of our national defence that has been taken since the Louisiana Purchase. Then, as now, considerations of safety from overseas attack were fundamental.

The value to the Western Hemisphere of these outposts is beyond calculation.

In addition to getting bases in the British Caribbean, the US acquired rights to build army, navy and air force bases on the Dutch islands of Curaçao and Aruba.

In March of the following year London and Washington joined together to establish the Anglo-American Caribbean Commission through which both governments co-operated in overseeing the politics of the region and gave some gentle encouragement to the most cautious social reforms. The Commission carried out a number of schemes which ranged from recruiting West Indian labourers for work in the US, to running a schooner pool and beaming US popular music and opinions to the region on the West Indian Radio Newspaper. In 1946 France and the Netherlands joined the Commission which was then renamed the Caribbean Commission.

With a weakened Britain fully stretched elsewhere in the world Washington at the end of the Second World War had undeniably become the paramount power in the region.

It was not long after the end of the war that the US became involved in the Cold War in the Caribbean. In 1951 Jacobo Arbenz was elected to the presidency of Guatemala and had, among his advisers, men of Communist sympathies. In 1954 he took delivery of a consignment of arms from Czechoslovakia and, later the same year, he was toppled by a right-winger with the assistance of the CIA.

Five years later Fidel Castro took power in Cuba and, shortly after, initiated a process which was to make Cuba the Soviets' closest ally in the Western Hemisphere. The then Vice-President Richard Nixon was the first to make a formal connection between Castro's challenge and Monroe's words. In *The Challenge We Face* Nixon wrote:

Recently there has been much concern expressed from time to time over the danger of Communism, in Cuba particularly, but also elsewhere in the American hemisphere . . . For Communism to come to any one of the American re-

59

publics is the very foreign intervention to which the Monroe Doctrine referred.

The following year President John Kennedy, who had criticised the Eisenhower-Nixon administration for being too soft in its treatment of Cuba, authorized the Bay of Pigs invasion of Cuba which ended so disastrously for the US. In 1962, raising the stakes, Castro agreed that the Soviet Union should install a missile base in the island. Kennedy this time won his encounter with Castro, forcing the withdrawal of the missiles in the autumn of that year.

As the confrontation with Cuba started in 1960, Kennedy delivered a warning about US willingness to act in the Caribbean which was to foreshadow many of the statements put out in Washington at the time of the invasion of Grenada.

'But', he said in an address of 20 April that year, 'a nation of Cuba's size is less a threat to our survival than it is a base for subverting the survival of other free nations throughout the Hemisphere. It is not primarily our interest or our security but theirs which is now, today, in the greater peril. It is for their sake as well as our own that we must show our will.'

British Guiana (since independence from Britain in 1965 known as Guyana) was in 1964 and 1965 the scene of Anglo-American co-operation in the halting of one Moscow-line Communist leader. Dr Cheddi Jagan, leader of the People's Progressive Party, won the election of 1961 but was removed from office by the British government after his refusal to resign in December 1964. Jagan did not accept that he had been defeated in the 1964 general elections whose rules had been altered from a first-past-the-post system to proportional representation, after much consultation between London and Washington, in order to favour Jagan's pro-Western rival Forbes Burnham. Burnham took his country to independence and, for decades continued to rule Guyana.

The events in Guatemala and Cuba – though not those in British Guiana which went relatively unnoticed by the US public – taken against the background of the consolidation of Stalinist régimes in the Soviets' client states in Eastern

60

Europe and the North Korean invasion of South Korea in 1950, served to raise the sensitivities of successive administrations with regard to the Caribbean. They also kept alive in those sections of US public opinion that took an interest in foreign affairs the belief that the area was 'Uncle Sam's backyard'.

In 1965 the Johnson administration had no hesitation in sending the marines into Santo Domingo in support of a right-wing junta. He did so in contravention of the Charter of the Organization of American States which Washington had been instrumental in setting up as a forum for hemispheric dialogue. Nor did it appear to matter to Johnson that in crushing the forces of Colonel Francisco Caamaño Deñó he was crushing a constitutionalist movement seeking to re-establish in the Dominican Presidency a man, Professor Juan Bosch, who had been fairly elected and unconstitutionally toppled by ambitious right-wingers.

Nor had Washington's ideological rivals forgotten the Caribbean.

With the consolidation of Soviet power, Moscow was not content to abandon the region to capitalism, as it made clear in the Comintern directives to the Mexican Communist Party of 21 August 1923:

> The capitalist development of North America and the backward economic and social development of the countries of Latin America determine the political attitude of the United States towards the countries of the South. The drying up of the purchasing power of Europe is forcing American products into the South American markets. In the American capitalist press one notices a stronger imperialist tendency towards the South than ever before. What has been done in the West Indies and in Central America, can be tried in Mexico and South America as well . . . But the conception is still lacking of the fight for freedom for all the oppressed masses in the West Indies, in Central America and in South America, against the imperialism of the oil magnates and

61

industrial barons of Wall Street . . . But the European revolution shall triumph.

We expect the workers of all American countries to contribute to this victory. We expect you to fight against the efforts of the counter-revolution to recruit the white and coloured fascisti and unemployed of America; the fight against the attempt to set the machinery in motion for the defeat of the European revolution; we expect you to control the railways and ships in order to prevent them from coming to the assistance of European reaction . . .

The Russian Revolution is the heroic prelude to the World Revolution. The victory of the working classes in the most important countries of Europe assures the victory of the proletariat in all countries. But the destruction of the last stronghold of capitalist imperialism, the overthrow of the North American bourgeoisie, is the task of the workers and peasants of all the American countries.

Having delivered themselves of those instructions the Soviets let the Caribbean part of the British Empire slumber on. Parties more or less compliant with Moscow's wishes sprang up in the Spanish and Portuguese speaking republics. In Argentina the party came into existence as early as 1918, in Chile in 1921, in Cuba in 1925. The Dominican Republic, however, could not field a Communist Party till 1942.

They did not change the face of Latin American society. For long periods most of them were proscribed. During the Second World War some struggled into coalition with non-Communist parties and achieved some glimmer of respectability as the USSR moved into alliance with the Western allies against Hitler. In some republics they tried to stage insurrections or putsches. In El Salvador an abortive rising in January 1932 was put down with immense ferocity by the right in a bloodbath which cost perhaps 20,000 lives and which left scars on Salvadorean society which are still present today. In 1935 Communists led risings in the poor northeast of Brazil and in Rio de Janeiro. They failed and brought the party little popular sympathy.

In the British-ruled Caribbean the Communists achieved little or nothing at all. The labour riots that Butler led in Trinidad and similar outbreaks in St Kitts and Jamaica owed nothing to Communist inspiration. Moscow, which had provided inspiration for Latin American Communists, seemed to have little to offer to the black workers and peasants of the British Empire. If they were political inspired by anyone – and most times they were politically inspired by no one – West Indian workers looked to trade unionists who could combine an ability to put a little more money in their pockets with a capacity to infuse in them some racial self-respect in a racist colonial society.

The appeal of Moscow's Communism was not helped by the feeling that revolutionaries in other parts of the world had a duty to subordinate their struggle to the preservation of Communism in the Soviet Union.

It was not until the advent to power in 1959 of Fidel Castro and his subsequent embracing of Marxism-Leninism that Communism began to take on a concrete appeal to the countries of what was beginning to be called the Third World.

One of the first steps on this road was the setting up of Tri-Continental Conferences.

The first Tri-Continental Conference was held in Havana in January 1966 and there Castro laid out his ideas for pushing ahead with revolution in the poorer countries. The Soviets gave the impression of being dragged along in the Cuban wake. Their delegate to the Tri-Continental Conference, S.R. Rashidov, struggled hard to maintain his country's credentials as an activist revolutionary power in the face of impatient criticism from the Cubans. When he addressed the Conference he said:

I wish to stress that the Soviet delegation has come to this conference with the objective of facilitating in every way the unification of the anti-imperialist forces of the three continents to lend still greater scope and still greater effectiveness to our common struggle against imperialism and neo-colonialism headed by the United States of America . . .

63

We express our solidarity with the struggle of the people in British, French and Dutch Guianas and the Antilles, with the struggle of the people of Puerto Rico. We are certain that the struggle of these peoples will lead them to their cherished goal, national independence.

A more theoretic approach to the question of revolution was set out in *Pravda* on 19 March 1968 by Professor Volsky of the Latin American Institute, which the Soviets set up in 1961 under the aegis of the Soviet Academy of Sciences. The Cuban revolution showed, he said, that 'the leadership of people's anti-imperialist revolutions in the developing countries can be assumed by revolutionary-democratic popular masses.' A touch patronisingly he continued:

However, the realisation of the far more complex goals and tasks of the socialist revolution and the profound reconstruction of the whole society on new principles calls for leadership on the part of the vanguard party of the working class, well armed with Marxist-Leninist theory.

Underlying Volsky's remarks was the assumption that Castro did the easy part in storming into Havana with the support of much of the population but that he was at a loss when it came to exercising the power he had won.

Among the ingredients for lasting success of a liberation movement, Volsky went on to say, were:

the strengthening and consolidation of the revolutionary political vanguard and its ability creatively to elaborate a correct strategy, a clear-cut and principled political line and flexible tactics:

the struggle for unity of action of the working class and the overcoming of dissociation into various trade union associations:

the overcoming of the gap between the struggle of the working masses of the city and those of the countryside and

64

the organisation of an effective alliance of workers and peasants:

the enlistment in active political struggle on the side of the revolutionary forces of broad strata of the population that are potential allies of these forces:

the expansion of co-operation between the progressive forces and those political trends that are followed by quite broad strata of the working population. The platform of such co-operation could be the struggle for profound social reforms, against the dominance of imperialism and for the broadening of relations with all countries in the world.

Castro's experience in government demonstrated the reasons for Volsky's emphasis on the need to get the praxis of ideology correct. Before he came to power in January 1959 Castro himself had not been a member of Cuba's Moscow-line Communist Party, the Partido Socialista Popular (PSP or Popular Socialist Party). He led the Movimiento 26 de Julio (M-26 or July 26 Movement) whose origins were in the youth politics of Havana. Castro's group was condemned several times as 'adventurist' by the PSP which for its part had had a history of tactical alliances with the right-wing Batista dictatorship which Castro overthrew.

A year after the January 1959 revolution all parties which did not support the Castro government were banned and the following year the PSP, M-26 and the Revolutionary Student Directorate were merged in the Organizaciones Revolucionarias Integradas (ORI or Integrated Revolutionary Organisations). In March 1962 the ORI was renamed the Partido Unido de la Revolución Socialista (PURS or United Party of the Socialist Revolution). This, in its turn, was reconstituted in October 1965 as the Partido Comunista de Cuba (PCC or Communist Party of Cuba). Years were to go by, however, before the PCC held its first party congress which had been promised for the end of 1966.

The various transmogrifications of the Castro movement did not alter the fact that the island was governed basically on the fiat of a revolutionary leader whose immense personality dominated every aspect of Cuban life. The early hesitancies about what the Cuban revolutionary government was, who was to run it and how it was to be run were to be repeated in Grenada after Maurice Bishop and the NJM took power there.

As might have been expected, the Soviets sought a greater formalisation of government in Cuba, particularly after the economic difficulties the island suffered in the early 1970s and Cuban calls for increasing amounts of Soviet aid.

In the early 1970s experiments were carried out in various Cuban provinces with the idea of Poder Popular (Popular Power), a network of local consultative committees created to monitor the work of government – though not, of course, to challenge its political power. The creation of a nationwide Poder Popular system coincided in 1975 with the calling of the first ever PCC party congress. It had taken revolutionary Cuba sixteen years to work out a formalised system of government and that after much Soviet prodding. And, even after 1975, Castro remained overwhelmingly the most important cog in the machine.

Whatever the state of Cuba's ideological health, Castro's commitment to fighting US influence, particularly in the Caribbean region, was clear from 1960. One of the earliest and most rousing declarations of revolutionary commitment, the First Declaration of Havana passed by 'The National General Assembly of the People', roundly condemned US policy and called for the liberation of Latin America from Washington's influence. It made no mention, however, of the European colonies in the Caribbean and did not specifically condemn the European colonialist powers.

That omission was partially corrected by Che Guevara in the speech he delivered to the UN General Assembly in December 1964, when he said:

We must as well draw attention to the fact that the principle of peaceful co-existence does not bear with it the right to mock the people's will, as is happening in the case of so-called British Guiana, in which the government of Prime Minister Cheddi Jagan has been the victim of all sorts of pressures and manoeuvres and the moment of giving it independence has been delayed in the search for methods which would allow the wishes of the people to be mocked and ensure the docility of a government different from the present one put there by shady dealings, so as thereafter to grant a neutered liberty to this piece of American soil.

Conscious perhaps that the smaller islands of the Caribbean were proceeding towards independence in a much more peaceful, not to say gentlemanly, way than Cuba herself got her independence from Spain, conscious perhaps also that there was little enough Marxist-Leninist straw in the region to make revolutionary bricks and aware that Britain, in particular, was at least as eager to lay down the burden of governing the Caribbean as some of the West Indians were to grasp their independence, the Cuban leadership never made a great issue of hurrying Britain out of the region.

Nevertheless, as the Gairy Government made its way to independence in 1974 harassed by the NJM opposition, all the actors in the regional drama – Cuba, the Soviet Union, the United States and Britain – were well rehearsed in their parts. Cuba saw the opportunity of eventually allying itself with the new political movements which sprang up in the 1970s, not just in Guyana and Grenada but also in Trinidad, St Vincent, St Lucia, Antigua and Jamaica. Governments friendly to Cuba would have reduced Havana's regional isolation. Just as important for Havana, they would bolster Cuba's position in the Soviet bloc where Castro had taken on himself the task of pushing the concrete and immediate interest of the Third World in a body which at times appeared all too preoccupied with the concerns of middlingly prosperous Eastern European countries.

At first Cuba moved cautiously, appearing to value diplomatic contacts with established governments in Barbados, Guyana, Jamaica and Trinidad over contacts with more radical groups.

The Soviet Union and Cuba, however, saw potential for making trouble for a US administration if Washington were ever tempted, for instance, to take too close an interest in the affairs of Eastern Europe. The US administration, conscious of how much electoral damage the Eisenhower Government had suffered for 'allowing Cuba to go Communist' was committed to halting the advance of Marxism-Leninism or indeed of any more mild régimes which might challenge Washington's hegemony in the area. At the same time, Washington had for centuries seen the British flag flying over most of the English-speaking Caribbean and was unused to thinking that a Commonwealth Caribbean country could be a source of trouble for a US administration.

Writing in 1972, as Grenada was in the run-up to its independence, Lincoln Gordon, a former Assistant Secretary of State for Inter-American Affairs under Johnson, commented:

Towards the newly independent or semi-independent units, however, there is ambivalence in American attitudes. This is true equally of the British Commonwealth Caribbean and the Netherlands and French areas. In the US Congress, for example, the question is often raised why, if external help is needed in the form of aid or special market arrangements, it should not come from the former or present metropoles in Europe rather than the United States.

Against that aloof view, there are factors forcing the development of American policy into a more positive mould than mere watchful waiting. The most important such factor is concern for strategic security. But there are also changing economic patterns tending towards increased American involvement: growing trade, investment, tourism, and to some extent migration. There are also growing cultural exchanges . . .

In the Commonwealth Caribbean, the result is an effort to develop a collective policy conjointly with Canada and the United Kingdom.

In the mid-1970s, when Grenada was going independent, Britain stood ready to do anything that would relieve her of Caribbean responsibilities and that did not cost too much. As far as Grenada in particular was concerned officials were privately worried about where Gairy with his record for irresponsibility, the activities of the Mongoose Gang and political cunning would take the country. At the same time they were relieved that the island was not going independent under the NJM which they looked on as excessively left-wing.

Gairy's achievement of independence for the island undoubtedly gained him support in Grenada, or at least prevented his stock falling faster than it might have done. Grenada was the first Associated State to achieve independence and its new status put it on a par, in theory at least, with Trinidad and Tobago and Barbados, and several steps ahead of St Vincent and the other small islands still dependent on Britain.

Gairy soon made it clear who his foreign friends were. Having secured Grenada's seat in the United Nations – where he sought the establishment of a study group on Unidentified Flying Objects – the Prime Minister sought membership of the Organization of American States, the *sine qua non* for entry to the Inter-American Development Bank. The IDB, like the World Bank to which Grenada was admitted, was seen as an important source of development funds.

In the event Gairy was disappointed. The application for IDB membership did not prosper and Grenada had to be satisfied with receiving funds second-hand through the Caribbean Development Bank.

Two years after independence Gairy went on visits to Chile and South Korea. In Santiago he asked General Pinochet for money though he did not submit much in the way of development projects. In Korea General Pak Chung Hee received him.

The following year relations with the Pinochet dictatorship blossomed. At 11.08 a.m. on Sunday 2 October 1977 a Chilean Hercules transport touched down at Pearls airport. Ten cases were unloaded, nine of them bearing the mark, 'Ministry of Health (Chile) to General Hospital Saint George (Grenada), Medical Supplies.'

Strangely, the acting chief medical officer, Dr Leonard Commissiong, denied any knowledge of any Chilean medical supplies and the storekeeper confirmed that none had been expected or received. Lieutenant-Colonel Winston Massanto, the head of the Grenada Defence Force, the chief 'Green Beast', commented 'All information relative to the Army is restricted.' The Ministry of External Affairs would not say anything and the Hercules flew off the next day. Bishop said the cargo was arms.

The Hercules arrived at Pearls within weeks of the appearance of the 3,673-ton barquantine *Esmeralda* with a complement of 340 men. On 30 August Captain Jorge Davanzo gave a reception for the Governor-General, Gairy and a hundred other guests in St George's harbour. One officer mendaciously but cheerfully denied that the ship had ever been used as a prison ship in the days following the military putsch against President Salvador Allende four years before.

Before long two members of the Grenada Defence Force, Fitz Abraham and Ian La Crette were in Santiago for training with a force which had the most noisome reputation for brutality in South America.

Gairy also strengthened relations with the Duvalier régime in Haïti.

As the relationship with Chile expanded St George's was host in July 1977 for the annual conference of the Organization of American States. As at the time of independence, the opportunity of parading their objections to the Gairy government was seized on by the opposition. Despite the government's decision not to allow the demonstration the NJM went ahead with its plans. The police broke up the protests with gunfire and the NJM acquired a second martyr, the 17-year-old Alister Strachan. As the police attacked protesters in Market Square in St George's they paid particular attention to Strachan. As they chased him he dived into the sea off the esplanade near the main police station and Gairy's men fired at him as he tried to swim away. His body was later washed up on the shore.

The Pinochet régime claimed the new relationship would help to counter Cuban aid to the Manley government in Jamaica.

Towards the end of 1976 the NJM acquired a new member who, from then on, was to leave an indelible mark on it. Bernard Coard was the son of a government official in St George's. He got a degree at Brandeis University in Massachusetts before moving to the University of Sussex in England where he worked at the Institute of Development Studies. While in Britain he wrote a report on the incidence of black children of normal intelligence in schools for the sub-normal.

As the most powerful intellect among the two score of full members of the NJM, on his arrival he had an immediate effect and he was quickly recognised as the ideological powerhouse within the movement.

It was his influence that started the shift of the NJM from the position of barely defined populistic nationalism that it had adopted at its foundation. Having been close to the British Communist Party during his time at Sussex he brought a good deal of Marxist-Leninist rigour to the political debate in Grenada.

Coard took care to gain the ideological and personal loyalties of younger members of the party. He invited them to take part in a Marxist study group, the Organization for Education and Liberation, OREL. Liam James, Ewart Layne, Leon Cornwall, Chris Stroude and John Ventour were among a group of about eighteen who gathered for regular readings of Leninist texts and discussion of Leninist praxis. In his task of instilling greater ideological content into NJM he was helped by his Jamaican-born wife, Phyllis, a member of the prosperous Evans family who are large shareholders in the company which produces the Tia Maria coffee liqueur. A strong feminist, plump and bespectacled, Phyllis Coard was the antithesis of the Gairy glamour-girl type of womanhood. She often appeared to care little for her personal appearance.

The roots of the OREL group are to be found, according to some Grenadians, in the classrooms of Presentation College and St Joseph's Convent, the bastions of Catholic boys' and girls' education in Grenada. The brothers at Presentation College did their best to foster self-reliance among their pupils

71

and the college was one of the first to introduce student councils where the boys were encouraged to take a share in planning the life of the scholastic community.

It was in such an atmosphere that there emerged in the early 1970s a group called the Joint Organization of Youth which came together spontaneously, without the promptings of the masters, to discuss the development of the life of the church. One participant recalled that the subject matter was advanced for the time, the application of the decisions of the Second Vatican Council and similar subjects which have since become commonplace but which in 1972 and 1973 were a few years in advance of their time. Among those who gathered periodically in a room underneath the Catholic cathedral, a few yards down the hill from the College, were Liam 'Owusu' James, Basil 'Akee' Gehagen and Ewart Layne's brother Raymond. JOY did not survive long but it gave the generation of teenagers who took part in it their first taste of discussion and study groups which they were continually to experience from then on. Before fading, JOY opened its councils to girls from St Joseph's and to boys from the Grenada Boys Secondary School.

JOY was only one of scores of youth groups which appeared to pullulate on Grenada in the mid-1970s and which came together annually in the Grenada Assembly of Youth (GAY).

James and Gehagen, joined now by Nazim Burke and Leon Cornwall, were to reappear a year or so later in OREL.

Among the members of the OREL group there grew up a sense of ideological and personal commitment which was to be enormously influential in the future of the NJM.

The impact of the arrival of Coard on the Movement was somewhat cushioned by the fact that he had not been a founding member and, absent from Grenada, he had not lived through the beatings and ill treatment that the others had suffered.

He had not acquired the fame that Bishop had acquired with his easy manner, oratorical gifts and work in the courts for those who fell afoul of Gairy. Though in no sense a dour personality, Coard did not have the gift of arousing spontaneous sympathy with his hearers that Bishop enjoyed.

Though Bishop was never a member of the OREL group

72

there is no reason to believe that he remained completely un-affected by the arrival in NJM ranks of this powerful new intellectual force.

In December 1976 new elections were called. The NJM decided to fight them as there seemed a reasonable chance that this time the electorate would finally turn against Gairy and the GULP. A coalition was formed between Blaize's GNP, the NJM and the United People's Party, a small group led by Winston Whyte who had once been a Gairyite but who had split with him when Whyte was not renominated to a con-stituency which he had several times won successfully for GULP. The three groups formed the People's Alliance, the NJM field-ing seven of the fourteen Alliance candidates, the GNP five and the UPP two. The distribution of the nominations dem-onstrated how the NJM had overtaken the GNP as the leading opposition force, despite the banning of its newspaper the *New Jewel* and its lack of access to Radio Grenada.

Once again GULP was able to demonstrate that it was able to command an electoral majority. Gairy, despite everything, still had a strong personal following and some Grenadians doubtless felt it more politic to vote GULP and work for the re-election of a man who had built himself up a position of great power in Grenada. The result gave the Alliance only 48.5 per cent of the vote and six seats, the NJM winning three, the GNP two and the UPP the remaining one. GULP took the remaining nine, some by only the slenderest of majorities. The opposition appealed against the decisions in a number of con-stituencies to the courts but the appeals were rejected. Though there was some degree of foul play, in the opinion of one lawyer who helped to prepare the appeals, their rejection was justified and it was difficult to prove that the amount of interference with the vote was sufficient to have swung the results away from the Alliance and in favour of GULP.

In any event Bishop was returned to Parliament and became leader of the opposition as member for South-East St George's, a seat which he won by a majority of 110 votes.

Bishop scraped home because he had decided to stand in one of the seats which was marginal as far as the NJM, or

73

indeed the Alliance, was concerned. The party considered it to be ninth on their list. The most promising seat, the town of St George's, was allocated to Coard. This was the NJM plum, as certain to return an NJM candidate as Carriacou was certain to return Herbert Blaize, a native of that island, for the GNP.

In later years Bishop's decision to take South-East St George's and leave the safer seat to Coard was taken as an example of Bishop's characteristic generosity. It is also the case, however, that OREL and Coard had had grave reservations about fighting an election anyway, certainly in such heterogenous company as the NJM allies in the Alliance, and the designation of Coard to the safest NJM constituency on the island may have been the price that Coard exacted for giving his blessing to an electoral campaign. At the same time it is also argued that OREL had no option but to accompany the NJM on its electoral path. OREL could not have survived on its own, Bishop supporters have argued, in isolation from the bulk of the NJM.

Parliament did not prove to be the platform for debate and denunciation that the NJM had anticipated. In its first seven months of life it met only once, to pass the budget. The party turned its attention to building up a trade union base which might eventually begin to match the Gairyite GMMWU and the Seamen and Waterfront Workers Union which had close links with the US AFL-CIO trade union confederation.

As NJM members sought positions within existing unions, Vincent Noel, a member of the NJM Political Bureau, formed the Bank and General Workers Union. This hoped to gather strength as workers at Barclays Bank went into dispute with their employers. But despite the wish of the Barclays workers to have the BGWU recognised as their negotiating body, the government continued to insist that the GMMWU was the recognized union.

The GMMWU, of which Gairy was President for Life, was acknowledged as the only representative for workers in the public sector.

As the fifth anniversary of independence came round in February 1979 the Grenada Council for Human Rights took stock of the first years and instanced a wide range of government violations of human rights:

opponents of the Government were beaten up when they met in public;

the ban by the Government on the use by the opposition of loudspeakers;

the muzzling of the press by reference to the post-independence Newspaper Act which demanded a deposit of EC$20,000 before any newspaper could be established;

the difficulties that people were experiencing in getting compensation for lands that the Government had taken over before and after independence.

The outlook, the Council said, was 'very sombre and gruesome'.

Economically the outlook was almost equally sombre and gruesome. In 1975 the current account of the balance of payments showed a surplus of US$500,000. By 1978 that had turned into a deficit of US$5.3 million. The flow of grants and loans to the Gairy administration was drying up and the foreign reserves were falling. The grant Grenada had been given by the British government on independence, some £2.5 million, was nearly exhausted. In December 1978 British officials went to Grenada to assess the economic situation and consider the case for more British aid. Gairy, however, had prejudiced his chances for more British aid by his involvement with the Pinochet dictatorship, not least because the British Minister for Overseas Development in the Labour government of the day, Dame Judith Hart, was an avowed opponent of the Chilean régime.

The mismanagement of the economy was recognised privately even by those merchants who on balance supported Gairy against the NJM or who were dependent upon his whim to maintain the prosperity of their businesses.

Gairy's drive to have the question of UFOs debated and examined by the United Nations certainly lost him credibility in the international financial institutions and among governments which might otherwise have given Grenada economic assistance. The amount of money the Gairy government was able to raise in grants and loans from abroad dropped from a peak of EC$8.7 million in independence year to EC$5.2 million in 1978.

As the first months of 1979 came, it was clear that the increasing corruption and brutality of the government – if not comparable in enormity to the conduct of Latin American governments in, say, Chile, El Salvador or Guatemala – was eroding the support Gairy had enjoyed for nearly three decades from the working people of Grenada. This erosion was all the more rapid now that the NJM had established itself as a credible alternative to Gairy rule.

For its part the NJM was on the alert for a moment in which it could bring about the fall of Gairy. Though now produced clandestinely the party newspaper, the *New Jewel*, sold well on the island and there was a nucleus of party supporters ready to fight if the occasion arose to eject Gairy.

The opportunity came on 12 March 1979.

CHAPTER FOUR

Revolutionary Monarchy

'It has to be admitted that the West Indian Negro is
ungracious enough to be far from perfect. He lives in
the tropics, and he has the particular vices of all who
live there, not excluding people of European blood.'
                    C.L.R. James
              The Future in the Present

At 4.15 a.m. this morning, the People's Revolutionary Army
seized control of the army barracks at True Blue. The barracks were burned to the ground. After half an hour of
struggle, the forces of Gairy's army were completely defeated and surrendered, and not a single member of the
revolutionary forces was injured.

Thus, in a broadcast on Radio Grenada, Maurice Bishop
announced the first *coup d'état* in modern times in the English-
speaking Caribbean and the advent of the Grenadian revolution
on 13 March 1979.
    The New Jewel Movement, six years old and with only forty-
five full members, had seized power from the hands of an
erratic and increasingly unpopular Sir Eric Gairy.
    Gairy had left the island the previous day for talks at the
UN in New York with Kurt Waldheim on Unidentified Flying
Objects and cosmic phenomena and Bishop felt sure he and
his NJM colleagues were about to be murdered. He said in
his first broadcast after the coup, 'The criminal dictator, Eric
Gairy, apparently sensing that the end was near, yesterday

fled the country, leaving orders for all opposition forces, including especially the people's leader, to be massacred.'

W. Richard Jacobs, for a time the Grenadian ambassador to Cuba and later the USSR, confirmed the existence of this fear by writing in September 1979, 'Gairy left Grenada for another one of his joy rides and issued instructions to his police, military, and paramilitary forces to exterminate the eight leaders of the NJM.' (But no one has ever shown that there was any truth in the allegation against Gairy.)*

Bishop, Coard and Whiteman went underground, changing their hideouts in St George's three times in three days. On 12 March the three met Austin and George Louison and completed plans for the following morning. That evening the 'defence wing' of the NJM was ordered to muster. Fifty of the seventy summoned appeared and forty-six were sent into battle.

On Monday 12 March Gairy flew to Barbados on the first leg of his journey to New York. At Grantley Adams International airport he was met by Frank Ortiz, the US Ambassador, before he boarded his plane for the flight northwards.

As he touched down the final hurried plans were being completed for his overthrow. As workers in the telephone exchange on the Carenage in St George's made sure the island was cut off from the outside world forty-six men were receiving their last instructions from the leaders of the NJM, Bishop, Coard, George Louison, Unison Whiteman and Hudson Austin, near the beach at Grand Anse. The operation was named Apple and had as its objective the capture of True Blue barracks, the principal base of Gairy's forces.

Austin had as his lieutenants Basil 'Akee' Gahagan and Leon 'Bogo' Cornwall. Einstein Louison and Ewart Layne were put in charge of small groups of men whose job was to cover the barracks from a distance while the assault went in under Austin's command.

In two cars and a small truck the group moved off. Eighteen of them had firearms – eight MI rifles, two .303 rifles, two

---

* (This sentence was included at the insistence of British libel lawyers. I did not write it.)

78

shotguns and a few revolvers were backed up by Molotov cocktails for those without guns. At four o'clock the attack went in, True Blue blazed and Gairy's men fled without firing a shot.

Leaving Gahagan and Cornwall at True Blue, Austin took his men off to capture Radio Grenada, a mile or so back towards St George's at Morne Rouge. Hearing the commotion at True Blue two of the three guards at the radio station fled and the one remaining quickly gave up his rifle on being confronted with Austin's tear gas pistol.

A desultory resistance was mounted at Fort George where policemen tried to defend their headquarters under the command of Gairy's particular associate, Senator Derek Knight.

They did not give in until 4 p.m. when they finally hoisted a white shirt on the flagpole of the fort. Five insurgents drove into Fort George where they found the policemen had piled their Second World War .303 rifles neatly in the inner courtyard and were willing to surrender. Austin saw to the strengthening of security at Fort George and gave out to his men some of the uniforms and boots that Gairy had received from Pinochet and, as a precautionary measure, Bishop ordered a curfew at 10 p.m. and the temporary closing of Pearls airport.

The coup was enormously popular with Grenadians and it seemed as if the whole of the island was coming out into the streets to celebrate.

By nightfall between fifty and sixty people were in custody. They included Herbert Preudhomme, Gairy's Deputy Premier who had broadcast a message that day calling on the supporters of the old régime to cease their resistance, nine other ministers, the acting commissioner of police, the superintendent of prisons and the manager of Radio Grenada.

With them were 'Hood', 'Spreeman', 'Heads', 'Pram' and Willie Bishop, members of Gairy's Mongoose Gang.

In his first broadcast, Bishop, who referred to himself as 'the people's leader', assured his listeners that 'all democratic freedoms, including freedom of elections, religious and political opinion, will be fully restored to the people'.

While Grenada rejoiced, there were immediate rumblings

from abroad. From New York, Gairy swore that he would soon be leading a counterattack that would put him back in the prime ministership which, he claimed, was constitutionally still his.

Milton Cato, Premier of the Associated State of St Vincent to the north, called on Britain to send troops to reverse the coup and put Gairy back.

By Wednesday a ministerial gathering was convened in Barbados to discuss the implications of the previous day's events.

Rejecting the Cato line the ministers of the Eastern Caribbean announced cautiously that there should be no outside interference in the affairs of Grenada but that 'the wider interests and unity of the area and of Grenada in particular require a return to constitutionality as soon as possible'. The following day George Louison, the emissary of the new government, was at the ministerial table in Barbados and there gave the ministers firm assurances that free elections would be held as soon as the electoral arrangements could be made.

That afternoon, Sir Paul Scoon, the Governor-General, made his first broadcast under the new dispositions.

Quiet, bespectacled, and in his mid-forties Scoon had only been Governor-General for a few months. He had been knighted only days before and transformed into Sir Paul Scoon, Knight Commander of the Order of St Michael and St George. Having fallen out with Grenada's first Governor-General, Sir Leo de Gale, who resigned in September 1979, Gairy had turned to Scoon as a trusty and discreet administrator who would occupy the post of a figurehead and would be unlikely to cause the Prime Minister any embarrassment.

Scoon's words were therefore listened to with particular interest. The fact that he uttered them at all was interesting in that it indicated that the People's Revolutionary Government was disposed to retain the monarchical system of government at least for the moment. In tones of ponderousness and well-honed euphemism which would have done credit to a small-town bank manager Scoon congratulated everyone on 'the calm and peaceful manner with which you greeted this period of change'. He added:

At the earliest time, and with the appropriate advice and co-operation, I shall do everything possible to ensure that we have a working arrangement of which all Grenadians can be justly proud . . . May God bless you all.

Ortiz was blunter. A letter from Barbados, where he was normally resident, said, 'We would view with displeasure any tendency on behalf of Grenada to develop closer ties with Cuba.'

The new Grenadian government was put out not just by this lecture from Ortiz (delivered within a month of it taking power) but also by US refusal to agree to block attempts by Gairy to get back into power. On 6 July 1979 *The Washington Post* carried a report that the National Security Council had considered a proposal to blockade the island. The establishment of diplomatic relations with Cuba on 14 April led to hostile references in the US press to the Bishop government and the State Department started warning travel agents that it was unsafe to go to Grenada.

The scene was now set for the playing out of that relationship between Bishop and Coard, the two chief men of the Grenadian revolution, which was to determine the course of the island's history up to the time of Bishop's murder on 19 October 1983 and, indeed, after.

The fact that Bishop, as we shall see, was to die at the hands of men loyal to Coard should not be extrapolated backward in time to colour judgements about the relationship between the two men and their ideas which was a subtle, complicated and shifting one.

As his first broadcast showed, Bishop considered himself the leader of the revolution. It was a revolution he had fought, thought, plotted, suffered and dreamt for. The New Jewel Movement was an organisation that no one had done more to create than he. His father had been killed by the opponents of the NJM, even though that father had never been a party member and can have had scant knowledge of its ideology. For nearly a decade he had been an important member of Grenadian society, recognized everywhere he went in St George's and in the countryside, beginning to be recognised in the streets of cities in other countries of the Caribbean. For nearly a decade he had appeared in court pleading the cases of clients, many of whom were in conflict with the Gairy government. He was confident of his powers of getting on with people and moving them to do what he wanted, whether that process of influencing them consisted in getting down to a good game of cards with them or orating at them from a public platform. Tall and handsome with a beautiful wife and two children he needed no convincing that he was attractive to women.

He was clearly vital to the NJM and its future development in Grenadian society. He was, however, neither a very acute political thinker nor a particularly good organiser. He was much more intuitive than he was intellectual, responding to people rather than ideas.

Coard was intellectually much the more powerful figure. He lived for Marxism-Leninism and was attracted to the form of it practised in the Soviet Union. He was as convinced of his intellectual powers as Bishop was of his physical powers. He was a man of many facets. He was capable of talking to almost any audience in terms they could understand and accept. In company he was affable and cheerful when that was needed. When he needed to be convincing and compelling he was able to demonstrate those qualities. He was able to command intense personal loyalty which matched anything Bishop could command. The youngsters whom he had recruited into his OREL study group were to be fanatically attached to him. He was single-minded and prepared to go to any lengths for the sake of the political ideals he believed in. Despite his undoubted charisma he did not have the island-wide following that Bishop had. His time at Brandeis and at Sussex had meant he had been absent during the heroic founding days of the NJM and its first battles. He was not recognised in the streets in the way that Bishop was.

During all but the last year of Bishop's life the two gave every sign of operating closely and harmoniously together. When opponents of Coard in the party tried to censure him in 1978 for 'recklessness' it was Bishop who came to his defence and helped to halt moves against him.

'Maurice charmed people: Bernard convinced them'. Thus a Grenadian friend of both men summed up their effect on others. Bishop told those he talked to what he thought and argued with them, if necessary, afterwards. Coard let his interlocutors speak, asking them questions about their opinions, before doing his best to convince them of the rightness of his own opinions. 'He always gave you the impression of taking your opinion very seriously and of not resting till he had got you round to his way of thinking.'

Yet, in this complicated relationship, it was inevitably Coard who influenced Bishop and the party while himself remaining impervious to influences from them. Coard was the grindstone and all the rest were so many knives to be sharpened – and blunted – as they came into contact with him. The trajectory of the party as it developed its increasingly Leninist character to the day when members of the Central Committee loyal to Coard gave orders for Bishop's execution bears witness to this fact. And, as an increasingly Leninist party was shaped by Coard, so the party shaped society, insofar as it could.

From 13 March 1979 to 19 October 1983 politics in Grenada were controlled by the New Jewel Movement. No other political grouping was allowed to organise or operate. The NJM was run by a Central Committee and the principal day-to-day decisions of the Central Committee were taken by a Political Bureau. Most, though not all, of those decisions were taken with the approval of one man, Prime Minister Maurice Bishop, who incarnated the revolution for Grenadians and foreigners alike.

Full membership of the party, which at the time that the NJM came to power included only forty-five people, was strictly controlled. The party itself chose those members of Grenadian society whom it wanted to recruit. Those the party wanted were invited to become applicant members. If their conduct was felt to be fitting applicant members were allowed to go forward as candidate members who, after two years' successful probation, would be accepted as full members of the party. By the end of 1983 the full members of the party numbered only about seventy. About 230 applicants and candidates were awaiting admission.

The Central Committee was made up of sixteen members and was officially the supreme policy-making body of the party. Its meetings took place in normal circumstances about every month. The eight man Political Bureau was, in practise, the governing body in Grenada, taking all urgent decisions. The NJM held no full congress during the time it ruled Grenada.

Throughout the Bishop era a handful of men took on themselves a growing number of increasingly complex responsibilities as they sought to extend the power of the state. The sheer amount of work this entailed and the psychological pressures it engendered was in large part responsible for the crisis and breakdown of the party in 1983.

The NJM was, therefore, structured closely on the model described by Lenin in the Soviet Union in 1920 and quoted by Daniel Shub in his biography:

We are afraid that the Party will be too large because to a ruling government inevitably gravitate careerists and scoundrels who only deserve to be shot. The Party is led by a Central Committee of nineteen people. The current work is done in Moscow by a small collegium, by the Organizational Bureau and by the Politburo . . . Out of this emerges a 'real oligarchy'! Not one important political or organisational question in our state institution is decided without the central committee of the Party.

As already noted, Bishop in his broadcast on the day of the coup described himself as the 'people's leader'.

To describe thus baldly the power structure in a party which controlled all government appointments and the forces of the state does no justice to the debate that ebbed and flowed within the NJM about the formal machinery that should exist to link the party with the mass of Grenadian society.

Within four days of the coup Bishop who, on the first day

had promised that 'all democratic freedoms, including freedom of election, religious and political opinion will be fully restored to the people', made it clear in the first press conference he gave that the process initiated by the NJM would be 'irreversible'.

From the first moment of its assumption of power the NJM showed itself desperately conscious of the dangers it ran of being forcibly overthrown, dangers it must have seen growing alarmingly as Reagan succeeded Carter in the White House and the US campaign against it grew.

In his first broadcast Bishop warned:

We know Gairy will try to organise international assistance, but we advise that it will be an international criminal offence to assist the dictator Gairy. This will amount to an intolerable interference in the internal affairs of our country and will be resisted with every ounce of our strength.

In his press conference on Friday 16 March 1979 Bishop again warned that Gairy had threatened to send a force 'by land, sea and air' to overthrow the revolution.

At the same time there was no move by the newly installed authorities formally to legitimise themselves in power either by the calling of a conventional election or by any swift move to set up the village councils which the NJM had put forward in its electoral programme at the 1976 elections.

Speaking on the first anniversary of the revolution to an audience in St George's which included Michael Manley, the hard-pressed Prime Minister of Jamaica and Daniel Ortega, co-ordinator of the Sandinista junta of Nicaragua, Bishop stated:

There are those (some of them our friends) who believe that you cannot have a democracy unless there is a situation where every five years, and for five seconds in those five years, a people are allowed to put an 'X' next to some candidate's name, and for those five seconds in those five years they become democrats, and for the remainder of the time, four years and 364 days, they return to being non-people

85

without the right to say anything to their government, without any right to be involved in running their country.

As to the establishment of some other formal system of assembly Bishop repeatedly said that the drafting of a constitution was a long and complicated process which demanded time and expertise that his government did not have. The NJM also advanced the argument that the process would involve discussion and inevitably dissension in a country which was menaced by the hostility of the most powerful nation on earth.

Such reasons were clearly not without their validity. The weightiest reason was, however, to be found perhaps in the fact that the party itself was balanced on the frontier between that Marxism-Leninism that Coard, its chief intellectual and principal ideologue, espoused and the more social democratic tendencies to be found in Bishop himself. The delicate ideological ambivalence was very clearly illustrated in the fact that the NJM sought admission to the international group of democratic socialist and labour parties, the Socialist International and, at the SI conference held in Madrid in 1981, achieved full membership while at the same time maintaining the closest political, economic and military relationship with an avowedly Marxist-Leninist government in Cuba. (Grenada voted on the Soviet side in the UN debate on the invasion of Afghanistan.)

In the economic sphere in 1979 no reasonable forecaster could have expected things to turn out better than they did. Despite heavy rains late in the year, which spoilt the outlook for some crops, and despite the damage that was done to tourism by the political upset and Washington's hostility, the island's economy grew by about 2 per cent.

Bernard Coard was a model of prudent caution at the finance ministry. A senior international banker who had dealings with him at this time recalled:

Affable and approachable, Coard was intellectually and operationally head and shoulders above his colleagues from the other islands in the Eastern Caribbean. Whereas even some of the more conservative governments in the region baulked at making the economic and political sacrifices demanded by the International Monetary Fund in exchange for its aid Coard was always willing to meet the IMF more than half way.

He also knew the way to get money quickly and efficiently out of the international lending agencies. While some of the other finance ministers would rant and rave about the bureaucracy of the lending banks, Coard saved his energies to understand the system and make it work for Grenada.

As a result Grenada, despite the hostility of the US, was not stuck for cash during the first year of the revolution.

A confidential memorandum prepared by the World Bank on Grenada circulated in May 1980 pointed out that the government had achieved a budget surplus in the first year of its revolution.

In exchange for a stand-by loan from the IMF which brought Grenada's borrowing from that source to EC$2.4 million the Bishop government got the IMF to train up new custom officers and tax inspectors. The government set up a budget division in the Ministry of Finance so that ministries should not spend more than was allotted to them. The IMF contributed an adviser here as well, with the result that Grenada's finances were better controlled than they ever had been. Monthly limits were set on departments' expenditure and every working day an account of what the government collected and paid out had to be submitted to Coard's ministry. Those government departments which by some miracle got away with overspending one month were reined in again the next.

As a result, the government 1979 budget registered a surplus of EC$2.6 million, compared with the EC$8.3 million deficit Gairy had chalked up the previous year and the EC$2.1 million surplus the World Bank had suggested. The government also cut the amount it had been borrowing from Barclays and other local banks and paid off some arrears that the Gairy government had owing to regional institutions such as the University of the West Indies. With the money it saved the government was able to finance capital projects which no one had thought Grenada would have been able to afford. In terms of good housekeeping the Bishop government in the first year of its revolution was doing a great deal better than many Western governments, the US included.

Conscious that the price of oil was higher than it had ever been in history and that every drop had to be imported the government set up an inter-ministerial committee which reported to cabinet on alternative energy sources and ways of saving fuel. As a result, in 1979 Grenada used 28 per cent less fuel than in the previous year.

Grenada's comparative poverty meant that little money could be spared to maintain school and hospital buildings and vehicles. The Bishop government spent what it thought it could afford on improving health and education.

The biggest development project of all, the Point Salines airport, was eventually got moving after decades of reports, assessments, reviews and other exercises in paper shuffling. The need had been clear for a long time. The World Bank memorandum pointed out:

> Last year's economic report identified air access as a major constraint on full utilization of existing capacity and further development of the (tourist) sector. Pearls Airport cannot accommodate international flights or night landings, and the LIAT feeder service is inadequate.

The cost of the project was US$45 million of which the Grenadians themselves were capable of providing only US$10 million. That sum of money was to buy Grenada a 'Class B' airport capable of taking medium- and long-haul jets such as DC-9s or Boeing 747s and 727s which could link the island directly with London, Toronto or New York and allow them to land at night. The runway was to be 9,000 feet long and 150 feet wide.

The new airport would not only help the tourist trade, it would also help the promotion of exports by allowing cargo aircraft to land and pick up Grenadian farm products and fly them to their destinations. It could also be of use to Trinidad as an alternative if that island's main airport at Piarco was shut. The ball started rolling after Bishop asked Castro for help on the project when he met him at the summit conference of the nonaligned movement in Havana in August 1979. Before the revolution was a year old the Cubans were landing their equipment on the island. Point Salines became one of the sights of Grenada. It became a favourite spot for weekend picnickers, the US medical students jogged round it and always attracted followers of that pastime of watching other people work.

For decades it had been realised that Point Salines, within a few miles of the capital, was the best site for an international airport. During the Second World War British engineers decided that the site was the best on the island but at the time Pearls on the east coast was chosen as the spot.

As the Grenadian tourist industry grew after the war the Point Salines site was again looked at and the British consulting engineers, Scott, Wilson, Kirkpatrick and Partners recommended it after conducting feasibility surveys. The fact that it was not built was one of the factors which disbarred St George's from being considered as the site of the capital of the West Indies Federation.

The Cubans, as they started work in 1979, were joined by Layne Dredging of Miami who employed thirty US technicians in building a causeway over the Hardy Bay section of the runway.

As the work progressed Grenadians were delighted. On 1 April 1981 a number of organisations, including the Grenada Chamber of Commerce, the Grenada Lawyers' Association and trade unions came together and passed a resolution to the effect that, 'Recognising the tremendous benefits and importance from an international airport, be it resolved that we, gathered here, wholeheartedly and fully support its construction.'

The Grenadians and Cubans were not the only ones interested in promoting the scheme. The Venezuelan government found some cash to help pay some labourers' wages and pledged a regular supply of diesel fuel, asphalt and petrol to help the project on its way. The British government's ears pricked up as it saw the prospect of a multimillion-pound contract in the offing for a British electronics manufacturer.

While the World Bank could not but give the government high marks for its enterprise and fiscal responsibility, it did its best to pressure the government away from left-wing policies. It expressed its disapproval of plans to set up state farms: the 1980 memorandum said:

> In the light of numerous experiences under widely different conditions in several countries, there is no reason to expect that the state-owned estates will achieve the economic development objective of maximizing productivity and output in agriculture.

On tourism the World Bank document remarked:

> The authorities have expressed interest in diversifying the tourism product to cater less exclusively to high income tourists seeking luxury-type accommodations. As a step in this direction, they propose to vest under a public corporation the hotel and other related properties confiscated from the former Prime Minister, and to operate them as medium-price hotels. At the same time the government is seeking financial assistance to construct two 300-room hotels to cater to the expected influx of visitors once the new airport is completed . . . The strategy to build large hotels remains to be justified.

On the government's relationship with private business the World Bank pressed the latter's case:

> Some actions of the government in its relation with the private sector have had the effect of increasing the lack of confidence about the government's attitude to private enterprise. Given that his outcome is undesirable in terms of the government's stated strategy for economic development,

it is urgent that a dialogue be established with the private sector, and that an investor's code be established.

In a broadcast on 18 September Bishop was able to claim some solid achievements for a revolution that, as he said, was only six months and five days old. More than 800 new jobs had been created, twenty miles of roads built and three new community centres started. The first fifty of 200 young farmers had completed an agricultural training course. Some 100 youngsters were about to leave for Cuba to be trained as fishermen and thirty-eight students would go there for university degree courses. Kenya and Tanzania had offered scholarships. Now that Grenada had paid some of its arrears to the University of the West Indies that institution would be taking more Grenadian students. One Grenadian in a thousand would be at university during the coming term. All children under five and all primary schoolchildren were receiving free milk. The number of primary schoolchildren receiving scholarships to secondary education had risen by more than half and the fees in secondary schools were being more cut by a third.

Women, Bishop claimed, were already benefiting from the proclamation of the principle of equal pay for equal work and everyone had benefited from the destruction of Gairy's Mongoose Gang and by better behaviour from the army and police. The northerly islands of Carriacou and Petit Martinique had benefited from better electricity supplies and improved health care.

'For the first time in the history of our country working people have the right to form or to join a trade union of their choice,' he added.

What to do with the fifty or so people taken into 'protective custody' by the revolutionaries on 13 March continued to be a headache for the government. Mortally anxious that they and others would combine with mercenaries such as those who had been active in Dominica or with the US government itself, the government was unwilling to let some of them out. Bishop announced on 16 March that more than half of them had been released the same day that they were arrested.

Others were kept in and were soon joined by more people whose actions the government had reason to fear.

From London, Amnesty International was soon expressing its concern about the situation. Bishop and AI had been in touch on penal matters for several years. The organisation in London had given help and encouragement to human rights groups in the island in Gairy times. The Caribbean Human Rights and Legal Aid Company with which Bishop was closely associated was involved with AI not only in questions of wrongful imprisonment but also with regard to the abolition of the death penalty. Under colonial laws the death penalty was mandatory for those found guilty of murder.

In April, July and August 1979 Amnesty expressed its concern about the continuing detention of people without charge by the government. Some were released but, with the commotion caused by the alleged conspiracy to stage an anti-Bishop coup in October and November, more people were detained.

A bomb blast at Queen's Park on 19 June 1980 caused another intake of detainees and the passing of People's Law 46, the Terrorism (Prevention) Law, 1980. Under this law the accused could be tried in the High Court by a single judge sitting without jury. Those convicted of causing deaths through the use of an explosive faced the death penalty. In the event four people were convicted and sentenced to death in November 1982. Bishop countered Amnesty's appeals to him to remember the days when he campaigned against the death penalty by saying frankly that he had changed his mind on the subject. One defendant, Roland Budhlall, acquitted on similar charges, was kept in detention after his acquittal.

The sentences were not carried out pending the outcome of action in the Appeal Court, a special court assembled from leading Caribbean lawyers when Grenada opted out of the West Indies Appeal Court. The Appeal Court had not delivered its verdict by the time the invasion came.

The main instrument used to detain suspects and keep them without charge was People's Law 8 which allowed the detention of anyone who 'has taken or has threatened to take or is reasonably suspected of intending to take action of a nature or on such a scale as is likely to endanger public safety or to deprive the community or any substantial portion thereof of supplies or services essential to life.'

Under the law a Preventive Detention Tribunal was established to make recommendations to the executive about the status of detainees. The Tribunal held hearings *in camera* and without legal representation being allowed to the detainee. The first sitting was held in April and May 1979 and a further one was held in September of the same year after which it was announced that it would meet every six months instead of every two months as originally planned. Another session was held in December 1980 but thereafter no more were held. The reviewing of cases was then done more informally by Bishop himself as Minister of the Interior.

Amnesty recorded at least one case of a detainee who had been released being picked up again.

On the last day of 1981, twenty-four detainees were released as a New Year gesture and on 16 November 1982 a further twenty-eight were released because the government declared they no longer constituted a threat to national security. About another sixty were released the following month. All those released had to surrender their passports and were to report to the police every two weeks.

By the time of the invasion there were around 100 people still in detention, though Bishop, in an interview with the *Trinidad Express* on 28 March 1983, had put the number at between thirty-five and forty.

The conditions the detainees were kept in at Richmond Hill Prison were said to be 'satisfactory but poor.' Allegations that the government was systematically ill-treating or torturing its prisoners which surfaced after the 13 March coup were later shown to be unfounded. Medical and dental visits were regularly provided though, after an escape attempt in December 1981, visits were banned and no religious services were allowed from then till April 1982.

It has been argued by opponents of the NJM that the Grenadian authorities were intent on keeping their enemies locked up whether there existed or not proof of their activities strong enough to convict them in a court of law.

At the same time there can be no doubt that the legal system in Grenada, as elsewhere in the Commonwealth Caribbean, was labouring under very great strains.

In his submission to the House of Commons Foreign Affairs Committee in May 1982 Professor Keith Patchett, a legal consultant to the Commonwealth Secretariat, commented:

It must be doubted whether any of these countries [the small island states of the Eastern Caribbean] is at present maintaining a legal service which is adequate to meet the constitutional and development demands of the individual states. More serious, there is clear indication that the present legal arrangements are totally inadequate for the fulfilment of their international responsibilities by those states which have achieved independence.

The technical difficulties of the administration of traditional justice were clearly, however, subordinate to the view that the revolution had its own justice. This was best expressed by Bishop on 19 June 1981 when he told a rally:

This is a revolution, we live in a revolutionary Grenada, this is a revolutionary condition, and there is a revolutionary legality, and they will have to abide by the laws of the revolution.

When the revolution speaks, it must be heard, listened to. Whatever the revolution commands, it must be carried out; when the revolution talks no parasites must bark in their corner. The voice of the masses must be listened to, their rules must be obeyed, their ideas must receive priority, their needs must be addressed; when the masses speak they must be heard. When the revolution orders, it must be obeyed. The revolution must be respected.

A gap was evidently opening up between the theories and rules Bishop had imbibed at Gray's Inn and the practise of law in revolutionary Grenada.

As the NJM struggled to get the country out of the chaos into which years of Gairyism had plunged it, it had high hopes that co-operatives would, with a little government assistance, be a major solution, especially for the unemployment problem. In 1980 People's Law 18 set up the National Agency for Co-operative Development (NACDA) to boost the co-ops. The idea was to encourage small groups of private entrepreneurs in the towns and put to use thousands of acres of idle land while at the same time offering a livelihood for the thousands of country boys who were out of a job.

It was a brave effort but it did not really succeed. Many co-ops which were started up failed and in the first nine months of 1982 eleven of the twenty-eight registered co-ops on the island closed. The remaining seventeen employed no more than 274 people. Despite the aid offered by the Canadian government and Oxfam, among others, there was not enough business and managerial expertise among the unemployed youth in the Grenadian countryside for the high hopes the revolution had of them to be fulfilled. The town workers who wished to set up co-operatives fared little better.

The credit unions, small savings and loan schemes, also favoured by the government, had a little more success. At the beginning of 1979 there were twenty-two co-operative credit unions with 5,000 members and assets of EC$3 million. At the time of the invasion the nineteen surviving credit unions had 6,000 members and funds of EC$6.5 million.

The government was never to lose the favour of the international financial institutions. The World Bank memorandum on the Grenadian economy in 1982 came as close to unstinted praise as that cautious institution was ever likely to come. It said:

The government which came to power in March 1979 inherited a deteriorating economy, and is now addressing the

95

task of rehabilitation and of laying better foundations for growth within the framework of a economy . . . Government objectives are centred on the critical development issues and touch on the country's most promising development areas.

In layman's language the government was tackling the country's problems and concentrating their efforts on those projects which were most likely to do the country good.

The World Bank praised Grenada for having set up a factory to process fruit and vegetables which before had gone to waste. It raised no objection to the immense effort being made to build the airport at Point Salines, it praised the efforts to push exports of manufactured goods such as garments and it was satisfied that all this was being done without the government running vast budget deficits. In terms of orthodox economic planning and good account keeping the Grenadian revolution was streets ahead of, say, the Chilean government in the time of Salvador Allende. The foreign debt was still minimal, well within what Grenada could afford to borrow. While the countries of Latin America, many with governments backed by the Reagan administration, got deep into such a morass of debt that they had to pay over almost all they earned in exports to pay the foreign bankers who had lent the money, Grenada in 1981 was devoting only a paltry 3.7 per cent of its export revenue to the servicing of the Government debt.

Nevertheless, as 1983 wore on and US hostility continued, the economic situation became tighter and tighter. 'The present cash situation is grim,' wrote Coard to the Cabinet from the Ministry of Finance on 31 March. The ministry, he reported, was barely able to cover the March salaries of the 9,000 state employees and Barclays Bank International were threatening to bounce cheques written in excess of the agreed limit of the government's overdraft. There was no way of printing new money – even if the cautious Coard had wanted to. The issuing of currency was the prerogative of the Eastern Caribbean Currency Authority which was controlled by the governments of St Vincent and the Grenadines, St Lucia, Dominica,

Montserrat, St Kitts-Nevis and Antigua and Barbuda jointly with Grenada.

In order to 'protect the credibility and credit-worthiness of the government' Coard urged the Cabinet to slash the recurrent budget by 20 per cent in order that four priorities could be met: civil servants' salaries, the debt service on government loans, 'inescapable recurrent expenditure' and the continuation of four sets of projects, the most important of which was the international airport. He ended optimistically, saying that he was aware that efforts were being made to raise new money abroad and the cuts could be revised if new cash actually materialised.

His cashflow projections for 1983, with a 20 per cent reduction in the last nine months of the year, were that the government would be spending EC$86 million and receiving EC$73.6 million – making up the difference by borrowing.

Ironically while the Reagan government itself had to borrow billions of dollars to finance its spending Grenada was, under Coard's guidance, living modestly within its means. While under the Gairy government not even the Pinochet dictatorship was willing to give Grenada ready cash the gifts of money came rolling in under revolutionary rule, thus helping to palliate the effects of the economic offensive being waged against Grenada from Washington. In 1977 and 1978 the Gairy Government received cash grants totalling EC$3.1 million from Britain, Canada and the EEC. In 1979 and 1980 the island received a total of EC$61.7 million from Cuba, the USSR, the Arab world, the UN and the western countries.

In August 1983 while the right-wing military governments in Brazil, Argentina and Chile were involved in painful battles with the International Monetary Fund which made little secret of the disgust it harboured for those countries' chaotic finances Grenada was able to raise a small IMF loan of US$14.1 million with the minimum of difficulty. After the US invasion the IMF promptly cut the loan off.

The churches had a chequered experience during the Bishop era. On 15 February 1980, as the revolution approached its first anniversary, the Prime Minister took the opportunity of wagging a stern finger at those who thought to use Christianity for counter-revolutionary purposes and also at the churches in general. He built a speech round a letter sent by a Dominican friar in Grenada to his brethren in England expounding a plan to bring to the island a group of left-wing Dominicans who would be able to exercise their ministry in a political climate increasingly tinged with Marxism-Leninism. Though the letter contained some unfortunate phrases and was never meant for the eyes of the government the thrust of the letter was unexceptionable and was summed up in the sentence:

Grenada offers them (left-wing English Dominicans) a tiny but significant field of experience in which to test out their theories and aspirations, an opportunity to preach the gospel in a predominantly Marxist-oriented society, while at the same time co-operating and assisting in the effort to construct a just human society.

Bishop took the letter as a religious attack on the revolution – which it clearly was not – and in that context prevailed on Bishop Sydney Charles, the head of the Catholic church, to suspend the publication of the *Catholic Focus*, a weekly news sheet, which Charles had committed the imprudence of having printed on the presses of *Torchlight*, the anti-revolutionary newspaper.

Bishop's decision to interpret the Dominican's letter, which had been passed to him by a disgruntled lay brother, in such a hostile way puzzled many church people who remembered the devout upbringing of the leader of the revolution. Whatever the explanation for Bishop's decision it was taken as a warning shot to those in the Catholic church, which claimed the loyalty of a majority of Grenadians, and to the Protestant churches and sects that they should not stand in the path of the revolution.

There was little evidence that the Catholic church at least was about to do so. Bishop Charles was not a dynamic church leader and gave his flock no particular guidance in the political matters of the day.

Despite this the revolution threw down a further challenge to the churches when in the course of 1982 and 1983 it began to place greater emphasis on the need for voluntary communal work, a practice which was well established in Cuba. Voluntary work was normally scheduled to take place between 7 a.m. and 12 midday on Sundays, the time when Grenadian church-goers were used to attending worship. The Ministry of Social Mobilisation clearly saw Sunday voluntary work as a way of identifying keen supporters of the revolution who were willing to give up their churchgoing for the sake of the revolution and separating them from those who put their religious practice first and from those who were apathetic about religion and the revolution.

Many parishes which met to consider whether they should change the times of Sunday Mass decided that they wanted to stick to the normal times and not change them for the sake of the community work.

One Catholic institution was happy to demonstrate its full commitment to the revolution. The Pope Paul Centre run by Grenadian former nun Judy Williams provided a convenient conference centre near Gouyave on the west coast where dis-cussions and conventions of Grenadians could be held and where the Grenadian revolution could be analysed sympa-thetically in the light of the liberation theology being developed in Latin America.

In addition to running the Pope Paul Centre with the help of donations from foreign charities, Williams organised the Grenfruit Women's Co-operative with the help of NACDA to start the production of dried fruit. When the co-operative was inaugurated in 1982, Williams naturally led the assembly in prayer after the political speeches were over.

The difficulty of the path Williams and other Catholics com-mitted to the revolution had to tread was exemplified by her treatment before and after the invasion. Coard's men ordered her arrest shortly before the killing of Bishop, presumably because of her known support of the Bishop cause; shortly after the invasion she was arrested by the invading forces and held in Gouyave police station under harsh conditions while the Centre was being ransacked by US troops. After her release she was evicted, her furniture and possessions being left at the side of the road. Appeals by her friends for support from Bishop Charles seemed to fall on deaf ears.

The churches' attitude to the revolution was summed up a fortnight after the invasion when all the members of the Grenadian Conference of Churches issued a joint statement giving thanks to God that 'our young country can look forward once again to a life of freedom and peace and to the hope of rebuilding our national institutions.'

It added, 'Our gratitude goes out also to all who made this possible by answering the appeal of the Governor-General, and particularly, to the American and Caribbean forces who responded to the call for help.'

As far as the Catholics were concerned Bishop Charles had clearly forgotten the pastoral letter that the Catholic bishops of the Antilles had issued after a meeting in Dominica in February 1982. In that document, which Charles himself signed, they quoted from the conclusions of the great congress of bishops from Latin America and the Caribbean held in Puebla, Mexico, in 1979 to the effect that:

Violence inexorably engenders new forms of oppression and bondage, which usually turn out to be more serious than the ones from which the people are allegedly being liberated. But, most importantly, violence is an attack on life, which depends on the Creator alone. We must also stress that when an ideology appeals to violence, it thereby admits its own weakness and inadequacy.

As the months went by and despite the successes obtained in many fields by the NJM, disenchantment set in. Grenadians, especially young Grenadians, appreciated the improved health facilities, the prospect of a new airport, Grenada's international posture, new educational opportunities and the sense of com-

100

munal self-help and co-operation that the PRG was attempting to carry out.

There were however murmurings about the lack of accountability of the NJM, the occasional arrogance of NJM members, some of whom felt themselves to be members of a new class, and the constant propagandising of the state controlled communications media.

The ability of the 'mass organisations' to mobilise Grenadians gradually fell. The Pioneer Movement, modelled on Cuban and Soviet organisations and designed for pre-teen schoolchildren did not have much success. The National Youth Organisation did better, catering as it did for the social needs of the teenagers and giving them a national ideal with which many of them could identify. The National Women's Organisation, after a first burst of enthusiasm from its founders, settled down to unspectacular growth.

Special difficulties were found with the Progressive Farmers' Union where a split developed in the leadership of what the government had hoped would unite the smaller farmers. Particular problems were found in the parish of St Andrew's. That parish was the site of Pearls airport and the prospect of the new airport opening up on the other side of Grenada raised the spectre of fewer jobs and the relegation of the parish and its town Grenville to a much lower status than it had hitherto enjoyed. In addition St Andrew's had been the place where much of the island's marijuana had been cultivated.

Under People's Law 39 of 1981 it was made an offence to grow marijuana or allow it to be smoked in premises. The law offended the Grenadian Rastafarian community who attributed sacred qualities to the drug, who had been ill-treated by Gairy and who had looked favourably on the advent of the Bishop era. It also upset many in St Andrew's who had been looking to the cultivation of marijuana as a source of a little extra income. The crackdown on the drug, justified as it undoubtedly was in part by the dangers it presented from racketeering, was not well received.

Despite everything the popularity of Bishop himself was not greatly eroded. He was accepted widely as the leader of Grenada, a man who had risked all in the service of right and justice, who did not spare himself in what he saw to be the cause of Grenada and who despite all kept his common touch. Virtually to the end Bishop maintained his sense of the occasionally ridiculous nature of political life and the craft of government. A British visitor rode with him one day in the back of his official car in which were three or four Kalashnikov rifles. As a soldier unloaded the rifles two shots were fired by complete accident.

'I'm glad they did not kill us,' Bishop remarked to his friend, 'It would have been awfully difficult for them to explain how we got killed here.'

The attractive sides of the personality of the Comrade Leader did a lot to compensate for the rigidities and failings of the revolution.

1. Mr (now Sir) Eric Gairy at the opening of the Grenada Constitutional Conference, Lancaster House, London, 1973. (Royal Commonwealth Society)

2. Maurice Bishop.

3.   Bernard Coard.

4.   Cuban technicians at work on Point Salines airport.

5. Che Guevara's portrait.

6. Road sign near St George's.

7. Maurice Bishop with Fidel Castro during the July 26, 1983
celebrations of the anniversary of the storming of the Moncada Barracks.

8. US patrol boat off Grenada

9. President Reagan in pyjamas confers with Secretary of
State George Shultz on Saturday October 22 about the Grenada situation.

10. USAF Galaxy aircraft at Grantley Adamas airport, Barbados, waiting to take off for Grenada.

11. Dead US helicopter pilot, Tanteen Field, St George's.

12. Safe conduct pass in the form of a Cuban 5 peso banknote bearing the picture of Antonio Maceo, black hero of Cuban independence. Distributed by US troops for use by Cubans during the October invasion.

13. A hooded Cuban prisoner is marched away by US paratroopers.

14. US marines with Grenadian prisoners.

15. Handcuffed Grenadian prisoner.

CHAPTER FIVE

The Split

'Woe betide us if, through a sectarian conception of
the Party's function in the revolution, we should try
to turn it into a material hierarchy, to fix in mechan-
ical forms of immediate power the governing appa-
ratus of the moving masses, to constrict the
revolutionary process into Party forms.'
Antonio Gramsci, 27 December 1919

The process which led to the fatal alignment of a small nucleus
of politicians, who wished to impose Leninist norms of conduct
and who were backed by the army, against a popular leader
backed by an overwhelming mass of politically conscious Grenadians was a long and complicated one. It was a process in
the course of which differences of ideological approach were
shot through, as they always are in politics, with clashes of
personality and shifting personal allegiances. The process is
all the more difficult to grasp in that the two principals in the
struggle, Maurice Bishop and Bernard Coard, espoused poli
cies from time to time which appeared to go counter to the
political strategies which each respectively represented. During the years the NJM was preparing itself for the exercise of
power Bishop advocated, or permitted, lines of action, which
contributed to the strengthening of a narrowly ideological outlook in the party. Coard for his part initiated policies which
apparently strengthened the capitalist complexion of the Grenadian economy.

With the advantage of hindsight one can see several milestones in the history of the NJM which marked the strengthening of the elitist 'vanguard' and, ultimately, anti-popular character of the NJM leadership.

The first milestone may be identified as the decision of the leaders of the NJM, after the reverses of 1973 and 1974 and the increasing use of physical force by Gairy's administration, to transform the membership of the party from a broadly based one, accessible to any Grenadian willing to subscribe to a wide set of political criteria and to pay a minimal fee for a party card. The limitations on full membership of the party and the relegation of most of the population sympathetic to Bishop and the NJM to the status of 'supporters' was to mark its future character deeply.

The return of Coard to Grenada brought with it in 1976 a strengthening of Leninist thought in the NJM and a reinforcement on ideological grounds of the tendencies towards that vanguardism which had been adopted two or three years before for reasons of practicality and empiricism. Coard and his wife set about strengthening the moves towards Leninism and strengthening their own personal power base in the party through the activities of OREL whose members, Layne, James, Cornwall, Stroud, Ventour and others, were to play key roles in the killing of Bishop and his comrades on 19 October 1983.

The recourse to fighting elections in December 1976, opposed as it had originally been by the OREL group, represented a temporary retreat from Leninism. It was not to last, however, as the events of March 1979 illustrated. While the toppling of Gairy proved to be popular with the mass of Grenadians the coup carried out by the NJM leadership and the score of armed militants they relied upon did not involve – could not involve – the whole population.

However justified the actions of 13 March were they cannot but have had the effect of reinforcing the self-regarding nature of the NJM leadership and its view that an élite group was needed to formulate and execute the wishes of the masses.

Bishop's assurance, issued in his first broadcast on the day of the coup, that the revolutionaries would be restoring 'all democratic freedoms, including freedom of elections', was

104

superseded, as we have seen, within days, when he declared at his press conference later that same week that the revolution was irreversible.

How serious he and his colleagues were on that score was demonstrated when, despite suggestions, even urgings, from their friends abroad, it was decided that no elections would be held and, therefore, the NJM would submit itself to no popular, effective accountability which might encompass the removal from power of the party leadership.

The island's growing involvement with the Castro government, despite the latter's repeated assurances of noninterference in Grenadian affairs, had its effects in many parts of Grenadian life. An NJM which was nervous of US hostility found a mentor in a government which had experienced two decades of a mutually hostile relationship with Washington. That mentor, in addition, took pride in an history of fighting which went back a century, to the time when Cuban patriots first took up arms against the Spaniards. Havana was willing to supply arms and ammunition and military and political training for the fledgling PRA. It was an ironic tragedy that it took a Cuban-trained and politically conscious army to kill a Grenadian political leader who had a close relationship with the leader of the Cuban revolution.

It was ironic also that the Cuban-Grenadian relationship should have been fostered by Washington, whose constant harping on the supposed strategic threat from a tiny Eastern Caribbean island caused the NJM to militarise their society more than they might otherwise have done.

The relationship with Cuba through the military links, the economic assistance and Bishop's close personal relationship with and regard for Castro brought with it an assimilation of Cuban political norms, many of them reflecting Soviet practise.

As Bishop was to say before a crowd of 1.5 million people on May Day in Havana in 1980:

Your revolution, Comrades, has also provided the region and the world with a living legend with your great and

105

indomitable leader, Fidel Castro. Fidel has taught us not only how to fight, but also how to work, how to build socialism, and how to lead our country in a spirit of humility, sincerity, commitment and firm revolutionary leadership.

In the background lay the political influence of the USSR itself. Both the Grenadians and the Cubans were conscious that Cuba's aid to Grenada was an indirect result of Soviet aid to Cuba.

Direct Soviet aid was not negligible either. Under the agreement signed with the Soviets in Moscow on 27 July 1982 by Liam James, Grenada was due to receive not only large quantities of arms and ammunition but training in the USSR and Grenada in their use. The 1982 agreement amplified the delivery of 5,000,000 roubles worth of arms and ammunition which was set out in the agreement between the Soviets and the Grenadians of 27 October 1980.

Despite the fact that the agreements specified the transfer of large quantities of war matériel they were not seen as sufficient by the Grenadian side. The day after the signature of the 1982 arms agreement Bishop wrote to Soviet Prime Minister Tikhonov to ask for further supplies of food, fuel, spare parts, transport, engineering kits, uniforms and other items. It is impossible to imagine that the supply of large quantities of arms that Bishop was keen to build up would not be accompanied by considerable Soviet influence on the still undefined Grenadian system of government.

A formal agreement between the NJM and the Communist Party of the Soviet Union was signed in Moscow, also on 27 July 1982, which looked to close collaboration between the two organisations. With Coard, the Cubans and the Soviets, not to mention the North Koreans and the East European governments, all promoting Leninism in Grenada it is not surprising that that ideology prospered to some extent.

Yet at no time did a Leninist theory of government carry the day completely. Whether out of personal conviction or out of a sense of prudence and the need to take out political insurance, Bishop maintained his island's links with the dem-

106

ocratic socialist parties of the London-based Socialist International. The high point of this relationship, apart from the formal entry of the NJM as a full member of the organisation at the 1980 congress in Madrid, was the holding in St George's of a meeting of the SI Regional Committee for the Western Hemisphere in July 1981. The Regional Committee, like the SI itself, contained parties of varied political outlooks. At one end were cautious parties such as Tom Adams' Barbados Labour Party or Luis Alberto Monge's Partido de Liberación Nacional of Costa Rica. There were also two small parties from the United States one of whose leaders, Carl Gershman, saw no contradiction in leaving his job and going to work for Mrs Jeane Kirkpatrick when she was appointed US envoy to the United Nations. At the other end of the spectrum were more radical organisations such as the Movimiento Nacionalista Revolucionario of El Salvador which was one of the constituent members of the Salvadorean FMLN guerrilla front. The Secretary of the SI Regional Committee, Héctor Oqueli, a member of the MNR, combined his post with that of the foreign affairs spokesman for the Salvadorean insurgents.

The SI meeting, which included delegates from the Canadian New Democratic Party and Antoine Blanca, the veteran French socialist and roving envoy for President François Mitterrand in the Western Hemisphere, was treated to a warm speech of welcome from Bishop. He said:

We certainly believe that the Socialist International is held in the highest esteem by progressive parties and forces of Latin America and the Caribbean because of the critical and crucial role that it has been playing over these past years in supporting and defending progressive and just causes in the region.

Bishop had a special word of praise for the President of the SI, former West German Chancellor Willi Brandt, and for the comrade Secretary-General of the Socialist International, Comrade Bernt Carlsson, 'an outstanding comrade, who has been over several years the leading force in the Socialist International administratively and in other ways'. The SI meeting was an indication that the NJM – or at least those parts of it closest to Bishop – was unwilling to break with the democratic socialist world whose parties were in government in France, Spain, Greece, Costa Rica and Germany and who were close to power in the Low Countries, Britain, Venezuela and Scandinavia. Equally importantly, the meeting signalled the fact that the SI, reaching out under Brandt's direction for a world role and seeking to efface the Euro-centrism of its postwar history, was keen to maintain and increase the links with Third World parties like the NJM.

The NJM also saw to it that the best possible relations were maintained with the European Economic Community, a process which entailed doing nothing that would call down on Grenada the wrath of any one of its members. This was successfully accomplished and the EEC gave Grenada in the years from 1979 to 1982 EC$8.2 million in capital grants.

The amount given by the USSR, which excludes the value of weapons and military training, came to EC$3 million in the same period. The maintenance of ties with the SI and the EEC must in large measure be credited to the work of Unison Whiteman who attended the SI meetings and who, for a year before Bishop's murder, was Minister of External Relations, a post he combined with that of Lands and Forestry and membership of the Central Committee.

As Grenada got deeper and deeper into the complexities of the new path the NJM leadership had chosen for it so the pressure on the leaders increased, and political life became more and more of a morass from which there was no escape. Bishop had his relaxations and he recharged his batteries by contact with the people of Grenada. Playing cards was one of his favourite occupations. At one session he was playing his favourite game – Peach. The score was being kept and Bishop's points were tallied under the initials PM.

'Do you know what PM stands for?' asked Bishop.

'Prime Minister,' his companions replied.

'No,' said Bishop laughing, 'It means Peach Master!'

Bishop also had a wandering eye. By 1981 his marriage with Angela was virtually at an end and they agreed to separate. He started living regularly with Jacqueline Creft, a graduate in political science from Carlton University, Ottawa, whom Bishop had known since she had been a member of MAP in the early 1960s. Creft was the mother of his son Vladimir. He enjoyed his gift of oratory and his easy contact with people.

Coard for his part was impatient for the emergence of an effective Leninist vanguard party on the small West Indian island. He objected to the way in which intellectual and theoretical problems were thrown at him by his fellow members of the Central Committee.

Not only was that physically and mentally exhausting for him but it meant that the less assiduous members of the Central Committee were able to shirk their responsibilities by leaving it all to him. He regarded it as a dangerous development in that if anything happened to him the party structure would be left very vulnerable.

In July 1982, therefore, he resolved to quit the Political Bureau, the Central Committee and the Organising Committee. It was a decision taken in private and communicated only to the members of the Central Committee. For the rest of the party it was said to be the result of Coard's deteriorating health. He retained his Deputy Premiership and his ministerial responsibilities for finance and planning.

There was perhaps another reason behind Coard's withdrawal from party posts which he did not communicate even to the Political Bureau. A master of the use of the tactical retreat, Coard doubtless wanted to impress his worth on the party and make his comrades all the more eager to see him back and to value him when he did come back.

In his absence, however, he made sure that his views would be represented in the Political Bureau and on the Central Committee. The Political Bureau, which, at the beginning of the revolution, had had eight members was, by the time of Coard's departure, down to five. Vincent Noel had been removed in

1980 and Kendrick Radix was removed when Coard left. The three vacancies were filled by Layne, James and Ventour, all three close supporters of Coard.

The departure of Coard from the inner councils of a party which had yet fully to define its own personality and ideology produced, as doubtless Coard had expected it to produce, great problems of identity for the NJM. The Coard loyalists of the OREL school, the influence of the Cubans, the Soviets and their allies and the experience of a party which had grown increasingly élitist and attracted to the theory of vanguardism pushed the NJM towards a Marxist-Leninist path.

At the same time the NJM did not have the organisational and managerial skills and the ideological commitment which might have allowed a more expert group of people to have carried out the political and economic changes that had been achieved in the Soviet Union and Cuba.

The forces opposed to a transition to a Cuban or Soviet model were meanwhile husbanding their strength. Within the party the democratic socialist trend which was represented by such as Lloyd Noel had suffered a defeat when Noel himself quit his post as Attorney-General in 1981 and was imprisoned without trial. The party was, however, not strong enough to do without the collaboration of democratic socialists and they could not be hounded out of the party – there might have been very little left.

Nor did the party have the assurance to make great inroads into the power of the private sector. Despite some officially tolerated land takeovers and squats the larger landowners were not expropriated wholesale. Despite the establishment of a state trading corporation the bulk of foreign trade was left in the hands of the traditional merchant houses such as Julien and Huggins. Despite the impatience of Leninists within the NJM to achieve ideological uniformity among the population the power of a conservative, if supine, Catholic church was still strong.

Not least important, Bishop's own reservations about a transition to a political model which would allow no popular accountability were still strong.

In such circumstances, and given the difficulties in domestic politics, great emphasis was placed on Grenada's international posture. A policy of hostility to the US had many clear advantages. The Reagan policy of support for murderous and retrogressive régimes and groups in Central America and Washington's hostility to long-awaited political change in the isthmus was not only condemned by most of the allies of the US but was also less than popular with Reagan's domestic constituency. In condemning US actions in Central America the NJM was joining its voice to that of the Cuban and Soviet Communist parties and to that of the Socialist International, many of the churches and many US Democrats and Republicans.

Condemnation of Washington's aggressive policies in Central America also served to rally Grenadians to the party. The party could justifiably say that Grenada might well be the next victim of the overbearing US attitude. As Washington's hostility to Bishop sharpened and the US government attempted to sabotage the flow of funds to Grenada from the EEC and the IMF, the process of representing Reagan as the island's principal enemy became increasingly easy for the NJM. Those who were pro-US could, without difficulty, be branded as disloyal to Grenada.

Hostility to the US, while justified and politically useful, did not, however, provide a long-term solution to the party's lack of political direction.

The process of making such a decision continued desultorily in the year following Coard's resignation from the central organo of the NJM. Coard himself was no less active with his ministerial duties than he had ever been. In May and June 1983 he made a month-long visit to the Soviet Union, ostenoibly for health reasons.

On his return journey from Moscow, Coard passed through London and took time to address a lunchtime gathering of the West Indian Committee, a venerable grouping of the old British plantocracy and more modern businessmen seeking business with the West Indies. About fifty of the most senior British business figures went to hear him speak at a West End hotel,

111

conscious that he was the 'hard man' of the Grenadian revolution. Coard exhibited once more his skilled touch and intellectual power.

'We went ready to throw tomatoes at him.' recalled one of those present, 'but I, as a Grenadian, came away proud of him.'

During the same stopover Coard spoke several times at the Institute of Education of London University. The normal audience of fifty or sixty was tripled as Coard, already well known in educational circles in Britain for his work on West Indian children, expounded his views on spreading the appeal of Marxist educational practice and explained the policies adopted by revolutionary Grenada. The atmosphere, as at the businessmen's gathering, was electric and he received an ovation.

He had clearly lost none of his intellectual force and none of his ability to bring it to bear with great effect on greatly differing audiences.

The policy of hostility towards Washington was meanwhile seen to be not without its drawbacks. The US government was in a position to blight the tourist industry by portraying the island as little less than an armed camp of the Cubans and the Soviets; it could discourage US firms from installing themselves in Grenada and older US citizens from going to live there in their retirement. There were a thousand ways in which the US government machine could make life difficult for Grenada and if the Grenadian government was often able successfully to counter Washington's ploys, that process demanded energy and imagination which were all too often in short supply among Grenada's hard-pressed ministers and officials.

At the end of February 1983 it was revealed in Washington that the CIA had considered mounting a covert economic offensive against Bishop in 1981 and Néstor Sánchez, the extremely conservative, former employee of the CIA who had become Deputy Assistant Secretary of Defense for Latin America and the Caribbean, announced to a gathering of Republicans in Florida that Grenada had become a 'virtual surrogate' of Cuba.

In a speech which helped to convince British diplomats that

112

the Reagan administration had become paranoiac about Grenada, Sánchez hinted that the Russians could use Grenada and Nicaragua as bases for a nuclear attack on the US.

Remarks by Reagan himself that Grenada represented a threat to US security, farfetched as they were, prompted a quick response from the Grenadian government. On 28 March Whiteman declared at the UN:

> Based on a careful analysis of evidence we are convinced that the Reagan Administration is planning an aggression. We believe the attack is imminent.

Two days later the PRA appealed to Grenadians to loan shotguns and air rifles to the militia for training purposes. The move might not have been strictly necessary from the military point of view, as there were ample supplies of arms in store on the island, but the political effect of the appeal weighed in Bishop's mind.

The continuing diplomatic hostility against Grenada caused some genuine alarm in St George's and prompted some change of tactics by Bishop. At the end of May he flew to Washington in a move billed as part of a campaign to promote normal and mutually respectful relations between the two countries. In a speech at the Organisation of American States he emphasised that the new airport was 'a civilian project vital to the economic development of our country.'

The Grenadian embassy in Washington sought a meeting for Bishop with Reagan. This was rejected and the State Department instead offered a call on William Middendorf, a businessman and political appointee to the post of US envoy to the OAS. The Grenadian head of government naturally rejected this and a compromise was reached under which Bishop talked to Lawrence Eagleburger and Kenneth Dam, Deputy Secretaries at the State Department, and Judge Clark of the National Security Council.

The following month Bishop was in Port of Spain where George Chambers, the Trinidadian Prime Minister, was host for a meeting of the Caricom Heads of Government. At that

113

meeting Bishop gave the Trinidadian assurances that a permanent constitution would be worked out for Grenada under which elections would be held by 1985. Shortly after, a constitutional commission was set up and the job of drafting a constitution given to Alan Alexander, a Trinidadian lawyer.

Though the Reagan administration had snubbed Bishop publicly there were those in the State Department who felt a *modus vivendi* could be worked out with the Grenadian leader and that he could be won away from what was seen in Washington as an over-reliance on Cuba and the USSR.

As Coard sought health care in the Soviet Union and Bishop sought a means of living with the Reagan administration and a draft constitution for Grenada, plans were laid for a series of meetings which would finally give some firm political definition to the Party.

At 1 p.m. on Wednesday 14 September there started an extraordinary meeting of the NJM Central Committee which was to initiate the Grenadian crisis. It was scheduled to end by 1 p.m. on the Thursday. According to the agenda prepared by Bishop, most of the time was to be given over to an evaluation of the collective work of the Central Committee and an assessment of individual members. In the event, Bishop's detailed seven-point agenda and its sixteen-item annex of supplementary reports was replaced at the insistence of Layne, Strachan, James and Ventour by a three-point work programme, an analysis of the party and the revolution, an analysis of the Central Committee and the way forward.

The way Bishop's agenda was tossed out of the way indicated that the Prime Minister did not have much chance of getting his way at the meeting. His only allies were George Louison, the Minister of Agriculture, Unison Whiteman, the Minister of External Relations, and Fitzroy Bain, President of the Agricultural and General Workers Union. One possible ally, General Hudson Austin, was out of the country, visiting North Korea. Against him were ranged nine more or less firm Coardites, Selwyn Strachan (Minister of National Mobilization), Lieutenant-Colonel Liam 'Owusu' James, of the PRA, John 'Chalkie' Ventour, Lieutenant-Colonel Ewart Layne, Phyllis

114

Coard (Bernard's wife), Major Leon 'Bogo' Cornwall (Ambassador to Cuba), Colville 'Kamau' McBarnette, Major Tan Bartholomew and Chris de Riggs (Minister of Health). Major Ian St Bernard was ill.

Layne led off the discussion. His job was to paint a gloomy picture of the state of the revolution which would make it seem imperative to recast the system of leadership in a new mould which would allow Coard to return and which would reduce the authority and executive power of Bishop.

The revolution was facing its most difficult test, he said, since 1979. The difficulties of running a state sector at a time of ecomonic pressure from imperialism were matched by the task of building a Marxist-Leninist vanguard party in a country which was predominantly petit bourgeois. A constitution had to be presented to the people.

The need was to develop the army and strengthen links with Cuba, the USSR, East Germany and other countries in 'the world socialist movement'.

In such circumstances, however, Layne argued, the party was falling to bits, the mass organisations were grinding to a halt and the Central Committee was showing no leadership. It was on a path of right opportunism.

Ventour supported that gloomy thesis. There was, he said, a serious drift away from the party by key supporters of the revolution and few comrades were prepared to fight reaction on the ground. The masses had gone backwards ideologically and people were beginning to get their views from the Voice of America. He agreed with Layne that the Central Committee was on a right opportunist path. He called for an ideologically clear and steeled Central Committee.

Bain added that the party had set too high standards for the people and that some of the revolution's firmest supporters were leaving the country. Bartholomew said that in some areas party workers who were trying to mobilise people had been chased away.

In her analysis Phyllis Coard said that the mood of party members could be graded as one or lower on a scale of one to five. The petit bourgeois elements in the party committees

115

were seeking to excuse themselves from criticism. The question that needed a decision was that of the ideological development of the Central Committee. If nothing was done, she said, the party would disintegrate within five or six months. No new members would come forward and the few remaining members would be overcome with work and frustration.

When it came to Bishop's turn to speak he agreed that the situation was bad but argued that much of the fault could be traced to the lack of strong links with the masses. There had also been a lack of concern for the material base in the country.

Louison, echoing Bishop's words, argued that there had been a clear lack of contact between some comrades and the masses.

Summing up a long debate Bishop proposed four main conclusions:

> there was a state of deep crisis in the party and the revolution;
> the main reason was the bad functioning of the Central Committee;
> the crisis in the party and the revolution had produced a crisis in the country and low popular morale;
> the crisis had been compounded by material weaknesses in such things as roads and electricity.

He went on to suggest five remedies:

> the improvement of the work of the Central Committee;
> the development of an outlook based on Marxist-Leninist criteria;
> deepening links with the masses;
> better communications between the leadership and the membership of the NJM;
> the development of 'structures for accountability' bearing in mind that comrades were demanding accounts from the party.

James started the discussion on the second item on the agenda. In his view the Central Committee was not moving forward.

What was needed was firm Leninism. The Comrade Leader had many strengths, the ability to inspire, the ability to command international respect for the party, the charisma to build confidence in the people and expound the positions of the party. He did not have what was needed to push the party forward. He had no Leninist level of organisation and discipline, no great depth of ideological clarity and no brilliance in strategy and tactics. The criticisms were taken up and expanded by speaker after speaker – Layne, Ventour, Cornwall, de Riggs, Bartholomew, McBarnette, Phyllis Coard.

Cornered, Bishop thanked the comrades for the frankness of their criticisms. He needed time to think out his own role and the problems surrounding it.

As the discussion and criticisms of the role of Bishop and the Central Committee flowed on, James tabled the first proposal aimed, he said, at marrying the strengths of Comrade Bishop and Comrade Coard. The former, he suggested, should take responsibility for direct work among the masses, the focus on increasing production and propaganda, for the organs of popular democracy, the working classes and youth and visits to workplaces in the town and the country, for the mobilisation of the militia and for regional and international work.

Coard, James said, should be given charge of the organisation of the party and the Chairmanship of the Organisation Committee; the development and formation of party members and strategy tactics.

Bishop should chair monthly Central Committee meetings, Coard the weekly meetings of the Political Bureau.

Bishop by this time had little alternative but to accept James' proposal for the division of powers between himself and Coard. It was a conditional acceptance, however. The formulation of criticisms implied that he had suffered a vote of no confidence, he said. No leader could be expected to inspire confidence in others if he had to look behind his back the whole time. Before accepting the division of power, he said, he wanted to consult Comrade Bernard. Louison also expressed reservations about the division. After more discussion, however, the formalisation of a joint leadership was accepted by a ma-

117

jority of nine to one with three abstentions, including that of Austin who arrived late at the meeting. It was further decided that the decision should be communicated to the NJM membership. Two meetings would be called: the first of full members and candidate members, the second of applicants. By nine votes to three abstentions it decided that the masses would not be informed.

Bishop suggested that the meeting be extended another day during his absence at the independence celebrations of St Kitts-Nevis during which the Central Committee could talk about the joint leadership with Coard.

Bishop went off with Whiteman, Jimmy Emmanuel, Permanent Secretary at the Ministry of Foreign Affairs, and Don Rojas, his press secretary, to Basseterre where under umbrellas at the Warner Park cricket ground he saw the twin-island state of 45,000 people emerge as the newest and one of the smallest independent states in the world.

The independence of St Kitts-Nevis was the triumph of Dr Kennedy Simmonds, the conservative Prime Minister of the new state whose policemen were, after some procedural hiccoughs, to take part a few weeks later in the invasion of Grenada.

Meanwhile the Central Committee met in St George's. Nine members gathered after lunch, Strachan, Austin, James, Layne, Ventour, Phyllis Coard, McBarnette, de Riggs and Cornwall. Bernard Coard was in attendance. Louison had gone to prepare Bishop's visit to Eastern Europe and Whiteman had accompanied Bishop to St Kitts so there was no voice favourable to Bishop's position to speak at the meeting.

Strachan took charge of the meeting and told Coard what he had already heard from his wife, that the Central Committee's leadership and unwillingness to adopt strict Marxist-Leninist norms, was leading to a deep crisis in the revolution. Coard was needed to put the Committee back on the correct path. Only he had demonstrated the qualities of ideological leadership over the years.

Coard in his reply agreed that the revolution was facing a crisis and that a petit bourgeois trend and a Marxist-Leninist

118

trend were at war with one another in the party. He formally expressed his willingness to return to the Central Committee and the Political Bureau providing that Bishop was agreeable.

Friday 23 September was fixed as the date by which Bishop should give his final decision about joint leadership and meanwhile Coard should work with the Central Committee on the planning of the future strategy of the revolution.

Throughout the subsequent week the Central Committee met in almost continuous session to hear the strategies Coard put forward to put the party on a firm Marxist-Leninist course. Coard, the newly returned member, chaired the meetings; Bishop, back from St Kitts, chose not to take part. As he saw the weight of opposition to him growing in the Central Committee he became increasingly troubled about his own political future. He was not sure how the joint leadership would work. He realised that he would be no more than a front man for Coard's policies and he pondered whether he should not give up politics for good, whatever the zealots of the Central Committee wanted.

On Friday 23 September, the day he was scheduled to give his answer to the Central Committee, he sent a message to say that he was unwell but would appear the next day.

There was, however, no Central Committee meeting on the Saturday; rather, a meeting was convened of the entire membership of the party on the Sunday. It met at 9 a.m. and did not break up for sixteen hours.

Bishop again failed to attend, saying he still had reservations on the issue of joint leadership. After a vote, a five-man delegation was mandated to go to his house and oblige him to come to the meeting. After an hour and a half's discussion with the delegation Bishop finally agreed to attend. Coard was absent when Bishop arrived. Having taken the lead in the Central Committee discussions the whole week he let it be known that he would attend only if the Prime Minister were there, lest it be thought that he was influencing the meeting too much. When Bishop arrived he spoke little but finally assented to the proposition of joint leadership for the sake of the unity of the party.

The next day he left for Budapest where Louison was already deep into the preparations for the visit.

In the course of Louison's stay in Budapest he got together with a group of Grenadians, including those on the delegation to Hungary and Czechoslovakia who had not been a party to the discussions at the Central Committee. He chaired the meeting which talked of events in Grenada. It was also attended by Unison Whiteman, though not by Bishop. The Coard group was to use this later against all three, despite the fact that Bishop did not attend.

The results of the East European trip were useful, particularly with respect to an agreement with the Czechs for the supply of electricity generation equipment which promised to put an end once and for all to the precarious shoestring operation of Grenelec which was always plunging the island into power cuts.

From Czechoslovakia the bulk of the party flew to Havana where, on Friday 9 October, they were the recipients of a powerful implicit message of support from Castro and his government. A reception was held for them which was attended by Fidel Castro, in his capacity as Commander-in-Chief, President of Cuba and head of the Cuban Communist Party, by his brother Raúl, the Minister of Defence and second man in the Cuban hierarchy, and forty members of the Central Committee of the Cuban Communist Party. Such a gathering was a great mark of respect.

It appears, however, that talk in Cuba did not hinge on the crisis in the party and that the bulk of the time was spent by the two leaders, who spent the day visiting projects around the city of Cienfuegos discussing agricultural problems, strange as that may seem in the light of the tensions within the party.

From Havana Bishop and his team set out the next day, 10 October, for Grenada and the final bloody dénouement of the crisis. In the course of their absence in Eastern Europe spirits at home in the Central Committee had got no calmer.

John 'Chalkie' Ventour, the Coard supporter newly appointed to the Political Bureau, went round openly saying that

Grenada was facing 'an Afghanistan situation' and that it might all have to end in bloodshed.

The meeting in Budapest chaired by Louison and attended by Whiteman had been reported back to St George's where the Coard faction took it, or at least decided to take it, as another instance of Bishop and his allies putting on one side the decisions of the Central Committee.

The decision by the Cubans to give the Bishop delegation such an outstanding welcome in Havana was similarly regarded as proof that Bishop was mobilising his powerful friends abroad against the decisions of the Central Committee, and might also be mobilising the Cubans in Grenada.

The Coard faction, for their part, had not been sitting on their hands while the Prime Ministerial delegation was away. As Minister of Finance Coard exercised his option to approve a pay raise for the PRA whose senior members had for months past been complaining not just about pay but also about the quality and quantity of rations issued to them.

Whether or not the decision to increase army pay in the absence of Bishop was coincidental or not – and there can be little doubt that it was taken after much deliberation – Coard, clever politician that he was, cannot but have realised the effect that a pay raise sanctioned by him in the absence of Bishop would have had in the ranks of the PRA.

The PRA, despite the critical role its soldiers were constantly reminded they exercised in the defence of a beleaguered revolutionary society, was not well treated economically. The average private's monthly wage was no more than EC$200 and a Lieutenant-Colonel took home little more than four times that amount. Rations were often no better than meagre and the Army as a whole was expected to supplement its fare from a 42-acre farm at Hope Vale, a mile or two south of St George's.

'It was aptly named,' a senior PRA officer commented after the US invasion. Given to the army as a piece of ground to put under cultivation it was never to prove much of a success as a food producer. Political considerations prevented the PRA being allotted any established farm which could be taken over as a going concern and the soldiers had to toil long and hard to raise their first unsatisfactory crop of maize and carrots. Hope Vale was never to make the contribution to feeding the troops and saving money that the originators of the idea had hoped it would.

'We were the worst paid toilers of the Revolution,' the PRA officer recalled.

Signs of the crisis were immediately evident as soon as the plane carrying Bishop landed at Pearls airport. The leader of the Revolution and Commander-in-Chief of the PRA who was returning from an important and successful trip to Eastern Europe and who had been seen off on his departure by Deputy Prime Minister Bernard Coard and many others was received on his return to the ramshackle airport by one man, Selwyn Strachan. The writing was on the wall in large letters.

The excuse the Central Committee gave was that they had received no message about the precise hour and time the party was returning from Cuba. That argument did not hold water as Bishop had sent word in advance about his party's arrival. Later it was argued by the Coard faction that there was no welcoming party because word had been received that Cletus St Paul, the Prime Minister's chief security officer who was travelling with him had been talking about killing Coard and there were fears he might do so as soon as the party stepped off the plane. It was strange however that no approach was made to Bishop to have St Paul arrested. He was not, in fact, detained until several days later.

Four days passed and both sides planned their moves for what was to be the last NJM deliberation. Before the Political Bureau met at 9 a.m. on Wednesday 12 October both sides had made their dispositions. Bishop had told Strachan that he wanted a review of the previous decision about joint leadership to be put on the Political Bureau agenda. In Bishop's mind, according to his supporters, was the wish to have a discussion on how joint leadership, now to be shared by him and Coard, could be concretely made to work. Bishop was not questioning the party decision about joint leadership itself.

Bishop's wish to have joint leadership put once again on the

122

agenda was taken by the pro-Coard majority on the Central Committee as a move by the Prime Minister to reopen party decisions and reject the concept of democratic centralism, or strict obedience to Central Committee decisions to which all party members were committed.

For the members of the party the tension in the days following Bishop's return was virtually unbearable. It was clear that a fight to the death between Bishop and Coard was on.

To the tension of trying to run an island under a new revolutionary system were added the tensions of worrying about the economic and financial plight of a country which was the object of a political and economic squeeze being imposed by the greatest power on earth. To pile Pelion on Ossa came the worry that the US, already doing its best to bolster the right in El Salvador and Honduras and perhaps on the brink of an invasion of Nicaragua might come round to invading Grenada. And the party itself was in a mess: militancy, despite the party's best efforts, had fallen throughout the island. The National Women's Organisation and the Nation Youth Organisation were in a mess, as were the Young Pioneers. On top of all this the party leadership was deeply and bitterly split.

It was no wonder that the party leaders found difficulty in sleeping, complained of ulcers and overwork and in some cases were on the brink of nervous collapse.

It was in such a mood that the leadership faced the Political Bureau meeting scheduled for 9 a.m. on Wednesday 12 October. Before the Political Bureau gathered the Coard faction took two last precautions.

At 1 a.m. that morning Major Keith Roberts of the PRA called together the security personnel of the government who were known not to be personally committed to Bishop. The selection of men in the compound at Mount Royal, which contained Bishop's and Coard's homes, where they were on duty was done so carefully that guards who might be trusted to obey the Central Committee were summoned to the meeting from the bunks in which they were sleeping without waking their less trustworthy companions sleeping above or below them in their quarters.

Roberts told them that there was a crisis in the party.

The Prime Minister, he said, was refusing to obey the instructions of the Central Committee. They, like the rest of the armed forces in the service of Grenada had to take their orders from the Central Committee alone and were to take no more orders from Bishop. They were to defend the working class as a whole and not the life of any individual leader.

The Coard faction called another meeting for 7 a.m. for all the NJM people in the PRA, full members, candidate members and applicants who together numbered about fifty-eight. Though he was still Commander-in-Chief, Bishop was not told of the meeting. There the same message was relayed as had been relayed six hours previously at dead of night. The meeting came out with a statement demanding that the Central Committee expel all those who were against the principle of joint leadership.

It ended:

> We clearly understand that party discipline is nothing less than the active struggle for the implementation of collectively adopted decisions such as the decision of the Central Committee on Joint Leadership which was ratified by our entire membership. Therefore we call on the Central Committee and the entire party to expel from the party's ranks all elements who do not submit to, uphold and implement in practice the decision of the Central Committee and party membership but are bent on holding up the party's work and spreading anti-party propaganda.

> The People's Revolutionary Armed Forces Branch of the NJM awaits the decision and order of the Central Committee!
> LONG LIVE THE NJM CENTRAL COMMITTEE – the highest body and authority of our Party and Revolution!
> LONG LIVE THE PARTY – NJM!
> LONG LIVE LENINISM!
> LONG LIVE OUR PEOPLE'S REVOLUTION!
> FORWARD EVER, BACKWARD NEVER!

The final NJM meeting at which the two principal creators of the party, Maurice Bishop and Bernard Coard, were present, gathered at 9 a.m. Under the chairmanship of Coard the Political Bureau gathered to consider three major items, the resolution passed just over an hour previously by NJM members in the armed forces, the question of the conduct of George Louison and lastly the present crisis in the party.

The first item was declared out of order. On procedural grounds it should have gone to the organisation committee before being presented to the Political Bureau as it had not come from a general meeting of the party but rather from one section of it.

There then followed two and a half hours of discussion about the situation of Louison. It was difficult to mount a strong case against him and it was clear to all in the Political Bureau that the attack was being made against him not principally for what he had done or had failed to do but because he was a supporter of Bishop. Nevertheless the Coard faction did their best with the accusation that, for instance, he had failed to rally the meeting in Budapest behind the decisions of the Central Committee.

The debate ended inconclusively at about midday after a resolution had been adopted convening an extraordinary meeting of the Central Committee that afternoon at 3.30 p.m. In one of those tactical retreats so characteristic of Coard he did not appear at the afternoon meeting which devoted the first seven hours of its deliberations to the question of Louison which had not been concluded at the morning session of the Political Bureau. At 10.30 p.m., however, a vote was taken and it was decided to strip Louison, a man who had served the party stalwartly as a founder and as a minister of government, of his membership of the Political Bureau and the Central Committee. As he left the meeting Louison gave his opponents notice that he would appeal against the move to the party as a whole.

In the course of the day, therefore, Bishop had been stripped of much of his personal protection, had had the PRA manipulated against him, its Commander-in-Chief, and had had one of his principal supporters stripped of power in the party. Never had Bishop been more vulnerable.

During the course of the day it became clear that the rumour was going round St George's that Coard was planning to assassinate Bishop. During the afternoon Cletus St Paul, Bishop's security chief, was called in by the Central Committee to answer charges that he and Bishop had collaborated in circulating the rumour. St Paul denied the charges but was arrested in any event.

Late that night, after the departure of the disgraced Louison Bishop faced a hostile majority of the Central Committee for the last time.

He was asked to do his best to dispel the rumours of that morning. He agreed to broadcast a message to the country in which he said that the rumour had been circulating that Coard had been planning to assassinate him, that this rumour was totally untrue, that there were indeed some differences within the party which would be resolved shortly and that the people should not listen to rumours but have faith in the revolution.

Bishop's message was broadcast three times on Radio Free Grenada between midnight Wednesday and 2 a.m. Thursday. Bishop also consented to write a letter to the woman who was said to have passed on the rumour about Coard plotting to assassinate him, Bishop, and asking her to collaborate with the Central Committee. The letter was dispatched as Bishop was talking on the radio.

Later that morning Maurice Bishop was placed under house arrest by the order of the Central Committee.

By this time, Unison Whiteman, the Foreign Minister, who had been on the mission to Hungary and Czechoslovakia and who had gone for consultations at the United Nations in New York was on his way back to the island. As he passed through Barbados he was contacted by Tom Adams, the Barbadian Prime Minister, and a fierce opponent of Bishop, the NJM and all it stood for. He told Whiteman of the latest reports of trouble in Grenada and urged him not to complete his journey but rather to stay in Barbados where he would be granted asylum. There is no doubt that the defection of Whiteman from a government and a party which he had done so much to create would have been a great feather in Adams' cap. Whiteman refused Adams' offer and went to his fate.

The news that Bishop had been put under house arrest went round Grenada with the force of a hurricane. For the first time for many Grenadians the depth and bitterness of the split between Bishop and his supporters and the majority on the Central Committee was revealed. The animosity against the Coard faction and the affection with which Bishop was held by very many Grenadians were not long in making themselves felt.

Against this wave of feeling the Coard faction did what they could. Party members were dispatched far and wide to explain the Central Committee line which was put to them at a special meeting of the party held later that Thursday. By all accounts the atmosphere at the meeting was vituperative in the extreme towards a man who had built up the party. In circumstances of extreme nervous tension the comradeship which had existed for years within the NJM and which had apparently been proof against the sharp internal controversies was now swept away in an orgy of *odium theologicum* against Bishop.

In such an atmosphere even those who were inclined to side with Bishop felt it wise to undertake to spread the Central Committee line. Under Coard's leadership the party had now taken leave of its collective senses and was embarked on that collision with the people of Grenada which was to bring about tragedy.

About 250 people were present at the meeting and thirty-one spoke. Some called for the execution of Bishop, some that he should be court-martialled. The final position was that he should be stripped of his positions and expelled from the NJM.

The temper of ordinary Grenadians was felt by the party as Strachan went to the *Free West Indian* to talk to the workers there. He was chased out of the building. Public outrage was such that Coard had to send word down to Market Square that he had resigned the Deputy Premiership. His place as Finance and Planning Minister was to be taken by Nazim Burke, a Coard supporter from the days of OREL.

127

It was in such circumstances that Hudson Austin came to the fore. Austin had had a continuous record of service to the party. He had taken his share of beatings during the Gairy days, he had taken the chief role in the heroic events of 13 March 1979 when his men stormed the True Blue barracks and routed the Green Beasts. He had played a crucial role in the building up of the PRA. Though he had become known as a supporter of Bishop he was now deciding to align himself with the majority in the Central Committee. At the Thursday afternoon meeting he was still sufficiently undecided to announce that the PRA would not be used against the people. Later that day he appears to have thrown in his lot finally with the Coard faction. The Coard faction needed him badly. The people would not accept a word Coard said, Strachan was seen to be Coard's man and only Austin had the prestige to be listened to with respect – for the moment.

On Sunday night at about 8 p.m. Radio Free Grenada announced that an important message would be broadcast at 10.30 that evening. The announcement was repeated several times in the subsequent ninety minutes. Then at 10.20 the announcer said it would be made at 11.30, one hour later than scheduled. At that appointed time the announcer merely told everyone to stay tuned. Eventually at twenty minutes past midnight Hudson Austin came on the air laying the blame for the present crisis squarely on the shoulders of Maurice Bishop who was proclaimed to be safe and well. No mention was made of the fact that he was under house arrest but Austin said that the Central Committee was now in control of the country.

It was a masterpiece of weasel words:

. . . the constantly growing desire of Comrade Maurice Bishop to exercise full and exclusive power and authority.
. . . Comrade Bishop had taken the position that no action can be taken to which he is opposed. At the same time he has become increasingly . . . suspicious that other members of the leadership of the party may be trying to seize power from him.

128

. . . the principled stand taken by the Central Committee of the party.

. . . the struggle of Comrade Bishop has been the struggle of one man to exercise unlimited power and that our party cannot and will not permit.

. . . No one loves Comrade Bishop more than the members of our own party but the decision on this matter must be based on principle alone.

Austin's midnight statement contained one outright lie. Bishop, he said, had been allowed to speak for forty-five minutes in his own defence at the meeting held the previous Thursday of the full membership of the party. He had also been given the chance of rebutting his critics and had refused to reply or even protest his innocence.

Austin, delivering a speech which few doubted had been prepared for him by Coard, called on Grenadians 'to maintain unity in order to ensure that imperialism does not take advantage of this moment of difficulty'. A more open indication to the US that now was the ideal time to stage an invasion could hardly have been conceived.

Having taken every move short of a lethal one against Bishop the Coard faction, now clearly victorious in the Central Committee, made an attempt to try and reach a *modus vivendi* with their defeated opponents which would allow a façade of party unity to be maintained. The recently arrived Whiteman joined Louison in hours of talks over the weekend with Coard and Strachan in an attempt to reach a compromise. While Bishop was locked in his residence under guards who were trusted to have understood the message that Major Roberts had given them at the meeting on early Wednesday morning the four plenipotentiaries of the two factions argued over the terms of an agreement. On Saturday after Coard called Louison at 2 a.m. to set up peace talks the conversations went on for one and a half hours, from 7.30 to 9.00 in the morning. The next day they went on for five hours and the day after for another five hours.

Whiteman and Louison argued that the imprisoning of Bishop was giving flesh to the rumour that had been going round since the beginning of the revolution that Coard had wanted to oust Bishop, a rumour which all the NJM leaders had done their sincere best to squash. They argued that the joint leadership was 'unscientific' and could mean the end of the revolution. Sure of their majority on the Central Committee and adamant that the Central Committee was the chosen vehicle of the NJM, which itself was sovereign in Grenada, Coard and Strachan argued that there could be no going back on the decision.

At this point it was clear to the Coard faction, as it was to their opponents, that the majority in the Central Committee would use force if necessary to impose their will. 'If the people won't accept it, the people will have to be made to accept it,' was the comment of one Coard supporter.

As the four talked the hours away crowds began to make their voice heard. People gathered at Pearls airport, schoolchildren, encouraged perhaps by teachers who, in their majority, were firmly anti-Coard, paraded through St George's. Hearing this, schoolchildren at Hillsborough on Carriacou turned out to protest. Everywhere the cry was 'No Bishop, no revo'. Years of popular suspicion of a clever man who had come late to the NJM and who was seen to be impatient at being in the shadow of the leader welled up.

As the peace talks were in progress on the Saturday the news came that Fitzroy Bain was organising the agricultural workers, of whose union he was President, to demonstrate against the imprisonment of Bishop. Meetings were being called in workplaces and some workers were calling for a general strike that would force the Central Committee to set Bishop free. Despite suggestions from Louison that Bain should call off or at least tone down the union protests, the demonstrations went ahead in St George's.

Julián Torres Rizo, the Cuban Ambassador, at this time offered his good offices to help towards a resolution of the problem but Coard, knowing the Cubans' partiality for Bishop, refused the offer. The ambassador, according to some accounts, temporized about whether Bishop could be given political asylum in the embassy.

By Monday it was clear that there was an impasse. The Central Committee had completely failed to bring round public opinion to accept the eclipse of Bishop and feeling in the country was running high against Coard and the Central Committee. In the tense world of the Central Committee feeling was running equally high against the people.

On Monday evening the Central Committee met for its last series of meetings, though Radio Free Grenada had been reporting that it had been in permanent session throughout the weekend.

In the course of the meeting, which was carried over to the following day, it was agreed that a six-point proposal be put to Bishop:

> that the party should commit itself to a Marxist-Leninist strategy and that Bishop should be required to do nothing to impede such a strategy;
> that Bishop should assume responsibility for the crisis in the party;
> that Bishop accept fully the principles of 'democratic centralism';
> that he remain an ordinary member of the NJM attending Political Bureau meetings in a consultative capacity;
> that Bishop accept the supremacy of the party over the state and
> that the post of Commander-in-Chief of the armed forces be abolished, the functions devolving on the Central Committee.

The party itself was beginning to disintegrate. Louison, Whiteman, and Lyden Ramdhanny, the Minister of Tourism, put in their resignations upon which Louison and his brother, Einstein Louison, the PRA Chief of Staff, were arrested.

George Louison was not in detention for long. At 6.30 a.m. on Wednesday 19 October he was summoned to a meeting with Bishop at which the Central Committee's six points were put to him.

Bishop, strengthened by the obvious manifestation of support and affection that had been shown him during his imprisonment, felt his position had improved rather than weakened over the weekend and felt strong enough to reject outright the suggestion that he should take on his own shoulders the full responsibility for a crisis which was clearly never all his own doing. He also stuck out for reinstatement on the Central Committee and the Political Bureau.

This was not to be.

It was the young Grenadians who were the first to show their rejection of the machinations of the Central Committee. The sporadic protests by schoolchildren in various parts of the main island and on Carriacou grew in intensity. By mid-afternoon of Tuesday 18 October a crowd of two to three thousand people were out in the streets of Grenville. Some were dancing and shouting slogans against Coard and calling 'We want Maurice Bishop'. Others were carrying rough placards reading 'We don't want Communism', 'We want democracy' and 'C for Coard, C for Communism'. While the police looked on from the front of the police station, members of the PRA with small arms patrolled quietly. The demonstration ended without incident by dusk and the crowd dispersed.

The effect of their demonstration, combined with a defiant interview given by Whiteman and broadcast by the powerful commercial Radio Antilles sited on Montserrat on Tuesday at sundown, got the schoolchildren of the capital into a ferment. The chief hotbed of pro-Bishop sentiment was the Girls' Anglican High School on Tanteen. The girls' student council met and decided on action sooner than anyone. By shortly after 9 a.m. on Wednesday morning emissaries were going out from the High School to Presentation College and St Joseph's Convent high up on Cemetery Hill, behind the Catholic cathedral of St George, and across the road to the capital's biggest school, the Grenada Boys' Secondary School.

At the Boys' school the students' council's seven delegates

were in feverish session under the chairmanship of 19-year-old Thompson Cadore, a tall, powerfully built boy from the village of Concord, a few miles up the coast. Word of their deliberations reached the ears of Victor Ashby, the Principal, who, while not being unsympathetic to their cause, was cautious about letting them out into the possibly violent streets of St George's. Ashby's instincts were proved to be tragically correct.

At about nine, however, the girls' delegation from the high school had arrived and the children of the two schools started pouring into the streets, to be joined shortly by the boys of Presentation College, who had similarly been spurred on to action, if that indeed had been necessary, by the girls from the adjacent St Joseph's.

Cadore, a popular boy from a poor home who was preparing for his examination for the General Certificate of Education, recalls how, as he travelled into school, he had the deep impression that the working people of St George's were hanging on every action of the schoolchildren, wondering if they would give the lead their companions in Grenville had given the previous day.

'We'll move if you move', was the remark he heard several times from adults as he came in from Concord and he felt that older people felt a massive demonstration would be safe if the youngsters headed it. The PRA, they argued, would never fire on them.

After milling around for a time in Market Square the crowd began drifting in ever-increasing numbers up the hill to Mount Royal, the gabled Prime Ministerial residence in the compound tucked behind Government House, Sir Paul Scoon's official house half a mile from the city centre.

At the gates of Mount Royal shortly after 10 o'clock the first face-to-face confrontation between the people of Grenada on the one side and the Central Committee and the Grenadian army on the other started. As the minutes went by the multitude swelled on the tarmac driveway of the Prime Minister's house, spilling over onto the bank covered with bamboos and tropical vegetation which rose to the right, and pressing against the chain link fence which marked off the drive from the ground which fell steeply away on the left to the capital below.

Beside the sentry box stood two armoured cars while a third was almost blocking a lane which skirted the residence and led down the hill.

As the shouts of 'We want Maurice', 'No Bishop, no school' and 'No Bishop, no revo', grew more insistent the tension grew almost to breaking point. As it approached 11 o'clock Major Leon 'Bogo' Cornwall, Coard's protégé from OREL days and now the Ambassador in Havana, came out to try to defuse the tension shouting, 'Maurice Bishop has betrayed the masses.'

He was unsuccessful and was booed and catcalled till he withdrew. Then from the high bank to the right the machine guns opened up over the heads of the crowds from the bank above causing hundreds to force themselves over and under the 8-foot chain link fence and down the slope below in panic.

The PRA, despite the firing, seemed irresolute and Cadore and a few friends decided that a flanking move from the rear would secure the object the crowds were seeking. Pushing past the single armoured car on the left they made their way round the back of Mount Royal and forced their way into the room where Bishop and Creft were.

Bishop, dressed only in a pair of dark green shorts, was strapped to one bed while Jacqueline Creft was bound to the other. Bishop's eyes were deeply sunken and as soon as he was released his friend realised that the crisis had taken its toll of his faculties and powers of concentration. He staggered for a moment till he was caught and supported and he seemed to have lost that power of command and that incisiveness that had marked him out in earlier days. Creft appeared in better physical condition and as both of them emerged on the arms of friends into the hot sun a great cheer of triumph and excitement went up from the thousands who awaited them.

They were half pushed, half carried by the stifling and jubilant crowd down the hundred yards of driveway to the main road where cars and trucks waited to bear them through the suffocating press of humanity down the road to the centre of town.

The normally decisive Bishop seemed unsure of himself. He and Creft first opted for one of the trucks which looked likely to be the most suitable vehicle for a triumphal descent on St George's. But then he changed his mind and decided to go in one of the waiting cars. Then he decided to go back to a lorry once again, finally settling for good on a car. Slowly the car set off through the jubilation of the throng down Tyrrell Street.

On the way the crowd surged past the house of Creft's mother Lynne. She ran out to meet her daughter who kissed her and murmured, 'Look what we've got ourselves into, Mum.' Lynne dashed back into her house to find some food for the pair but by the time she emerged with bread the stream of people had moved on. She was not to see Jackie again.

They went past the traffic point to the junction with Church Street where Wesley House and the party headquarters stood side by side across the road from Bishop Charles' house. From that crossroads the street led steeply down to the Market Square where Norris Bain, the popular and respected Minister of Housing, was listening to Boysie Charles' suggestion that a minister of religion should be found to lead the assembled crowd in a prayer of thanksgiving for the liberation of the Prime Minister.

But Bishop and Creft, more conscious than their supporters of the dangers still presented by the Coard faction, chose to turn left along Church Street which leads past the lawyers' chambers, St George's, the Anglican church and the offices of the Organization of American States and the cubbyhole which served as headquarters for John Kelly, the representative of the British High Commissioner. For them the priority was a recovery of physical security from attack and that security could only be found within the walls of Fort Rupert.

Leaving the puzzled and impatient crowd to wait in the sun in Market Square, two cars carrying Bishop and his closest friends drove on past Barclays Bank and up the slope between the St James Hotel and St Andrew's Presbyterian kirk to an outbuilding of Fort Rupert and they went up the stairs to the

135

first floor balcony. Bishop who, according to Dr Roger Radix who had seen him for a few minutes previously, gave every sign of having been without food and water for more than a day, cupped his head in his hands and rested it on the balcony rails in exhaustion and bewilderment as a new crowd began to form around him.

His Grenada was around him. The fort he had renamed after the father who had died for his cause, the people who were celebrating his release, the mottoes – POLITICS, DISCIPLINE, COMBAT READINESS EQUALS VICTORY, and FORWARD TO POLITICAL AND ACADEMIC EDUCATION FOR 1983 – which he had caused to be painted up on hoardings at the entrance to the fort. Wearily and confusedly he indicated that the first priority must be to get within the walls of the fort proper. The small PRA garrison was nonplussed, not knowing whether to resist as the Central Committee had recently been commanding or to give up to the Prime Minister and to the masses to whom the army was always taught to defer.

The garrison, seeing the crowds and seeing that some of the Bishop supporters were armed, opted for the second course though one woman soldier had to be thrown to the ground before she would give up her AK 47.

As the way lay open Bishop quit the veranda and moved across into the operations room of the PRA on the first floor of a building on the outer courtyard of the fort where the Central Committee had used to gather for meetings. Scores of friends moved into the operations room with him as the courtyard quickly filled with the crowds who had moved up from Market Square when they realised that Bishop was not going to address them down there.

Peter Thomas, an immigration officer, asked Bishop if he should set seats round the big table for a meeting and the Prime Minister nodded absently. Grasping for coherence Bishop told Thomas to take a vehicle and some men and collect the weapons kept at the immigration department next to the fire station on the Carenage. Thomas dashed off, returning within a quarter of an hour with automatic rifles and light machine guns. By that time Major Einstein Louison, the PRA Chief of Staff and Bishop's only supporter in the army command, had appeared, having broken out of the house arrest. Bishop told him to get to the fort's armouries and start giving out weapons to the crowd so that they could defend themselves in case of attack.

By now the attack was on its way, for careering down the road from Fort Frederick came four PRA vehicles. The first was an armoured car commanded by Lieutenant Iman Abdullah, a 24-year-old from the parish of St David's who had been baptised Calixtus Bernard but who, following the vogue of a few years before, had decided to adopt a Black Muslim name. He had been serving as the chief of the PRA on Carriacou.

In a second armoured car came Officer Cadet Conrad Mayers who, because of his experience of three years which he spent in the US army which included service in the West Berlin garrison, was in charge of the column.

The third armoured car was commanded by Lieutenant Raeburn Nelson, while the rear was brought up by a squad of PRA soldiers in an East German truck. As the column sped down Tyrrell Street along the route Bishop had travelled an hour before many of the crowd cheered them as reinforcements for Bishop. From his house Dr Radix had his premonitions. The four vehicles sped by a group of young boys out celebrating in the road and as the small convoy passed at speed one of the soldiers cursed them for being in the way. 'Push 'em out. Push 'em out,' he roared. Radix mused that they might not be so friendly after all. He drove away from what he felt was impending trouble as fast as his car could take him.

Down Church Street the four vehicles sped, nearly crushing a car which got in their way at the crossroads outside Barclays Bank. Fifty yards past the bank as Church Street climbs up to the fort the convoy halted a moment between the kirk and the hotel. Mayers gave his final orders. It was 1.03 in the afternoon.

The troops dismounted from the truck and fanned out up the incline to the right, the engines of the three armoured cars

137

revved up and the cars shot forward into the courtyard in front of the operations room and they began firing.

Vince Noel fell dead on the veranda of the outbuilding Bishop had been occupying less than an hour before. The cry of panic and the groans of the dying and the wounded were almost effaced by the sound of hundreds of people rushing to escape wherever they could.

Some ran down the incline back to town, others ran for cover in the General Hospital tucked below the fort, others threw themselves over the battlements to death or injury below, like so many lemmings. From vantage points in St George's the rest of the population looked on, horror stricken. Some of the PRA were disgusted with the job they were ordered to do. According to some evidence, Mayers was shot by a soldier from the third armoured car whose occupants were unwilling to take part in the killings.

Within the operations room Bishop gave the order to stop any return fire on the attacking forces. In the last cry of anguish his followers were to hear he moaned, 'Oh God, Oh God, they turned their guns against the masses.'

In the courtyard there was a lull in the firing for a moment while a soldier called over Simon Alexander, a 15-year-old fourth former from Grenada Boys' Secondary School. He gave him a parcel wrapped in paper and told him to take it down to Market Square and leave it. As firing started again Simon ran off, stumbled and fell, detonating the bomb he had been given. He was killed instantly. He had been a quiet, friendly, rather retiring lad.

As the armoured cars ceased fire a second time Bishop gave the order to those in the operations room to give themselves up. They filed out onto the balcony and made their way back down to town, the lucky ones, that is.

As Thomas filed across the courtyard he was aware of the blood dripping from the gash a bullet had caused on the left side of his head and sensed he was being watched by some hostile figure from the bushes growing out of the battlements to his left. As Bishop's senior colleagues filed out last they were turned back and ordered into the courtyard of Fort Ru-

138

pert's central citadel. Keith 'Pumphead' Hailing from the Market and Import Board was turned back. As Evelyn 'Brat' Bullen, a business supporter of Bishop's was stopped, a voice said, 'Go back, youse a boojwa!!'

Evelyn Maitland of Maitland's Garage was turned back. Unison Whiteman, the creator of the original Joint Endeavour for Welfare, Education and Liberation in the pioneering days in St David's, was turned back. Norris Bain, the 53-year-old Minister of Housing, was turned back. Fitzroy Bain, the 32-year-old President of the Agricultural and General Workers Union, was turned back. Jackie Creft was turned back, Maurice Bishop was turned back. They went through the tunnel from the outer to the inner courtyard and their friends never saw them again.

Petrified with fear Thomas made his way as steadily as he could back down past the kirk and St James Hotel, turned right at the corner by Barclays Bank and walked, blood still dripping from the gash in his head down to the Carenage while the moans of the injured rose from the heaps of people below the battlements. As he reached the water he heard two prolonged bursts of machine gun fire. Seven men and a woman had been murdered next to the basketball net in the inner courtyard of Fort Rupert. The followers of Bernard Coard had aborted the Grenadian revolution.

At Fort Frederick the initial reaction was one of exultation rather than remorse. A communiqué was immediately composed to the PRA in which it was specifically stated that the unit sent that day to Fort Rupert acted under the orders of the Central Committee. It said:

Today our People's Revolutionary Army has gained victory over the right opportunists and reactionary forces which attacked the Headquarters of our Ministry of Defence. These anti-worker elements using the working people as a shield entered Fort Rupert.

Our patriotic men, loving the masses and rather than

139

killing them since we understood that they were being used, we held our fire . . .

Comrades, these men who preached for us that they had the interest of the Grenadian people at heart did not have one member of the working class controlling their criminal operations. These elements although they used the working class and working people to gain their objective did not have any confidence in them and therefore had only businessmen, nuns, nurses and lumpen elements in the operations theatre . . .

Comrades, today Wednesday 19th October, history was made again. All patriots and revolutionaries will never forget this day when counter-revolution, the friends of imperialism, were crushed. This victory today will ensure that our glorious Party the NJM will live on and grow from strength to strength leading and guiding the Armed Forces and the Revolution . . .

The following day a more detailed version of Wednesday's events was issued by the PRA Main Political Department. 'Maurice Bishop and his other petty bourgeois and upper bourgeois friends,' it said, 'had deserted the working class and working people of Grenada.'

The city lay stunned and it took an hour or two for news of the massacre to seep to the outside world over the telephone. Until 4 p.m. Caribbean radio stations were reporting merely that shots had been heard from Fort Rupert and that smoke could be seen rising from there. Shortly after 4 p.m. the CBC station in Barbados flashed the news that Bishop had been shot, but that was shortly afterwards retracted as inaccurate. Within St George's confusion and tension rose.

Radio Free Grenada which had been silent returned to the air about 5.30 p.m. and after playing a few records announced that all retired nurses and Salvation Army personnel were being asked to report to the General Hospital 'to assist with the care of patients'. In that institution the staff were struggling as best they could with the flood of mangled flesh.

A moment later Radio Free Grenada added that free transport would be provided to and from the hospital for any volunteers.

The suspense heightened as the radio announced that Hudson Austin would be speaking to the country at 8.30 that night. At 9.10 he was heard.

Unsteadily and nervously he started to recount how a sixteen-man Revolutionary Military Council had been set up at 3 p.m. after the killing of Bishop at Fort Rupert. The dead Prime Minister, he strongly implied, had thrown in his lot with imperialism and counter-revolutionaries. A four-day curfew would be imposed during which offenders against it would be shot on sight.

The RMC consisted of sixteen of the most politically active officers in the PRA. Under Austin served two Lieutenant-Colonels, Liam James and Ewart Layne, as joint vice-chairmen of the Council. Six majors included Leon Cornwall, Ambassador to Cuba and Nicaragua, Tan Bartholomew, Chris Stroude, Keith 'Chicken' Roberts, the security chief, and Basil 'Akee' Gahagan, Captains Lester Redhead and Huey Romain, First Lieutenants Ashley Foulkes and Rudolph Ogilvey and Iman Abdullah and Second Lieutenants Kenrick Fraser and Raeburn Nelson. It was announced that the body had full legislative and executive powers though there was no mention of any move to make the country a republic or expel Scoon from his post as Representative of the Head of State.

The unnamed but key figure in the Government was Coard who guided the strategies of the Council from behind the scenes. On Friday and Saturday Austin went to great lengths on the telephone to assure me that he did not know where Coard was, that his Council was looking for him and that he could have left the island. He also laid great emphasis on the fact that Coard had nothing to do with the RMC. Those statements were not true and, throughout the short life of the Council at meetings in Fort Frederick which became the Council's headquarters, Coard counselled the RMC and directed its strategies.

The first strategy was to secure the physical safety of the members of the Council. In this the imposition of a curfew was a vital factor, even though all members of the RMC realised what an unpopular move it was, especially for those who did not have enough to eat or drink in their houses or who had animals to tend.

Under cover of the curfew opponents were arrested and the corpses of those killed at Fort Rupert were disposed of.

Major Keith 'Chicken' Roberts, the security chief, meanwhile gave orders for those who had helped to organise the morning's demonstration of support for Bishop to be rounded up. Under cover of the 24-hour curfew which was imposed that evening the RMC sent out patrols in all directions to hunt down their adversaries. The experience of two such adversaries exemplify the lot of scores of Bishop supporters in the succeeding days.

Boysie Charles of Birch Grove, St Andrew's, the largest inland village in the island, had been part of that bedrock of support upon which the NJM was built. A prosperous black Trinidadian married to a Grenadian, he farmed cocoa and other crops while at the same time running a small liquor store, bar and general shop on the outskirts of the village. Originally a supporter of the GNP and Herbert Blaize, he had become a follower of Bishop since hearing his speeches at the time of the nurses' strike in 1970. A full member of the NJM up to 1975, when the party became much more selective about the militancy and full-time commitment demanded from full members, Charles continued an active supporter of Bishop. He helped enthusiastically in the mobilisation of Bishop supporters on Wednesday 19 October travelling himself into St George's at around 11 a.m. He rushed back home to his shop in Birch Grove after the massacre which he heard from the Market Square.

Just after 3 a.m. on the Thursday morning he was awoken by the arrival of two vans and a squad commanded by his neighbour Gellineau James who had two days earlier been appointed Minister of Agriculture to succeed the man to whom he had been acting as secretary, George Louison. He put on the light outside the flat over his shop but was roughly told to turn it out before it was shot out.

The squad identified themselves as the security forces and told him to come out. He was bundled into one of the vans and asked whether he had any firearms. When he replied that he had a legally registered pistol James dispatched a member of the squad to take it from his wife nervously waiting in the flat. In the van he recognized an acquaintance, Billy, from the town of Grenville, who had been wounded in the groin during the firing the previous day at Fort Rupert.

Then started the ride along the twisting potholed road in the dark to St George's and detention. From time to time the small convoy would stop as James sought other suspects. Desslyn, a girl in her mid-twenties who was one of the principal organisers of the NJM in Grenville, was not at her home. James, however, found Johnson Chase, a Bishop supporter and a director of the Grenada Nutmeg Board.

A mile or so further on James stopped at Adelphi to pick up Silvia Belmar, another Bishop supporter whose 19-year-old daughter Gemma had been killed the previous day at Fort Rupert. Silvia too was not at home but James, as dawn got closer, picked up another Bishop supporter, Kentus Alexander.

As dawn was breaking the little convoy reached Richmond Hill Prison where the men, including Billy who was now in agony from the wound in his groin, were stuffed into the Goat Pen. Over the next few days new opponents of the RMC arrived so that at one point the Goat Pen, a cell about 6 feet by 10 feet and containing four bunks, held seventeen people. They were provided with some milk and one and a half bread rolls per meal and two buckets for their urine and excreta. Other detainees included Alister Hughes, the journalist, and Cletus St Paul, Bishop's former bodyguard.

Over the weekend the stifling fetid crush was relieved as some of the prisoners including Charles were transferred to the infirmary on the orders of Deputy Superintendent Thomas of the prison service.

On Monday afternoon, the eve of the invasion, word came that they were about to be released. First was to come a political exhortation by a member of the RMC. As Charles was being transferred from the infirmary he caught sight of Joan Ventour, who ran the pharmacy in Grenville and who was the wife of his next door neighbour in Birch Grove, Theobald Ventour.

Joan received her admonition from Austin himself. Charles claims that Austin, with whom he had been on intimate terms since his boyhood, avoided contact with him out of shame. Charles's admonition came from Major Chris Stroud who told him to listen carefully to the message that Einstein Louison was going to deliver at 7 p.m. that Monday night.

He was back at his home in Birch Grove by 5.30 p.m. where he found the distraught wife of Norris Bain who asked him anxiously if he had seen Norris at Richmond Hill. Bain had been dead for five days but his wife was not yet willing to accept that fact.

Lalla, a former member of the PRA and former member of the ministerial bodyguard, had a more adventurous experience. He, like Charles, had taken a hand in mobilising the crowds to go into St George's on Wednesday to help release Bishop. Having organised buses and cars for people wanting to go to St George's from the west coast area near his home at Grand Roy, Lalla took a leading part in freeing Bishop himself. After the massacre he fled back to Grand Roy where he hid in a mango tree near his house. Before dark on Wednesday he pushed on to the next village of Gouyave where he made himself conspicuous in the knowledge that this would be reported to the RMC.

Then with a colleague he made his way by night up gullies and through the forest towards Birch Grove. The two fugitives hit the road as dawn was breaking and just as a PRA patrol was approaching. They froze in their tracks. Had they moved they would certainly have been spotted but the Coard supporters passed by without noticing them. In Birch Grove they lay up in an outhouse belonging to a relative who fed them until the invasion was in full swing and they felt it safe to emerge.

Einstein Louison attempted similar tactics. On his way to the armoury in Fort Rupert at the moment the armoured cars were approaching he abandoned his job of issuing arms to the people and with the others hurled himself over the battlements

144

where he injured his hip. He limped into hiding in St George's but his hip was so painful that he was forced to seek medical assistance at the General Hospital. There he was picked up by 'Chicken' Roberts' men on Friday 21 October. Under arrest once again he was asked to make a statement which could help to rally all Grenadians to the RMC flag as the danger of US invasion became more immediate with the approach of naval vessels.

He refused to make a statement but did give an interview. It was not broadcast as delivered. Over the weekend editors did their best with the tape recording and there emerged a statement in which Einstein Louison apparently took on the guilt of organising the arming of the people and seemingly justified the attack on Fort Rupert as a vital military operation. The resulting discourse was so disjointed, however, that few of his hearers did other than think the words had been forced out of him under duress.

From Barbados, Bishop's sister Maureen and Creft's sister Coleen appealed to Austin to hand over Maurice's body to Allan La Grenade, his uncle, and that of Jackie to her mother Lynn. Whiteman's and Bain's bodies, they said, should be given to their wives. They received no reply.

La Grenade was one of the few members of Bishop's family, apart from Alimenta, his mother, whom the RMC had allowed to stay at liberty. The rest, including Bob Evans, a technician working on the airport project and the late Prime Minister's cousin, were confined, despite the protests of the Cubans working at Point Salines. They stopped work during the curfew. There was in any case little they could do. Orders were given to block the main runway with barrels, vehicles and whatever else was at hand lest it be used by invading aircraft. The senior representative from Plessey, the British firm overseeing the equipping of Point Salines, told Austin that his company was ceasing work at the airport because of *force majeure*.

From Brampton in the Canadian province of Ontario a word of mourning came from Bishop's wife. Angela, who had at one time been a junior minister for tourism in the Government, had been separated from Bishop for about two years and at

145

the time of his death was working in a bank. As he died she was having to deal with the serious illness of their 16-year-old son John.

'He was a very great man,' she said. She confessed she had had forebodings of his early death. 'Ever since the day of the revolution, 13 March 1979, I have been waiting for it. My husband was a determined man. I hate to think what will happen now the force of the people has been taken away.'

She had last seen him alive in New York in mid-1983 and had spoken to him on the telephone two days before his death.

Dispositions were meanwhile made for the best use to be made of the physical supplies in the island. Food and other stores were taken from civilian wholesalers for the use of the PRA and contingency plans made for the priorities in the allotment of power supplies and fuel in the likely event of a shortage. The island's consumption was small, 110,000 barrels of oil a year. But storage space was also small and supplies needed to be topped up by visiting tankers every eight weeks. An emergency programme of government was worked out to be put into effect by a small council overseen by a commission drawn from all parts of the administration. In the energy sphere as audit of fuel stocks was ordered, arrangements worked out for electricity load shedding and gas rationing and the likelihood of obtaining new supplies of oil 'legally or illegally'. The possibility of a shutdown of telecommunications with the outside world was considered in the light of the possibility of an international boycott.

Preparations were made to try and halt action against the RMC in international organisations and it was decided to 'contact countries on whom we can hope to depend in the coming period. As soon as possible we must contact them. At whatever stage our emergency programme had reached we must inform them of our needs and seek assistance.'

The RMC resolved to apply for banknotes from the Eastern Caribbean Currency Board to maintain the supply of cash in Grenada, seek meetings with LIAT, the regional airline which was the only air carrier which regularly linked Grenada to the outside world and contact the Organisation of Eastern Caribbean States and Caricom, the Caribbean regional grouping.

As the US warships anchored on the horizon, Cornwall ordered all state-owned vehicles to be concentrated on Tanteen Field in St George's, at Grenville Police Station and at Sauteurs Police Station. The safety of drivers making deliveries of vehicles during the curfew was guaranteed and they were promised transport to return to their homes.

'Anyone who resists in any way or another this directive of the Revolutionary Military Council (RMC) will be dealt with in the strickest (sic) manner,' he warned.

Within their homes the Grenadians sat, mourned, sweltered and worried. The RMC announced a lifting of the curfew from 10 a.m. to 2 p.m. on Friday but Radio Free Grenada went on to warn that anyone found violating the curfew would be dealt with severely. While the Grenadian radio station was mute about the events of Wednesday, apart from putting out the RMC declarations, Grenadians tuned in and heard the worldwide condemnation of the Wednesday massacre from the many regional stations which could be picked up; Radio Antilles, the Voice of America, the BBC, the stations in Barbados and Trinidad, St Vincent and many other islands. It was not until Friday that Radio Free Grenada announced that the death toll in the Fort Rupert shooting was 17, a figure which was widely disbelieved in Grenada.

The telephone lines within Grenada and between the island and the outside world buzzed with report and rumour.

On Saturday CBC Radio in Barbados, which set up a special news service to cover the crisis, announced, 'A United States task force including battleship is now heading for Grenada to evacuate US citizens if the necessity arises.'

The next day curfew prevented churchgoers attending services, a constraint which irked thousands who resented being stopped from praying in public for the best outcome from the clash which they felt was now inevitable.

From abroad the first reactions started to come in. The one from the declared opponents of the revolution were predictable. From Barbados, Prime Minister Tom Adams declared, 'I was horrified at these brutal and vicious murders – a most vicious act to disfigure the West Indies since the days of slavery . . . I for one will not be able to sit down at any table with these disgusting murderers.'

From Jamaica, Prime Minister Edward Seaga said, 'The government of Jamaica, while not in sympathy with the ideology of the Bishop government, is repulsed by the tragic death of Mr Bishop and his colleagues under the new régime of Cuban-trained Army generals and other Marxist ideologies . . . One thing is certain and that is that Jamaica will not participate in any Caricom meetings with the present régime in Grenada.' Eugenia Charles, the Prime Minister of Dominica who, as chairman of the seven-nation Organization of Eastern Caribbean States, was destined to take a key part in the unfolding of the invasion, announced that her government would have nothing to do with the Austin régime.

But condemnation was not confined to opponents of the left in Grenada.

In London, Shridath 'Sonny' Ramphal, Commonwealth Secretary-General and former Foreign Minister of Guyana sensed that a US invasion was a possibility and said, 'I share the sense of horror which is widespread throughout the Commonwealth at the loss of life in Grenada, including that of the Prime Minister and Ministers of the Government', adding that he felt the will and the interests of the Grenadian people should be respected 'and the integrity of the island-state preserved.'

Michael Manley, former Prime Minister of Jamaica, counsellor of the NJM and leader of the opposition People's National Party, said the killings were a 'squalid betrayal of the hopes of the ordinary people of our region'.

Reverend Allan Kirton, General Secretary of the Caribbean Council of Churches which had followed a line of critical support for Bishop's aims, announced the CCC was cutting off all relations with the régime in St George's.

Colonel Deysi Bouterse, the erratic left-wing leader of Surinam in whose country there had been a massacre in December 1982 in Paramaribo, deplored the murders and warned that

Grenadians were at 'a serious and perilous phase of their development which may lead to serious consequences for the development for the entire region'. He was later to expel the Cuban ambassador to Surinam.

In Washington, Larry Speakes, the White House spokesman, said that the situation in Grenada 'raises our concern to the highest level'.

It was left to the taciturn Prime Minister of the Republic of Trinidad and Tobago, a country which had for decades been the most immediate El Dorado for Grenadians and where tens of thousands of them worked and lived, to strike the first effective blow against the Austin régime. On Thursday he announced he was horrified at 'the importation of such executions in the English-speaking Caribbean.' With immediate effect, he said, no Grenadian would be allowed into Trinidad and Tobago without a visa, the trade concessions granted to goods from Grenada under the Caricom economic co-operation treaties would be suspended and Grenadian registered vessels disbarred from using the facilities at the Caricom jetty in Port of Spain.

As Austin and Coard awaited the reaction from Havana they could take comfort only from the Soviet reaction. A brief dispatch from the state news agency TASS said:

A tense situation has formed in the country following sharp differences and a split in the leadership of the New Jewel Movement.

An armed clash took place which claimed the lives of the Prime Minister and several ministers. The Revolutionary Military Council assumed full power in the country. It stated its determination to uphold the cause of the revolution.

Moscow was not ready to condemn the killing of Bishop.

In Havana the news of Bishop's murder sounded alarm bells straight away. The Castro government was faced with a problem of enormous complexity and seriousness. In the first place Bishop had been seen off from Havana only days before having been accorded some of the highest marks of esteem. In the

149

second place there were strong personal bonds between Castro and Bishop. In the third place Bishop had been promoted as something of a popular hero in Cuba itself. Cubans remembered how on 27 July that year he had been present with Castro at the inauguration of a new textile mill in Santiago de Cuba, an occasion at which the Grenadian leader had presented Castro with a rifle used on 13 March 1979 in the overthrow of the Grenadian government. Ordinary Cubans remembered too that Grenada was the source of supplies of spices which suddenly became available in the shops. They remembered the Grenadian turmeric which they had not seen for years and which went far to flavouring the rice that was one of the staples of their nutritious but often monotonous diet.

In the fourth place the overthrow of Bishop, the Cubans strongly suspected, would be taken by the Reagan administration as a signal for US intervention in Grenada. If the worst came to the worst it could be the signal for US landings not just in the Eastern Caribbean but in Nicaragua and El Salvador and perhaps in Cuba itself. In the fifth place the putsch must of necessity affect the standing of Cuba with revolutionary movements throughout the region.

Havana had to move fast to limit the damage caused by disaster in St George's. It had to distance itself from the RMC while doing its best to dissuade Washington from invading Grenada. The task of working out a coherent political line in a very thorny situation was hampered by the fact that Ricardo Alarcón, the Deputy Foreign Minister with responsibility for the Western Hemisphere, was in a meeting in Montreal.

If Austin and Coard had any real hope that Cuba would come to their aid that hope was dashed when, the day after Bishop's murder, the Cuban Communist Party and the government put out a statement which left no doubt about Havana's condemnation of the events. It was strong enough to preclude any help being offered to the RMC from Moscow either without it becoming clear that there was a deep rift between the Soviets and the Cubans on the Grenada question.

In unequivocal language the statement said:

. . . Bishop was one of the political leaders best liked and most respected by our people because of his talent, modesty, sincerity, revolutionary honesty and proven friendship with our country. He also enjoyed great international prestige. The news of his death deeply moved the Party leadership and we pay the most heartfelt tribute to his memory.

Unfortunately, the division among Grenadian revolutionists led to this bloody drama.

No doctrine, no principle or proclaimed revolutionary position and no internal division can justify atrocious acts such as the physical elimination of Bishop and the prominent group of honest and worthy leaders who died yesterday.

The death of Bishop and his comrades must be cleared up. If they were executed in cold blood, the guilty should receive exemplary punishment . . .

Castro's anger could hardly have been made more plain.

The Cubans promised that they would not halt their aid to Grenada but warned that Havana's relations with the new leadership in St George's would 'have to undergo profound and serious analysis.'

In response to the insistent appeals for military help from the RMC Castro himself drafted a reply which Torres Rizó was on Saturday afternoon ordered to pass on verbally to Austin and Layne. The sending of reinforcements was 'impossible and unthinkable'. Castro also passed on a Council of Perfection to the effect suggesting that the RMC should seek a reconciliation with the people and punishment for those responsible for the massacre. He further counselled the RMC to offer every facility for the evacuation of US, British and other nationals.

Such was the seriousness of the situation that this succession of public and private slaps in the face did not dissuade the Grenadians from renewing their calls to Havana for help. Cuba must send troops to help in the repulse of an invasion and Cubans and Grenadians must fight shoulder to shoulder under Grenadian command to push the invaders back into the sea. This must be formalised in a defence agreement.

151

The Cubans, however, would not budge.

On Monday Tortoló flew with Carlos Díaz Larrañaga, the 41-year-old Party expert on Grenadian affairs, from Havana to St George's. Their task, apart from instructing the Cubans what to do in the event of an attack, was to make it clear to the RMC that the roles of the Cubans and the Grenadians would be different. The Cubans would not attack US troops but merely defend themselves within the perimeter of their workplaces. Cubans would not serve under Grenadian command and there could be no co-ordination of their actions. The Cuban perimeter was defined as the runway of the Point Salines airport up to the Hardy Bay filling and the area between Point Salines itself and Morne Rouge. The Cubans told the Grenadians that it would be better if soldiers were kept away from the St George's University Medical School so that it should not become a battleground and justify any invasion.

There would be no formal agreement between the RMC and Havana and, the message finished tartly, 'the instructions regarding what the Cuban personnel is to do in case of war can only be issued by the government of Cuba.'

Farce accompanied the RMC efforts to contact the British government. Britain had no resident High Commissioner in St George's, the British envoy being based in Barbados. At the time of the crisis he was represented in Grenada by John Kelly, a member of the British Foreign Service born in Tuam, in County Galway. Kelly's office was a tiny set of cubicles on the ground floor of a building next to the Anglican church in Church Street. Together the cubicles were hardly more spacious than some of the snack bars to be found in the Grenadian capital. He was provided with a telephone installed in the air conditioned cubicle he occupied but telex services came by courtesy of the much more imposing headquarters of the Organisation of American States which occupied the floor above. Kelly was helped in the office by his wife. He received periodic visits from the staff of the High Commission in Barbados and despite his straitened working conditions was well informed about Grenadian affairs and active on behalf of British interests.

On Saturday afternoon Kelly received the visit of David

Montgomery, the Deputy High Commissioner, who shared a charter flight to Grenada with political counsellor Ken Kurze and Linda Flohr of the US Embassy in Barbados. Though the US had not broken diplomatic relations with revolutionary Grenada, Washington had never accredited any ambassador to the Bishop government and did not maintain even the sparing official presence that Britain afforded.

Montgomery and Kelly toured the island by car after having obtained the necessary safe conducts from the RMC and interviewed various British residents. He found that between thirty and forty of them wanted to leave the island. During his stay he talked to Bogo Cornwall who assured him that the curfew would be lifted as promised on the Monday morning at 6 a.m.

Montgomery's interview with Cornwall was followed by the dispatch of two successive messages by telex to London. On Sunday afternoon the RMC reported that a US invasion was imminent and requested the British government to do what it could to forestall it. The message was accompanied by the text of a telex addressed to the US embassy in Barbados appealing for any hostile action to be called off.

The following day an even more urgent message went to London. In this the RMC announced that the invasion was about to get under way and appealed to Britain to raise the matter in the United Nations and 'to condemn publicly this planned invasion which is a blatant violation of international law'.

The RMC's persuasiveness was, however, lost. Dialling an old Foreign and Commonwealth Office telex number in London, the Council did not realise this had been reallocated to a plastic bag manufacturer at South Molton Street, in the West End of London.

The staff at Scanplast, realising the urgency of the material they saw on their telex machine on Monday morning, telephoned the Caribbean and Atlantic Department of the FCO to ask what to do. 'Put them in an envelope', was the reply. Worried, Scanplast asked if they should be hand delivered and to whom they should be addressed. 'Leave them at the front

153

door,' came the laconic reply. The plastic manufacturer decided to save effort and dispatched the material by post.

When the second appeal was found on the telex on Tuesday morning Scanplast once again telephoned the Caribbean and Atlantic Department and offered to dictate the message. His interlocutor said she could not take shorthand and promised that someone who could would call back. By the time anyone did the invasion was under way.

There is little doubt that the US forces had some contingency plans prepared for an invasion of Grenada. The joint chiefs of staff would have been failing in their duty had they not considered what steps they might eventually take, particularly in the light of Reagan's claim that Grenada was a threat to US security. In August 1981 as part of the Ocean Venture '81 military manoeuvres an exercise called Amber and the Amberines was staged in the island of Vieques, off the eastern shore of the US possession of Puerto Rico. Three hundred men from the 75th Ranger Battalion were used in the mock attack on the island which was staged, according to Rear-Admiral Robert P. McKenzie, to rescue a group of US citizens held hostage by an unfriendly government. The use of the code name Amberines was strongly reminiscent of the Grenadine chain of islands, sovereignty of which is shared between Grenada and St Vincent. British and Dutch vessels took part in the exercise.

On 26 October 1983 in a French television interview in Paris, Evan Galbraith, the US Ambassador to France, said that the Reagan administration had been planning the invasion for the previous two weeks, i.e. since before the house arrest of Bishop on 12 October, a fact later confirmed by Assistant Secretary of State Langhorne 'Tony' Mottley who chaired the first planning meeting.

On the same day in Barbados, Adams in an address on Barbadian television said that his government had been approached 'at a low level' by a US official about the possibility of a rescue mission being mounted for Bishop with the aid of a US transport aircraft.

154

Quite clearly there were those in the US government who were fully prepared to move in some sort of operation in Grenada as the political crisis in St George's came to a climax.

The formal start to the invasion preparations came on Monday 17 October when an inter-agency group, chaired by the State Department and the Central Intelligence Agency, among others, met for the first time to discuss the possible repercussions of Bishop's arrest.

Discussion centred on the fate of the thousand US citizens in Grenada. The Pentagon, thinking back to the Amber and the Amberines exercise, favoured an Entebbe-style operation in which highly trained troops would be sent in on a specific rescue mission and rapidly recalled. Defence was opposed to anything more elaborate because it was already fully engaged in the Lebanon crisis and was unwilling to engage in possibly futile future planning if there was not a firmer indication from higher up in the government that such plans could be of real use.

The same group met two days later in the afternoon to discuss the new, but not unexpected, news of the death of Bishop but details of the events were still sparse. The machine was, however, beginning to pick up speed. Langhorne Motley, the newly appointed Assistant Secretary of State for Inter-American Affairs, was called that evening to brief Secretary of State George Shultz on the Grenada situation and to receive the majority opinion of the inter-agency group that contingency plans should be extended to cover an outright invasion. The generals on the group were still holding out against doing unnecessary work if Reagan himself did not appear Interested in a major operation. At this point Reagan was brought into the discussions and was immediately receptive to the idea of an invasion.

With the President's interest now plainly aroused, the Government machine went into top gear. Reagan asked Vice-President Bush to chair a meeting of the National Security Council. The Council met in the Situation Room, the windowless sub-basement under the Oval Office in the White House, a command bunker equipped with all the control monitors and communications equipment needed by a President during wartime.

The hawkish view of the State Department was forcefully put by Lawrence Eagleburger, the Deputy Secretary of State for Political Affairs, who raised the spectre of the Tehran hostages and argued that if the US did nothing to rescue the citizens who had, he said, been taken hostage in Grenada then the Reagan administration would lose face in the Caribbean and Central America at the very time when toughness against the left-wing challenge in Nicaragua and El Salvador was the order of the day.

Shultz and Motley arrived late for this meeting after briefing congressmen on Capitol Hill and the meeting broke up having made a recommendation that a naval task force then steaming for the Mediterranean with replacements for the Marines stationed in Lebanon should be diverted towards Grenada.

At the State Department preparations were going ahead on the instructions to be given to Milan Bish, the US Ambassador to the Eastern Caribbean, resident in Barbados, where the heads of government of the Organization of Eastern Caribbean States were due to meet on the evening of the next day, Friday, to discuss the Grenada crisis.

The chair at the OECS meeting was to be taken by a good friend of the US, Miss Eugenia Charles, the Prime Minister of Dominica.

The assistance of the small islands of the Eastern Caribbean was vital if legal justification for an invasion was to be found. An invitation from Grenada's neighbours would be of inestimable value in the diplomatic fallout that the State Department saw as inevitable after the US action.

With the help of Charles, of John Compton, the cautious Prime Minister of St Lucia, of Vere Bird, the Prime Minister of Antigua and Barbuda and his son Lester, the Foreign Minister, of Kennedy Simmonds, the conservative Prime Minister of St Kitts-Nevis which had been independent of Britain for only a month, and of Milton Cato, the right-of-centre Prime Minister of St Vincent and the Grenadines, there would be little difficulty in getting a consensus. The young and inexperienced John Osbourne of Montserrat, as an Associated State still dependent on Britain, would scarcely present an obstacle.

Any waywardness on the part of the OECS – an unlikely situation – could be dealt with by Tom Adams who the previous week had shown himself not averse to US plans for an incursion into Grenada.

Legal minds in Washington were not unaware that the articles of the 1981 treaty which brought into existence the OECS offered scant justification for any invasion of Grenada, invited or uninvited.

Paragraph Five of Article Six of the OECS treaty was transparently clear. It read:

The Authority [the Heads of Government who were to meet on Friday in Barbados] shall have power to make decisions on all matters within its competence. All such decisions shall require the affirmative vote of all Member States present and voting at the meeting of the Authority at which such decisions were taken provided that such decisions shall have no force and effect until ratified by those Member States, if any, which were not present at that meeting, or until such Member States have notified the Authority of their decision to abstain. Such decision by the Authority shall be binding on all Member States and on all institutions of the Organization and effect shall be given to any such decision provided that it is within the sovereign competence of Member States to implement them.

In laymen's language this meant that the OECS could take no action until the Grenadian authorities had signified they had no objection to it. And it was difficult to see in any case how a number of neighbours could ever have the right to call for an invasion of another state under any circumstances. The RMC would obviously never agree to permit the invasion of their own country.

As Friday afternoon came and the six members of the seven-member OECS authority arrived at the Dover Convention Centre overlooking the sea a few miles south of Bridgetown,

157

the Barbadian capital, they were in a dubious mood, despite the encouragement given to them by Bish and Charles 'Tony' Gillespie, the Deputy Assistant Secretary of State for Caribbean Affairs, who was on hand in the island to help forward the discussions. The presence in Barbados of as senior a figure as Gillespie underlined the extreme seriousness with which the US was taking the OECS meeting.

The meeting started shortly after lunch amid the strictest security measures ever seen in Barbados. Soldiers of the Barbados Defence Force mixed with uniformed and plainclothes policemen while the Barbados coast guard vessel *George Fergusson* stood a few hundred yards out at sea. No flags were flying at this very secret meeting and reporters pressed fruitlessly to get comments out of the OECS Prime Ministers. The normally expansive Adams arrived at the Conference Centre by a back door half way through the discussions as night was falling and emerged from the conference room once with Charles to make a telephone call. He pushed his way through reporters calling out, 'No time to talk now. No time to talk now.' Among the press corps was a member of the staff of the British High Commission in Barbados, Denis Healy with his wife, carrying a tape recorder and doing his best to look like a reporter, a fact that illustrated the British anxiety to get as much news as possible from a meeting from which Britain was excluded.

It was becoming clear in Barbados that an invasion was a clear possibility – even a likelihood – and diplomats and journalists swapped conjectures about how a landing could be effected with the minimum loss of life and least danger to the Grenadians and to the US medical students. In the likely event of the overthrow of the RMC all agreed that Sir Paul Scoon would be called to play a key role as representative of the head of state and the residual fount of authority in Grenada.

The meeting of the OECS merged, with the arrival of Adams, into a meeting of the Eastern Caribbean Defence Community, of which Barbados but not Grenada was a member.

Late that night the heads of government broke up and the OECS announced sanctions against Grenada; the cutting off of further supplies of banknotes from the Eastern Caribbean

158

Currency Authority and the suspension of all air and sea contacts between the OECS countries and Grenada.

The measures followed closely those called for before the meeting by Compton. No mention was made of the fact that in the absence of a Grenadian representative the whole exercise was illegal.

In the course of the OECS meeting objections were made to the invasion by Lester Bird, the Deputy Prime Minister and Foreign Minister of Antigua and Barbuda. He was unhappy with the plan which, he thought, would bring his little country nothing but trouble. He was to be overruled. Bish, hearing the news, telephoned his father Vere Bird, the Antiguan Prime Minister in St John's, the island's capital, and persuaded the old man of the rightness of the US case and the error of his son Lester's ways. The tiny Antiguan contingent of policemen was mobilised for the invasion forthwith to the chagrin of Lester.

In Washington Friday proved to be one of those reasonably relaxed days that Ronald Reagan enjoyed. A weekend of golf beckoned at Augusta, Georgia. The idea was to build up the somewhat dented image of Secretary of State George Shultz by having him partake of a few days of intimate relaxation with the President and a party which was to include Treasury Secretary Donald Regan, Nicholas Brodley, former New Jersey senator, and their wives. Reagan got behind him the unpleasant duty of telling Jeane Kirkpatrick, Ambassador to the UN, that Robert McFarlane, not she, was getting the job of National Security Adviser.

Before taking off for the championship course at Augusta Reagan agreed that the convoy heading for the Mediterranean should be diverted to Grenada. Thoughts of invasion in the mind of the media were played down and a US Navy spokesman told *The New York Times*, 'There are not going to be any landings or anything like that. This is not to be construed as a provocative act.'

The golfing party was not destined to be the relaxing affair the participants had looked forward to.

At 2.45 a.m. Shultz was awakened in Augusta with the

159

results of the OECS meeting and the news that the Eastern Caribbean states, after conversations with Gillespie and Bish, were now appealing for US collaboration in an invasion of Grenada. Unless Washington moved quickly, the message read, the news would leak out and the Cubans and Grenadians would have time to prepare their defences. Speed was essential and Sunday would be the best day to go in.

In the early hours Shultz discussed the outcome of the OECS meeting with the newly appointed McFarlane and Vice-President George Bush convened a meeting of the National Security Council at the White House where the Pentagon still held out against any rushed operation in Grenada. The earliest reasonable time for that would be Wednesday or, at a pinch, Tuesday.

Legal or not, the governments of the Eastern Caribbean had moved with amazing speed against the RMC and, by Friday night, less than sixty hours after Bishop and his companions had been murdered, the RMC faced a grim situation indeed. They were about to be blockaded and shortly run out of fuel needed to maintain essential services on the island; transit for passengers to and from the outside world was problematical; Grenada's principal and nearest ally, Cuba, had not only turned its back on them but had called for their punishment; work had stopped on the Point Salines airport; little help could be expected from the Soviet Union; popular wrath against them, muted now by a twenty-four hour curfew, could not be muzzled indefinitely; the sanctions their immediate neighbours had imposed on them were likely to be extended after the heads of government of Caricom met the next day, Saturday, and the US and Britain were sending warships to their waters.

As a black weekend approached, Coard and the leaders of the RMC, meeting now in Fort Frederick, overlooking the silent St George's, did their best to appear conciliatory.

Arrangements were quickly made for the reception of Montgomery, Kurze and Flohr and curfew passes were rapidly issued to Kelly and his wife and the staffs of the Venezuelan, Cuban and Soviet embassies. Such courtesies had their advantages as the acceptance of RMC documents by resident

160

diplomats constituted, it could be argued, diplomatic recognition of the RMC by the countries they represented.

On Saturday afternoon Major Chris Stroude, a member of the RMC and an alumnus of OREL read on Radio Free Grenada a statement of intention by the Council. It said that a new Cabinet would be appointed within ten to fourteen days in which all classes and interests would be represented and which would work for peace, national unity and national reconciliation. Economic construction would be the most urgent task to be tackled by the new Cabinet. Agriculture would be encouraged as would tourism. While Grenada would continue to pursue an active foreign policy, 'efforts made recently to better relations with the United States government would continue'.

Three days too late the RMC sent out its appeal for tolerance:

In the future, the Revolutionary Military Council will permit no harassment, intimidation or victimization on any persons or social groups in Grenada. Our country cannot be built on the basis of hatred or bitterness . . . Let us now, in an atmosphere of calm and of love for one another, unite as one people. Long live our Grenadian people. Long live our unity as one people. Long live the revolution. Forward ever, backward never.

The broadcast convinced few, if any, Grenadians of the benign nature of the RMC and betrayed the fact that while the ruling group was worried it was not yet ready to pledge itself to hold new elections.

Instructions meanwhile went out that the US students should be treated with the utmost consideration by the PRA. Vehicles and escorts were provided for them to shuttle between their two campuses at Point Salines and Grand Anse.

Before even the OECS Heads of Government had finished their session, plans were going forward for a meeting of Caricom leaders which would consider the situation in Grenada.

161

The involvement of the large countries of the Commonwealth Caribbean in any action against the RMC would greatly strengthen its apparent legal justification. As far as international public opinion was concerned the members of OECS could hardly be expected to carry much weight. After all, few newspaper readers in North America or Europe would have much idea of the political complexion, geographical location, or even the very existence of such newly independent states as St Kitts-Nevis and even the formidable Miss Charles, well known though she was in the West Indies, was hardly a world figure.

The addition of Jamaican Prime Minister Seaga to the list of supporters of any invasion would give it much increased legitimacy. The supporters of an invasion would also be able to claim a majority in Caricom. There were obvious dangers for the promoters of the Caricom summit. A number of heads of government, including notably President Forbes Burnham of Guyana, might be expected to speak out against any move against Grenada. It was important, therefore, to have a sympathetic location and a skilful and committed chairman to steer the project through possible shoals.

Barbados was the ideal location and Adams was the best chairman, as far as the hawks were concerned. On Friday morning, therefore, it was put about in the Barbadian capital that the Caricom ministers were about to set out for a meeting in Barbados. Compton, perhaps not wanting Adams to take too preponderant a role in the operation, suggested Port of Spain as the venue and George Chambers, Prime Minister of Trinidad and Tobago, as chairman for the emergency meeting.

The US task force was sailing south and HMS *Antrim*, the British cruiser with her supply ship *Pearleaf*, headed towards Grenada from the Colombian port of Cartagena where she had been on a good will visit as the Caricom heads of government gathered in the Trinidad Hilton hotel built on a hill overlooking Port of Spain and its busy docks.

Having expected to preside over Caricom talks being held in his country Adams decided not to go to the Trinidadian capital and sent his Minister of Foreign Affairs, Louis Tull.

The OECS leaders, Lester Bird, Charles, Osbourne, Simmonds, Compton and Cato arrived en bloc from their meeting of the previous evening. They were accompanied on their flight from Barbados by Seaga who had snatched some time to co-ordinate his position with Adams in Bridgetown. The single-minded but retiring George Price, Prime Minister of Belize, arrived as did Sir Lynden Pindling, Prime Minister of the Bahamas and a man under whom the scattered archipelago off Florida had made a handsome, if at times dubious, living from offshore banking and gambling.

A picture call was announced for 8.15 p.m. at which press photographers would be allowed access to the leaders in their meeting room. For fifty-five minutes the eleven leaders waited for the twelfth guest. They chatted desultorily for half an hour, unwilling to sit down and reveal at the table that their consultations were being delayed by an absent guest and the only leader among them who was also a head of state. The atmosphere in the meeting room grew sulphuric.

Compton remarked testily, 'Where's the General? He's probably putting on his–' and he pointed to his right shoulder in a mute reference to the epaulettes which the Guyanese President favoured with his full dress. At 9 p.m. sharp Lynden Sampson Forbes Burnham, President of the Co-operative Republic of Guyana, appeared and proceedings could commence.

As the Caricom leaders were making their way towards the Trinidad Hilton a small tragi-comedy was being played out at the golf club in Augusta. Reagan was out on the fairway when an unemployed worker at a paper mill drove his pick-up truck through an unguarded gate at the clubhouse, pulled a pistol and held seven men hostage while he demanded to talk to the President. The man was overpowered before he could make contact with Reagan. The incident would have provided a good excuse to return to the White House but Reagan chose to play on.

'I want to play another round of golf,' he said, 'I want the weekend to end on an "up" note.'

His wish was not to be granted. At 2.27 a.m. on Sunday morning he was roused from his bed in Augusta by McFarlane and told that a guerrilla on a suicide mission had driven a lorryload of explosives into the US Marine Corps headquarters in Beirut and that 46 marines were already known to have lost their lives with many more probably dead in the rubble.

By 7.30 that morning Reagan was heading back on Air Force One to Washington in a state of some exhaustion to preside over two National Security Council meetings, the first on Beirut, the second on Grenada.

In the Trinidad Hilton the Caricom meeting had adjourned wearily at 3.06 a.m. on Sunday morning. Chambers was confident that a consensus had been reached. Caricom was agreed, he understood, on four points:

> there should be no outside involvement in the resolution of the Grenada crisis;
> the crisis should be handled within Caricom;
> Caricom should act within the dictates of international law and the United Nations Charter;
> and all efforts should be bent towards restoring normality in Grenada.

In restoring normality conversations should, it was agreed, be carried on through Scoon lest the RMC were given the idea that they were being accorded recognition by their neighbours. The Commonwealth Caribbean should, through him, push for a broad-based government of national reconciliation which would hold elections at the earliest possible date. A fact-finding mission of Caricom notables should be dispatched to Grenada. Arrangements should be made to safeguard foreign nationals on the island and their evacuation where desired. The Grenadians should further be persuaded to accept a peacekeeping force on the island composed of contingents from Caricom countries.

Before the meeting broke up, names were bandied about the table of those who might form the fact-finding mission. Chambers himself was entrusted with the task of pursuing the initiatives. It was agreed that the number, terms of reference

164

and composition of the mission would be decided later that morning after everyone had had some sleep.

As the leaders went to their beds, the only major point at issue was what should be done if the RMC held out against the Caricom proposals. Seaga and others argued that force should be used with whatever military help could be found from outside Caricom. Chambers, supported by Burnham, Price and Pindling, said that force should not be used, at least in the first instance. Chambers added that he for one would have to consult parliament before sending his islands' troops to war in Grenada.

The talks at the Trinidad Hilton did not end, however, after the formal meeting broke up. The same night and into the next morning the hawks, Seaga, Charles, Tull on behalf of the absent Adams and an unhappy Lester Bird, took counsel about how to get the idea of an immediate invasion as favoured by the State Department back on track. From Bridgetown Adams gave his own advice about how to handle the situation.

The Caricom meeting, it was agreed, had gone worse than expected for them. It was decided that the invasion should go ahead on the basis of the State Department's willingness to invade and that the US action should be supported by Jamaica, Barbados, Antigua, Dominica, St Lucia, St Kitts Nevis and St Vincent. When the meeting reconvened after breakfast, an hour later than originally scheduled, Charles merely tabled the proposals of the OECS meeting for peaceful sanctions against the RMC for approval by the Caricom leaders while Seaga surprised everyone by tabling a plan for the restructuring of Caricom itself. The hawks declared that there had been no consensus the previous night and that it was otiose to continue talking about the actions proposed at the earlier session

The final upshot of the meeting was that a majority of Caricom leaders decided to suspend Grenada from their organisation and to support the OECS sanctions against the RMC which had been suggested by the Eastern Caribbean states at their session in Barbados two days before.

As many of the hawks travelled back to Barbados on Sunday afternoon they took pains to cover their tracks and give no

165

hint of the impending invasion. At her seat in the first-class compartment of the Pan Am flight from Trinidad to Barbados Charles told reporters, 'If there is an invasion of Grenada the left in the Caribbean will kill us.'

The Prime Minister of Dominica was fast developing into a ruthless international operator. (She already had on her record the rare distinction of having discomfited Margaret Thatcher, her British counterpart. Thatcher arrived late for a meeting with her at 10 Downing Street and Charles never let her forget it.)

By the time that the aircraft carrying the OECS leaders landed at Grantley Adams airport in Barbados, Antiguan troops had already arrived and men of Barbados's own Defence Force had been told to pack their bags ready for action and not to tell anyone what their orders were. Also waiting in Barbados was Francis McNeil, former Ambassador to Costa Rica who had come with the message that the Caribbean leaders would have to submit a written request for US help before the invasion would go ahead.

Uncomfortable news for the invaders was, however, also on its way to Barbados. Montgomery, Kurze and Flohr had to report that the US students in Grenada were, for the most part, unwilling to leave or be evacuated. They were too intent on their studies for these to be disrupted by the little local difficulties on the island. Kurze said he had not advised US citizens to quit Grenada.

The previous day Bob Dickerman of the US Information Service had done his best to point up the anxieties of two new young German students, Ludger Kreilkamp and Thomas Stein, who had left Grenada on Friday by boat. Dickerman met them at the airport and they gave their story to eager reporters at a press conference at the Holiday Inn. More blood would flow, they forecast.

Besieged by reporters at the airport, Montgomery said the situation in Grenada was 'calm, tense and pretty volatile' but he added that he had no idea if there would be violence when the curfew was lifted on Monday morning. He reported that he had got Cornwall's word that Pearls airport would be open

166

the following day, Monday, and that any British, US or Canadian citizens who wanted to leave would be free to do so. In the Bayshore, New York, office of the St George's University Medical School, Charles Modica, the school's Chancellor, repeated that his students were in no danger.

Modica's words were echoed by Dr Geoffrey Bourne, his British deputy still in Grenada. That night Dr Joseph Damon of Winchester, Virginia, talked by telephone to his 30-year-old son, Joseph, a student at the school, who told his father that he did not consider he was in any danger and that he did not want to go home. Eloise Litman of Pomona, New York, was told the same thing by her 23-year-old son Steven, also a medical student.

Don Atkinson, a retired US businessman who had lived in Grenada for twelve years, recounted afterwards that there had been no threats whatever to US citizens before the US assault.

On the day of the invasion Modica, talking on an NBC broadcast, said Reagan had been 'very wrong' to have charged that US lives were in danger in Grenada.

Meanwhile leave had been cancelled for the 75th Ranger Battalion and, throughout Sunday and Monday, the troops received detailed briefings about the invasion at Hunter Army Airfield outside Savannah, Georgia.

It was late afternoon before Reagan finally made up his mind to agree to the operation. Far from holding the invasion up the deaths of so many US marines in the Lebanon made the President even firmer that his country would not be seen to be giving in to what he considered terrorism.

On Sunday evening McFarlane drew up the National Security Decision Directive, the document needed before US troops can be committed to military action.

Preaching at St Michael's Cathedral, Bridgetown, Dean Harold Crichlow, took his text from the fourteenth chapter of Jeremiah, 'We look for peace, and there is no good; for a time of healing and behold trouble.'

'I cannot see how we can have a military intervention in Grenada since we would not sanction such interference in our own affairs,' he said.

His words reached neither President Reagan nor Prime Minister Adams.

Expectations in Barbados rose that the invasion would take place within the next few hours and, late on Sunday night, the Voice of Barbados told its listeners to stand by for a special announcement. It never came. Before he left Trinidad, Burnham hit out at the decision taken by his colleagues to suspend Grenada from Caricom. He said:

It's not binding because in the first place it is not a decision of Caricom, because one of the constitutents of Caricom was not invited, Grenada.

Secondly, even if it were a Caricom decision, the fact that Guyana was opposed to any suspension or expulsion makes any majority decision worthless in terms of the Caricom treaty which on an issue like this calls for unanimity.

Guyana was unhappy with the outcome, he added:

First of all Guyana was distinctly interested in two things: one, that before we get too far in condemnatory statements we should have a fact-finding mission or body from Caricom to make contact with and visit Grenada to ascertain what really happened and, secondly, we were and still are completely averse to any military intervention, especially from outside the region.

Burnham's complaints and Chamber's protestations, (voiced in good faith but, in fact, inaccurate) that Caricom was not contemplating any interference in Grenada's internal affairs, availed nothing. The invasion, in the course of being approved by Reagan and supported by Adams, Seaga, Bird, Compton, Simmonds, Charles and Cato, was going ahead.

Shortly after the invasion, Seaga charged that some member of Caricom had been treacherous enough to warn the Grenadians that an invasion was being planned. His reference was widely taken to mean Burnham. In any event by Sunday eve-

168

ning Radio Free Grenada was frantically repeating a communiqué.

Member countries of the Organisation of Eastern Caribbean States, along with Barbados and Jamaica, this afternoon took a decision to send military forces to invade Grenada and to call on foreign forces also to invade our country. The decisio was opposed by Guyana, Trinidad and Tobago, the Bahamas and Belize. However, some islands have already sent armed forces to Barbados as a jumping off point for this invasion of Grenada and units from Jamaica and Antigua are on their way to join them. At this time a warship is only seven and a half miles from Grenada, well inside our territorial waters. An invasion of our country is expected tonight.

Reflecting the ebbing hope of the RMC that some negotiated solution to the crisis could be found, even at this last minute, the announcement added that Grenada was 'prepared to fight to the last man and woman to defend our homeland, though it is equally prepared to hold discussions with any of these countries to find a peaceful solution.'

As Monday dawned in Grenada Coard and the RMC did much to try and get things back to normal – though that did not include the release of Alister Hughes and other opponents of the régime. Having closed Pearls airport on the day of Bishop's murder to keep out intruders the military group now faced the task of tempting traffic to use the airport. Kelly tried his best to arrange transport for a group of British and Canadians who wanted to leave the island and for a group of technical experts working for the Organisation of American States. He and his colleagues at the British and Canadian High Commissions in Bridgetown were unsuccessful. The governments of the countries of the OECS, having taken a decision to isolate Grenada, were unwilling to allow Leeward Islands Air Transport, LIAT, the regional airline, to land on the island. The British and the Canadians tried diplomatic persuasion on the toughest opponent of any flight by LIAT to Pearls, the government of Antigua, and Vere Bird finally agreed that an exception should be made on humanitarian grounds for the sake of the refugees.

By the time the permission finally arrived from St John's, the Antiguan capital, it was too late to find a crew for the LIAT aircraft. Four flights were, however, made to take out that small minority of medical students who wanted to quit Grenada. The OAS experts were able to climb aboard one of these flights. But contrary to the position during the previous week those who wanted to leave Grenada were being locked out of neighbouring countries by the OECS ban on air travel from Grenada, rather than being stopped from leaving the island by the Grenadian authorities. As the population emerged from three days of house arrest to talk and buy food Coard and Austin did their best to tempt people back to their jobs, though they did add that a nightly curfew from 8 p.m. to 5 a.m. would continue. For fear of new demonstrations by the schoolchildren the RMC decided to keep the schools closed for another week.

In the White House, Reagan went over the invasion plans with Defense Secretary Caspar Weinberger and the Joint Chiefs of Staff for an hour and a quarter after lunch and finally, at 6 p.m., signed the directive that McFarlane had prepared the previous day.

The green light had been given to the invasion forces who had already taken up their position round Grenada.

One government was kept out of the fun. John Osbourne, Chief Minister of Montserrat, the one member of the OECS which was not independent but still a British crown colony, was peremptorily forbidden to send forces of any kind to assist in the invasion of Grenada. For Montserrat to have been allowed to do so would have implicated the British government in the operation and that the Foreign and Commonwealth Office was not going to permit under any circumstances.

In Barbados on 23 October the *Sunday Sun* printed an interview its reporter Tony Best had had with Gairy in Washington. The former Prime Minister had quit his exile in the US and gone to Barbados in August. He held a press conference and said that he considered himself 'the duly elected, constitutional Prime Minister and head of the Government of Grenada, Carriacou and Petit Martinique'. He was, he added 'in temporary exile'. Adams quickly cancelled his permit to stay in Barbados and he was bundled off the island back to the US capital.

The day after Bishop's murder Gairy called at the British Embassy in Washington. His hopes of returning to Grenada were rising and he wanted British help to get back. In his interview with Best Gairy insisted that Britain had an obligation to restore him to the position he had occupied before the revolution. The countries of the Commonwealth Caribbean, he said, should band together with 'the bigger democracies' and take positive, aggressive and meaningful action against the RMC.

The British for their part were at this time doing their best in Washington to read the Reagan administration's mind at a moment when that mind was being made up. The British diplomats in Washington, Barbados and Trinidad were fully conscious of the hawkish thoughts of the State Department and of some of the Caribbean leaders.

Giles Bullard, the British High Commissioner in Barbados, had been called in by Adams on Friday to be told that Barbados favoured an invasion. Adams claimed that the original idea had come from Compton. After the joint approach by Adams, Charles and Seaga to Bish on Friday Bullard was told by Adams that British help would be welcome. The Foreign and Commonwealth Office in London was against the invasion plan but was very keen to know what Reagan would finally decide to do.

Reports in the British Sunday papers of an impending invasion aroused increasing interest in London. In the *Observer* Austin's remarks to me, accusing Britain and the US of collaborating in an assault on the island were carried prominently on the front page and the following day in the *Financial Times* I reported the arrival of Antiguan troops in Barbados. Other newspapers also carried full reports of the growing crisis.

Sir Geoffrey Howe, the Foreign and Commonwealth Sec-

171

retary, was obliged to make a statement in an excited House of Commons at 4 p.m. on Monday afternoon. Reporting on Montgomery's visit to the island Howe informed the House that he had found the island calm but tense but that neither Scoon nor members of the British community appeared to be in any imminent danger. HMS *Antrim* was on hand nevertheless if it was necessary to evacuate British subjects.

As he sat down, Denis Healey, the Labour foreign affairs spokesman, rose from the Opposition front bench and asked him a question that Howe was destined to rue. 'Can the Foreign Secretary assure us that there is no question of American military intervention on the island? It could only make the position worse.'

Rising for a second time Howe answered, 'I know of no such intention.'

Twice more he was pressed by Labour MPs George Foulkes and Jeremy Corbyn on the question of an impending US invasion. To the former he replied, 'I have no reason to think that American intervention is likely.' To the latter he said rather testily, 'I have already explained twice the presence of the United States naval vessels is not prompted by the consideration that the honourable gentleman has in mind. The vessels are there for the reason that the United States government and we have given. There are more than 1,000 United States citizens and several hundred British citizens on Grenada. It is only prudent that when governments of democratic countries are faced with such circumstances they take steps to provide for the rescue of their citizens if necessary. That is the reason for the presence of the naval vessels.'

With such a reply Howe, never wholly at home in parliamentary debate, saw his reputation as Foreign and Commonwealth Secretary buried, perhaps for good. The reply was also the signal that Reagan was willing to allow the Thatcher government, the strongest US ally in Europe, to suffer great embarrassment in the cause of the secrecy surrounding his pursuit of Washington's own ends in the Caribbean. The US government was willing to invade a Commonwealth country which shared the same monarch as Britain without informing the

British government. The Reagan administration had gone farther than that – it had deliberately misled the British.

While British diplomats were gathering intelligence as hard as they could in the Caribbean the Foreign and Commonwealth Office in London took the understandable view that nothing the Caribbean mini-states supported would come to pass without the approval of the US President. The efforts of Sir Oliver Wright, the British Ambassador, and his staff in Washington were therefore bent to finding out what Reagan's decision on the matter would be. From every senior official they tackled in Washington they got the word that no invasion was contemplated. British conviction that this was the case was not ruffled even when word reached the FCO from Bullard on Monday that an invasion was imminent. After all, Wright had been told that afternoon in Washington by Lawrence Eagleburger, Under-Secretary of State for Political Affairs, that all was calm. The Foreign and Commonwealth Office was totally hoodwinked, a hoodwinking made all the more bitter by the fact that the US government took into its confidence the governments of small independent Commonwealth Caribbean countries and the administration of the British Crown Colony of Montserrat.

Thatcher was told only after Reagan had signed the order. At 10.30 p.m. on Monday she received word of the invasion as she was dining with John Louis, the US Ambassador at the table of a member of the Royal Family. Thunderstruck and extremely angry, she hurried back to Downing Street where senior officials gathered to meet her shortly before 11 p.m. Louis, displaying the imperturbability he exhibited in 1982 when he continued his holiday in Florida after the invasion of the Falklands, stayed at table for coffee. Despite two telephone conversations with Reagan, the British Prime Minister could not get the invasion plans cancelled.

CHAPTER SIX

The Aftermath

'If we had to do it over again, I believe we would not
change a thing.'
Milan Bish, US Ambassador to Barbados, 13 December 1983.

In the political confusion which followed the invasion Reagan
was to win the domestic battle, the one which he perhaps felt
was the most important one to him as he weighed his chances
of re-election to the Presidency of the US. US citizens in the
majority were to be convinced that the invasion was right and
justified.

Internationally the balance would not come out in his favour.
The invasion of Grenada, like US actions against the Nicaraguan government and in favour of the extremely brutal oli-
garchies of Central America, raised the temperature of politics.
In doing so it gave legitimacy to radically anti-US forces in
the Caribbean whose cause would otherwise have found little
favour among politically easygoing West Indians. The embitterment and radicalisation of Caribbean politics cannot be in
the long-term interest of the US.

It also strained relations between Washington and its principal European allies and increased distrust among Western
leaders of Reagan's handling of international affairs. It even
muted what might otherwise have been a major public row
between Havana and Moscow on the question of Bishop's
death.

While Reagan was winning at home he was losing out abroad.
On the morning of the invasion, he moved quickly to cull

what he hoped, correctly, would prove to be a harvest of popularity and gratitude from the people of his country. He appeared at a press conference early at the White House in the company of Eugenia Charles who had flown up to Washington the night before.

In contrast to his later claims the President did not link the invasion to any battle with the Cubans or the Soviets in the Caribbean. He gave three reasons for the US action:

First, and of overriding importance, to protect innocent lives, including up to 1,000 Americans, whose personal safety is, of course, my paramount concern.

Second, to forestall further chaos.

And third, to assist in the restoration of conditions of law and order and of governmental institutions to the island of Grenada where a brutal group of leftist thugs violently seized power, killing the Prime Minister, three cabinet members, two labour leaders and other civilians, including children.

Pressed by a questioner about Speakes' statement the previous day that US citizens in Grenada had been in no danger, Reagan claimed that 'several hundred' wanted to leave. 'But the airports were closed. There was no way of leaving.'

Charles was asked if there was evidence of a Soviet and Cuban takeover of Grenada. Embroidering the truth she answered, 'Yes, we do have this information. I can't give you all the details because of the safety of the people concerned.'

On President Reagan's right Weinberger and Shultz looked on pensively.

Reaction in the US was initially guarded. The newspapers of the following day were sceptical of the rightness of the President's decision. The excuse for invasion, *The New York Times* said, was 'flimsy' while *The Washington Post* said the White House justifications were 'hardly adequate'. The *Minneapolis Star and Tribune* wrote sarcastically, 'President Reagan has shown that the tiny nation of Grenada cannot push the US around.'

As the hours went by the popular support for the invasion

175

grew. Central to the increase in acceptance in the US was the arrival back in the US on the night of Wednesday/Thursday of the first US medical students. The action of the first who disembarked was to kiss the ground and this touched a chord of folksiness among TV viewers and was almost by itself sufficient to swing the country behind Reagan's action. 'I don't want to hear anyone criticise those American soldiers. They saved our lives, man,' he said.

The suppression of mention of desperate resistance by some Grenadians to the invasion of their country coincided with accurate reports coming from Grenada that the invaders had been welcomed with open arms by other Grenadians.

In order to ensure support for his action Reagan now began to change the justification for the invasion. The day after the US landing White House officials began to argue that Washington had been principally concerned with the Cuban and Soviet presence on the island and that it could not afford 'another Nicaragua'. The President had had to move, it was argued, to avoid another crisis such as that of the US hostages in Tehran.

Reagan himself publicly argued this position on the Thursday. In a television speech he said:

The events in Grenada and Lebanon, though oceans apart, are closely related. Not only has Moscow assisted and encouraged violence in both countries, but it provides direct support through a network of surrogates and terrorists.

We got there just in time.

At 3.30 p.m. on the day of the invasion the Foreign and Commonwealth Secretary rose in the House of Commons to address a gathering from which he was to emerge, according to one parliamentary observer, 'more like a strangled chicken than a minister of the Crown'.

The morning's news had revealed to all what the British government had learnt with horror the previous evening – that it had been kept in the dark. In his opening statement Howe said the administration in Washington had told Britain that it was giving 'serious consideration' to a request from the OECS for help with a military intervention. He went on:

We put to them a number of factors which we thought should be carefully weighed before a decision was taken to intervene. Early this morning they informed us of their conclusion that, for the United States and for those Caribbean states which had proposed it, intervention was the right course to pursue.

For the Labour opposition Denis Healey, the shadow Foreign and Commonwealth Secretary, rose to deliver the hammer blows such as had already made him the terror of the Government and the *bête noire* of many members of his own party.

Yesterday, the Foreign Secretary told us that there was no reason to think that American military intervention was likely, and that he knew of no American intention to invade. That is an extraordinary statement by a representative of a government who pride themselves on being America's most loyal ally . . . The American decision has already split the Commonwealth states in the Caribbean. It represents an unpardonable humiliation of an ally. I must ask the Foreign Secretary, indeed the Prime Minister, to protest directly in the clearest possible terms.

Amid one of Howe's confessions of ignorance about the situation the outspoken Labour MP Dennis Skinner – known familiarly in the press as the Beast of Bolsover – asked ex-asperatedly, 'What does the Foreign Secretary know?'

Andrew Faulds, a former actor turned Labour MP, asked:

Does not the Foreign Secretary think that it is time that he and the Prime Minister reconsidered their attitude of underwriting American policies across the world, particularly when that business is conducted by a bunch of ignorant businessmen led by a president who is a dangerous cretin?

Conservatives were also unhappy at the government's posture and a leading Conservative backbencher asked Howe:

Is my right honourable and learned friend aware that there are people in all parts of the House who will believe that this is no way for the Americans to treat their closest ally?

The encounter ended with prolonged shouts of 'Resign!' from Opposition benches.

Nor was this the end of the matter for the Thatcher government. Eugenia Charles at the UN had claimed that Scoon had sought to get a message through to the Queen – presumably on the Sunday morning during the course of the meeting he had had at Government House in St George's with Montgomery. In a rare public statement a spokesman at Buckingham Palace denied any such appeal had been received. In fact Scoon had been in touch with both Buckingham Palace and Sonny Ramphal at the Commonwealth Secretariat on the Friday and Saturday after the murder of Bishop. In the course of these conversations he made no reference to the need for outside intervention. Indeed he speculated about the composition of the civilian government the RMC was trying at that time to put together.

The lack of correct intelligence about the invasion had placed the Queen in a position of considerable embarrassment. Her role as the Head of State of a number of countries whose governments could, and did, have divergent or even mutually hostile policies was always a delicate one. In the present crisis she was, for instance, Queen of Belize, whose government opposed the invasion, and Queen of the Bahamas, whose government likewise opposed the invasion. She was, however, at the same time Queen of Jamaica, whose government supported the invasion and Queen of Barbados, where the government also supported the invasion. She was likewise Queen of St Kitts-Nevis, St Lucia and St Vincent and the Grenadines all of whose governments supported the invasion. She was not Queen of the Commonwealth of Dominica, whose Head of

State was a President and whose government favoured the invasion or of Guyana and Trinidad and Tobago, republics whose governments opposed the invasion. All the governments, however, from Belize to St Kitts-Nevis and from Guyana to Dominica recognised her as Head of the Commonwealth.

She was indisputably Queen of Grenada. She was indisputably represented in St George's by her Governor-General, Sir Paul Scoon. But Scoon was bound to take his decisions from his ministers. He was in the same position as the Queen herself was as constitutional ruler of the United Kingdom, bound to act in British matters only in accordance with the advice offered to her by her British ministers.

Had Scoon, in fact, got a message through to her saying he favoured an invasion? If he had, on whose advice had he acted? Bishop was dead. The RMC? He had not publicly challenged its authority. Moreover the British government and the Reagan administration had *de facto* recognized the members of the RMC by negotiating with them about the visit of Montgomery, Kurze and Flohr to Grenada and about the evacuation of British and US nationals from Grenada. But the RMC clearly did not want an invasion.

If the Queen had acquiesced in an invasion of Grenada that was a serious matter. If she had had no knowledge of the invasion it was an equally serious matter.

In any event she had been let down by the Thatcher government. Her courtiers let it be known that she had cancelled the usual Tuesday audience with Margaret Thatcher. It was a sign of great displeasure, one of those gestures which in the rarified atmosphere of the British Establishment is the equivalent of a punch in the kidneys by a prize fighter or a Bronx cheer by a Chicago baseball crowd.

The continuing British dismay at Reagan's action forced Thatcher to distance herself even more from the US administration, a highly embarrassing operation since US cruise missiles were about to be installed in England and for months she had been arguing passionately that the British people could have full confidence that the weapons would not be fired by

179

the US forces who controlled them without the permission of the British government.

As the fighting stopped, apparent normality returned quickly to Grenada. Few buildings in the centre of St George's had been damaged. The most notable signs of destruction were to be found in the ruins of the mental hospital from which workers were still removing the bodies of the inmates killed by the US air attack a week after the event.

The shops which had been looted during the Wednesday and Thursday when St George's was virtually a no man's land were quickly boarded up and traders resumed their business. After a week or so the telephone system was reconnected to the outside world.

Those with the means to do so started making money out of the troops and police of the invading force and the hundreds of foreign journalists who swarmed through the island a week late in search of the story they had missed.

The Caribbean troops and police who had not been seen during the invasion made their public appearances as they mounted joint patrols with US troops through the city.

Losing their fear the forces began to relax and enjoy the warmth of the welcome of thousands of Grenadians who saw them as the men who had saved them from the horrors of the RMC.

Around checkpoints that the US troops set up on the main roads there gathered groups of excited or absorbed children. The troops fraternised and were careful to mind their manners. 'Have a nice day' was the almost invariable postscript to a US soldier's search of a car or check of documents at the roadside. Dalliance had its day.

In little more than a week after their arrival the marines were gone again and Queen's Park tried to return to its original role as a sports field and forget its time as a military headquarters. On Tanteen Field the remains of the helicopter shot down by the Grenadians on the first afternoon of the invasion were tidied away leaving nothing more than a scorch mark on the turf.

The US authorities did their best to seize and maintain a public relations initiative in the island, not least because it would justify the invasion in the eyes of voters in the US and blunt foreign criticism.

An office was set up on the Carenage to receive claims for damage done by US forces accidentally to Grenadian property outside battle situations. Well produced lapel badges of crossed Stars and Stripes and Grenadian flags appeared for use within days of the landing. Anonymous advertisements appeared in newspapers in Barbados asking supporters of the 'rescue mission' to write and tell their friends abroad of their reviews. Radio Free Grenada, silenced within hours of the first landing, stayed closed, superseded by 'Spice Island Radio' transmitted by the US forces.

Organisations hostile to the revolution were quick to express their gratitude to the forces. A typical statement came from the Grenada Employers' Federation. On 8 November the management committee of the Federation announced:

> The Grenada Employers' Federation joins with other private sector organisations in the country in expressing its support for and gratitude to the liberation forces of the Caribbean and United States of America over timely and effective intervention in our time of crisis. Following the massacre of 19 October and subsequent take-over of the country by the Revolutionary Military Council which held the entire population hostage, the events of the few days following provide convincing evidence that only an intervention by international military forces could have solved our problems . . .
>
> The Federation appeals to the Caribbean Employers' Confederation, Caribbean Congress of Labour and trade unions both within and outside the Caribbean to investigate objectively without delay the factors relevant to the present Grenada crisis before forming conclusions and passing judgements . . .

The statement was signed by representatives of the principal firms operating in Grenada including Geo. F. Huggins, Bryden and Minors, Jonas Browne and Hubbard, Geest Industries and Phillips Estates.

Businessmen were responsible for paying for the most prominent banners which appeared at strategic positions in St George's calling on the US forces to stay and condemning the Thatcher government. Businessmen were also responsible for a fund which was collected to defray the costs of a mass demonstration of 'thanks to the US and Caribbean Forces for rescuing us from oppression.'

The demonstration was scheduled to leave Market Square at 1 p.m. on 7 December. Employers were encouraged to give time off to their workers to participate in what was billed as 'a mammoth rally'. In the end, however, permission was denied by Scoon. The holding of one rally might have encouraged Bishop supporters to try and organise their demonstration. The invasion forces had in their first broadcast to the island on the morning of the landings demonstrated their hostility to Bishop. It would have been embarrassing to the authorities if the pro-US rally had attracted fewer people than demonstrated for Bishop on the day of his death.

Within a month of the invasion the *Grenadian Voice* was again publishing, two and a half years after it had been closed down after one issue by the People's Revolutionary Government. The editor was Leslie Pierre assisted by Alister Hughes, though the latter was much in demand for press conferences arranged by the US government which he participated in in Barbados and the US itself.

The first number of the *Grenadian Voice*, which was produced in the offices that until a month before had been occupied by the Cuban Government news agency Prensa Latina, carried a full-page advertisement from Geest Industries congratulating it on resuming publication 'so swiftly after the liberation'.

Less publicised was the quiet offensive carried out by the forces to catch and neutralise those who appeared likely to attempt to criticise the invasion. Soon after the fighting stopped Austin was picked up by men of the 82nd Airborne in a house on the smart residential estate at Westerhall. Coard and his wife were among others arrested. Initially Austin and Coard were flown to a US warship for questioning. At the beginning of November they were transferred back to Grenada, photographed bound, blindfolded and stripped to the waist, and consigned to Richmond Hill Prison. There they were in the charge of the men of the Jamaica Defence Force but their questioning by US intelligence agents continued.

The interrogation of the rank and file of the PRA, militia and supporters of the NJM was carried out at Point Salines.

The traditional methods of interrogation, initial isolation of prisoners, questioning, sorting into batches, mixing of more with less co-operative prisoners, occasional physical violence, reward for information given, were augmented by use of a computer which logged the details of all detainees. For a time some prisoners were confined in wooden structures, similar to packing cases, at the airport. Those wanting to relieve themselves were able to attract attention by poking sticks through the bars.

In the days which followed the end of the fighting the political battle restarted. The key to political legitimacy, it had been clear since the previous week, was Scoon, the Governor-General. Whatever his other qualities and defects, he had proved himself a survivor. Appointed by Gairy, tolerated by Bishop, allowed to continue in office by the RMC, it was ostensibly in his name that the invasion had been carried out. To be able to influence him was the key to controlling Grenada's future.

He relished his newfound prominence. There had been days, as the *Observer* recalled in its profile of him published on 23 October, when his colleagues would pass him in the corridors of the Commonwealth Secretariat and not feel it incumbent on them to break their step. Those days were long passed. He was now as close as he would ever get to being a monarch, not just reigning in representation of the Queen of Grenada, but almost ruling. It brought out those Hanoverian qualities which had been latent in him for years.

One of his first acts after the invasion was to make contact

183

with Buckingham Palace and to receive news that the Sovereign had expressed concern for his safety.

In day-to-day life, however, he had to work closely with the US authorities who held a very strong hand of cards. Recognising the political challenge of the Grenadian situation the State Department designated Gillespie, who had been a quiet but vital factor in the planning of the invasion, as Ambassador to Grenada. He set up his office in the Ross Point Hotel, not far from the US army headquarters at the Grenada Beach Hotel. The Governor-General and the ambassador were obliged to work closely with each other and this gave rise to remarks by wits in St George's that the Governor-General should be re-christened Sir Paul Gillespie.

That was scarcely just. While Scoon shared the conservative instincts of the Reagan administration he was keen that his prerogatives were not infringed too much. In his first proclamation on 31 October he announced the formation of an Advisory Council which would assist him till the calling of elections. While the step in itself was welcome enough to Gillespie its composition was hardly dictated by Washington.

Scoon after all had at his elbow the Commonwealth Secretariat whose Secretary-General Shridath 'Sonny' Ramphal, no great friend of the US, had been firmly opposed to the invasion. Ramphal had proposed that the Commonwealth should take care of Grenada – he was more conscious than most of the danger of the Commonwealth Caribbean splitting on the issue – and he quietly pressed for the quickest withdrawal of the US troops. The Commonwealth Secretariat and the US government indulged in weeks of quiet contest for the ear of Scoon.

Ramphal was delighted when Scoon offered the post of Chairman of the Advisory Council to one of the most prominent Grenadians in international life, Alister McIntyre, Deputy Secretary-General of the UN Conference on Trade and Development (UNCTAD). McIntyre had had a brilliant career as a development economist, had worked in Caricom and had been a driving force in the establishment of the International Bauxite Association which tried to do for producers of bauxite

184

what OPEC had done for oil producers. Another appointee was Dr Patrick Emmanuel, a university lecturer who had been in sympathy with many of Bishop's strategies and who had on one occasion been banned from entry to Trinidad and Tobago for his unconventional views.

In the event a combination of health and bureaucratic problems led McIntyre to turn down the offer after conversations with Scoon at Government House and his place was taken by Nicholas Brathwaite who had been director of the Commonwealth Youth Centre based in Guyana.

The advisory council was less than perfect from Washington's point of view. Controversy between Gillespie and Scoon surrounded the former's announcement that elections would be called within a year. Many in Washington thought that at least two years should elapse in which new parties could be formed and time could erode the image of Bishop.

In the wings lurked Gairy who let it be known several times before the end of the year that he was on his way back to claim a Prime Ministership which was still rightfully his. He finally returned on 21 January 1984, promising not to stand for office again. From Barbados Francis Alexis, one of several leaders of a Grenada Democratic Movement which had been encouraged by the US to set itself up in exile as an opposition group to Bishop, said at a press conference he called at the Holiday Inn in Bridgetown on the day of the invasion that, 'It would be somewhat irresponsible of me if my country needs my services to say no.'

From his political stronghold in Carriacou Blaize announced that he had not retired from politics. The NJM itself riven by the events of the year was silent though, as the weeks progressed, surviving supporters of Bishop, particularly Kendrick Radix and George Louison made discreet soundings about the possibility of launching a successor movement. There was no lack of contenders to enter the political arena in Grenada, however bloodstained it was.

A manhunt was mounted for missing members of the NJM and for several weeks a number of revolutionaries tried to

maintain a clandestine existence. Those who had been inter-
rogated and released were given a document attesting to this
and told to go home and keep quiet. This did not stop many
of them being rearrested, harassed and otherwise molested by
the invasion forces.

With the departure of the marines and the thinning down
of the naval presence, command of the forces devolved from
Admiral Metcalf to Major-General Jack B. Farris Jr, Deputy
Commanding General of the XVIII Airborne Corps, who had
seen service as a battalion commander in Vietnam. On 12 and
13 December the bulk of the US force flew off and on Wednesday 14 December the *Cygnus*, an enormous roll-on roll-off
vessel of the Lykes Lines, steamed out of St George's Harbour
with much of the transport and other impendimenta that the
US troops had brought. Farris handed over command of the
force to Lieutenant-Colonel Delroy Ormsby of the Jamaica
Defence Force. Colonel Ormsby, who had attended the Royal
Military Academy at Sandhurst and the Military Staff College
at Camberley, had his headquarters in the house that had been
Bishop's official residence and had seen some of the momen-
tous events of October.

Several hundred US troops remained, carrying out police
duties with the Caribbean forces. Paramount in importance
now, however, were the scores of civilian officials in the embassy of a power which, until the day of the invasion, had not
thought it worthwhile to station one resident vice-consul in St
George's.

The rest of the world was unwilling to give the US President
the benefit of the doubt and then the credit that his own people
gave him. As the news of the invasion came to the UN headquarters in New York, Victor Hugo Tinoco, the Nicaraguan
envoy led moves to convene an emergency session of the Security Council. Tinoco wrote to Abdullah Salah, the Jordanian
President of the Council, seeking an urgent meeting to consider
'the invasion of the Republic of Grenada by United States
troops'. Despite the inexactitudes of his reference to the is-

land's constitutional position the Council met at 11.11 p.m. on Tuesday night to debate the crisis.

By that time, more than fifteen hours after fighting had started, the principal powers had made their attitudes known. In Moscow Tass had accused the US of having pulled of 'a bandit-style armed intervention'. The French government had declared it could not 'appreciate the reasons which provoked this surprising action in relation to international law'. Hans-Dietrich Genscher, the West German Foreign Minister, expressed Bonn's 'great concern'. In Brussels the EEC decided on an immediate freeze on its aid programme to Grenada.

In Madrid Felipe González reported he had had talks with the Presidents of Colombia and Panama about the invasion which he opposed. From Venezuela came a condemnation of the invasion from a government which had backed Reagan's support for right-wing régimes in Central America.

For three and a quarter hours the Security Council debated a question about which the world's mind had already been made up. The first speaker was Porfirio Muñoz Ledo, the infinitely experienced and subtle Mexican envoy. That evening he was not subtle. Mexico, he said, unequivocally condemned without reservation the intervention and military invasion which were without any justification.

Tinoco followed. He ridiculed US legal justification for the invasion. Since when, he asked, had it been legal to get together and decide to invade another country with which they were not even at war? The Council, he urged, must condemn this flagrant violation of international law.

That got Jeane Kirkpatrick pressing for the right of reply. At around midnight she showed she had not lost her own gift of invective. Nicaragua, she said, was trapped in the fantasies of dictatorship and was wont to produce 'hysterically distorted analyses of history'. The United Nations, she said, echoing Reagan's impatience with a body which produced an anti-US majority on many issues of interest to Washington, was 'an outdated institution'.

For Grenada itself Ian Jacobs, one of the island's brightest intellects, read out the telex the RMC had sent to the US Embassy in Barbados on the day before the invasion. If the US was allowed to invade Grenada without condemnation then international law would collapse into anarchy, he said.

The Cuban delegate, Raúl Roa, was also in good voice as he referred to US justification of the invasion as 'squalid little footnotes they used to cover up their disgusting acts.' As Roa finished, a draft resolution sponsored by Guyana was circulated to the members of the council condemning US action and calling for an immediate withdrawal.

It was a ritual gesture. Everyone in the chamber knew it would be passed by a large majority only to be vetoed by Kirkpatrick. The session wound on into the small hours and Ali Treiki for Libya said that the US had celebrated United Nations Day by invading Grenada. 'Where will it stop?' he asked rhetorically. Oleg Troyanovsky for the Soviet Union took up Kirkpatrick's earlier point. This same terminology had been used in the 1930s by fascist Italy, Japan and Nazi Germany in talking about the League of Nations. (He made no mention of the Hitler-Stalin pact.)

At the end of the session at 2 a.m. Kirkpatrick took the floor again, now in less truculent mood than before. The US was in Grenada to protect US citizens, to help evacuate those who wanted to leave, and to support the OECS, she said.

The session restarted at 2.25 p.m. later that day and the Caribbeans on the invading force fought back. Charles, now a media star after her experience in a supporting role at the White House the previous day, put up a spirited resistance to criticism. Scoon, she reported, had called for assistance and the OECS and the US, Barbados and Jamaica were doing no more than answering an appeal. Sir Egerton Richardson for the Seaga government pushed the offensive even further. The former Bishop régime was illegitimate and never held elections. The OECS countries were democracies. For Antigua and Barbuda Lloyd Stone Jacobs went even further and appeared to start a process of rehabilitation of Gairy's régime which he implied had been a constitutional government. At the death of Bishop, he said, and with the backing of Cuban and Communist troops 'a few madmen seized power and foisted on the backs of our black brothers and sisters a revolutionary junta.' At 7.47 p.m. the company retired, exhausted by its own oratory.

The combatants convened the next day at 5.15 p.m. They continued through the night and broke up at 3.03 a.m. on Friday morning after a vote of condemnation of the invasion which was supported by eleven countries and vetoed by the sole vote of the US. Britain joined Togo and Zaïre in a blushing abstention. The world had delivered its judgement on the intervention in Grenada.

The following Monday, 31 October, the US delegation, following the lead given by Scoon in Grenada who sought to withdraw the credentials of all Grenadians representing their country abroad, sought to have Taylor Caldwell removed from the seat of Grenada in the UN General Assembly.

'If someone wants to remove me from Grenada's seat, they will have to do it physically', he replied with defiance. He got a round of applause.

The Cuban stand of support for the dead Bishop and a call for punishment of his murderers infuriated the Soviets who let it be known to Western journalists in Havana that they held the Cubans responsible for 'losing them a country'.

Despite Havana's strong statement the day after the massacre at Fort Rupert the Soviets clung to the line that it was nothing more than a falling out of revolutionaries and that the action of Austin and Coard was understandable given the need for greater discipline and ideological clarity wthin the party.

The normally well hidden points of friction between Moscow and Havana burst into the open at the beginning of November when, at the last minute, it was made known that the celebrations of the Soviet revolution, usually one of the high spots of the diplomatic calendar in Havana, was cancelled as the Soviet diplomats would be devoting the day to voluntary labour. It was not clear whether the Soviets cancelled their celebrations as a mark of unhappiness with the Cubans or whether the Cubans announced that they would not be attending in their usual force at the annual cocktail party, so forcing the Soviet ambassador to cancel the occasion.

On 14 November Fidel Castro drew together a crowd of a million in the Plaza de la Revolución in Havana and delivered a speech (see Appendix 1) in which he once again extolled Bishop and condemned Coard and Austin, members of what he called the 'Pol Pot Group'. It was a *tour de force* of a man who had seen the work of years in Grenada blown away during the massacre and the invasion and who was fighting to re-establish the credentials of his revolutionaries after a series of stunning blows.

The continuing Cuban eulogies of Bishop did not influence the Soviet line and the November edition of the Soviet Communist Party theoretical magazine *Kommunist* carried an analysis of the Grenada situation entitled 'Grenada, Victim of US Imperialist Aggression' by D. Muravyev. In the blandest of moods it recounted:

In these exceptional circumstances the serious problem of the revolutionary process facing the leadership caused divergences of opinion within the party itself. These problems did not touch on the main principles of internal and foreign policy but on the management of the economy and other spheres of party and governmental activity. They also concerned the delineation of relationships between party and state organs. Unfortunately the differences of opinion in the leadership of the NJM party, closely bound up with current affairs, took a tragic turn.

On 19 October as the result of an armed conflict in a district of St George's, Grenada, Prime Minister Maurice Bishop together with several ministers and trade union activists, perished.

Echoing Soviet criticism of Cuban political and economic management in the 1960s Muravyev claimed that the organisation of the NJM had 'lagged behind the needs of the revolution'.

Unlike the Cuban statement of 20 October, the article did

not call for the punishment of those responsible for the massacre. The inclusion and omissions strengthened the feeling that Moscow regarded Coard as 'their man' and thus above criticism, whatever he did.

Muravyev went on to use the Grenada issue as another opportunity to berate the Reagan administration and to warn the Western Europeans of the dangers of accepting cruise missiles.

The impression left was in the mind of the reader that the Soviet government was unable to bring itself to criticise Coard for in doing so it might indirectly be criticising its own policies. The other impression was that Grenada was somewhere to the back of the Soviet government's mind and useful only as a focus through which to consider more serious matters relating to Europe and super-power relationships.

CHAPTER SEVEN

The First Casualty of War

'Eventually the American air attack reduced Fort
Rupert to a smoldering shell with only one full wall
left standing.'
Newsweek, 7 November 1983

As the government in Grenada staggered towards its nemesis
no hint was given in its public pronouncements of the struggles
which were going on inside the government about the future
path the island society should take. In the planning and execution of the US led invasion the US authorities and their allies
proved to be equally reticent about trusting the public with
the facts.

Given the long history of reticence about its own affairs, a
reticence that at all times bordered on secrecy, and given its
unwillingness to tolerate public criticism of its policies, such
attitudes by the authorities in St George's came as no surprise.

After the Revolution opposition voices were accorded little
more shrift than they have been given under Gairy.

In mid-June 1981 the Newspaper (Publications) Law – People's Law 18 of that year – was promulgated which, for a
period of a year, banned the publication of any new 'paper,
pamphlet or publication containing any public news, intelligence or report of any occurrence or any remarks or observations thereon or upon any political matter, published for
sale distribution or any other purpose.'

Of the established press *Torchlight* was the first to go under.
Partially owned by Ken Gordon, a Trinidadian entrepreneur

who had interests in the *Trinidad Express*, the Barbados *Nation* and the *St Lucia Voice*, *Torchlight* made no secret of its opposition to the New Jewel Movement and Bishop's coup.

In a speech to a gathering of Caribbean journalists held in St George's in April 1982 Bishop was to accuse *Torchlight* of being 'a base of slanderous and destablising operations here in Grenada'. Despite this later judgement Bishop was known at the time to have been opposed to the action against *Torchlight* which happened in his absence. In his book *Grenada: the Struggle against Imperialism* Chris Searle, an enthusiastic supporter of the Bishop cause, claimed:

> The *Torchlight* soon became a continuous source of destabilisation and ally of almost every force that was trying to turn back the Revolution. It promoted an anti-communist editorial position, attacking the Cuban technical assistance and casting aspersions on Cuban internationalists like the medical teams who were making life so much better for the working people of Grenada . . . there was a striking headline, quoting one John Harrell, the 'Founder of the Christian Conservative Churches', and declaring that 'Communism is the boiled-down evil of all the generations.'

Before the year end *Torchlight* was closed down. In August 1981 the Torchlight company, Grenada Publishers Ltd, was taken over the employers who claimed large quantities of back pay and who turned it into a co-operative.

An attempt to start another opposition journal, the *Grenadian Voice*, was no more successful than *Torchlight*'s attempts to criticise the revolution. In May 1981 a group of Grenadians, calling themselves the Committee of 26 and including Alister Hughes and Lloyd Noel, who had not long previously resigned from the post of Bishop's Attorney-General, produced the first number of the newspaper. While some of the first issue managed to circulate, the whole printing of the second number was seized.

The venture was described by the government as having

been backed by the US Central Intelligence Agency. Bishop in a speech on Heroes' Day said:

It is no accident then, bearing this in mind, that so many elements of the 'Committee of 26' come from the biggest and most unpatriotic landowners in the country, those who are opposed to land reform, those who are opposed to workers' participation; those who are opposed to the Trade Union Movement.

Shortly after the closure of the *Grenadian Voice* Lloyd Noel was detained without charge and put in Richmond Hill Prison from which he was released only on 26 October, the day after the US invasion.

If the government acted toughly against the opposition press it maintained a theoretical commitment to free speech. The first publication of the Centre for Popular Education the Foreword to which was signed by George Louison, Minister of Education, Youth and Social Affairs, and which was designed as a simple political primer, attacked the former government. Under suitable drawings the publication said: 'Gairy has smashed the right to free speech' and 'Gairy had smashed the right to print newspapers and the right to read literature of one's choice.'

Grenadian efforts to control and supervise the flow of information on the island were puny in comparison to those being made by the administration in Washington to portray Grenada as first and foremost a potential base for Cuban and Soviet ideological and military operations in the Caribbean and Latin America.

Not long after the Bishop government was established persistent reports started coming out of Washington that a Soviet submarine base was being constructed on the south coast of the island near the Point Salines airfield. The report was given wide currency in the US and abroad. It was not until 1983 that the report was shown to be fallacious when Ed Cody, a correspondent for the *Washington Post*, visited the supposed

194

site and demonstrated that no submarine base could possibly be constructed in an area where the sea was so shallow.

Despite the fact that, as we have noted, the project of a new airport at Point Salines had been accepted by many foreign governments and international development institutions as sound, indeed vital, for the long-term development of the tourist trade, US spokesmen continued a barrage of misrepresentation in which they pounded away at the theme that it would serve as a staging post for the Soviets and the Cubans.

In the war of words that the US and Grenadian governments waged on each other the first casualty was the truth.

On 22–24 June 1981, a month after the closure of the *Grenadian Voice* the US International Communications Agency held a three day seminar in Washington in which one of the principal topics of discussion for the invited Caribbean editors was the issue of press freedom under the Bishop government. This resulted in a crop of editorials and news reports attacking human rights violations on the island and the pressures on press freedom.

On Sunday 27 September principal newspapers throughout the Commonwealth Caribbean printed an identical editorial in which they joined 'in a common expression of condemnation of the behaviour of the People's Revolutionary Government'.

Bishop reported to a conference of journalists at St George's in April 1982 the results of a survey he said the island's Media Workers Association had carried out on the contents of nine Commonwealth Caribbean newspapers in the period from June 1980 to December 1981. Sixty per cent of the 1570 articles examined were negative to the revolution and only 5 per cent of the rebuttals sent out by the government were published.

A special target of Bishop's wrath was the Inter-American Press Association which he charged with being in the pay of the CIA. The Association, which groups the more conservative newspapers of the Western Hemisphere, has for decades been the object of sharp criticism from the Latin American left which charges that its members are quick to condemn violations of the rights of right-wing newspapers but are usually supine when left-wing organs come under attack.

Reading the edition of the government-controlled *Free West Indian* which appeared on 12 October, a week before the murder of Bishop and the others, no one would have sensed the great debate going on within the councils of the NJM, all burning issues of national policy were suppressed. The front page of the sixteen-page newspaper was justifiably given over to accounts of the results obtained by Bishop in his visits to Hungary and Czechoslovakia which he described as 'extremely successful'. The main front page article was devoted to an agreement with the Czech government for the supply of three new electricity generators to a total value of some US$3 million. It was not clear, however, whether this equipment was being provided on normal commercial terms or as a gift, though the inference was that the Czechs were acting generously.

The alert reader would have noted the Prime Minister's special references to the abilities of his two particular allies contained in the mention of 'the performance of the entire delegation, especially the skilful negotiations of the Agriculture Minister, George Louison who led the advance delegation and Foreign Minister Unison Whiteman, who led discussions on the exchange of views between countries.'

A full-page advertisement announced that the Grenada-Venezuela Co-operation Centre was celebrating its first anniversary with a series of events which ranged from a regatta to the showing of a documentary on Simon Bolivar and a Mass at Grand Anse prior to the inauguration of a public library at the centre.

The newspaper's editorial was devoted to the contradiction the newspaper saw between the blowing up by the CIA of a Cuban airliner in October 1976 and the US reaction to the recent shooting down of a Korean Airlines Boeing 747 by the Soviet Union.

The bursting out into the open of the crisis with the detention of Bishop, the announcement made by Strachan and reported by Alister Hughes, that Bishop had been replaced by

196

Coard, the demonstration lead by Radix for the freeing of Bishop and Radix's own subsequent resignation from the Government, presented the authorities with new challenges. They accepted them.

The five principal foreign reporters on the island were picked up on 15 October by men in plain clothes who identified themselves as security police and were sent off the island by plane.

Before being taken to Pearls the reporters were told by the chief of immigration that they had arrived at an inconvenient time. 'This is an inter-party problem,' the official said, 'we don't want anyone reporting it until it is finished and then you will be invited back in'.

Radio Free Grenada for its part played down the party struggle reporting that Coard had resigned his portfolios so as to make it 'abundantly clear' that rumours that he and his wife Phyllis were plotting the assassination of Bishop were untrue.

No reference was made to Strachan's announcement that Coard had replaced Bishop. Radio Free Grenada did, however, mention the resignation of Radix.

The expulsion of the foreign journalists who included Nat Carnes, a reporter from the Puerto Rico office of the Associated Press, Linda Prout of *Newsweek* and Charles Hackett, the photographer of the Barbados *Sunday Sun*, were not as successful as they might have been. Hackett was able to smuggle out in his sock a roll of film containing pictures of the pro-Bishop demonstration which were displayed prominently in his newspaper in its issue of 16 October.

Hackett's reporter colleague Neville Martindale evaded arrest and made his own way back to Barbados via St Vincent and Trinidad and was able to write of the demonstrations and report the public protests on 14 October in which demands were made for the newspaper to print news about Bishop's whereabouts.

The expulsion of foreign journalists did not prevent the outside world knowing what was going on in Grenada. CANA, the Caribbean news agency which has a working relationship with the British Reuters news agency, continued to receive at its Barbados headquarters dispatches from Alister Hughes, its

197

correspondent in St George's. Hughes, however, was arrested late on the day of Bishop's murder. Two security officers, one in uniform, the other in plain clothes, called at his house in the centre of the city late on the Wednesday evening. They waited patiently while he took off his pyjamas and dressed and then took him off to Richmond Hill Prison where he was to be lodged for a week.

After Hughes' arrest all the news agencies were in the same boat and, with the rest of the media in the islands adjacent to Grenada, kept themselves informed by a constant monitoring of Radio Free Grenada and by gleaning news from travellers who continued to leave Grenada by air and by sea up to the day before the invasion.

The day after the killing of Bishop the Barbados *Nation*, the daily sister newspaper to the *Sunday Sun*, distinguished itself with an extraordinary Grenada special evening edition which combined the latest information from Grenada with accounts of the careers of the principal actors in the Grenadian drama, living and dead, and regional and world reaction to the killings.

The maintenance of international telephone links was crucial for the continuing flow of news out of Grenada. Indeed on Friday and Saturday I was able to speak to Austin himself by telephone. He said that Britain and the US were seizing on the pretext that their citizens' lives were in danger to mount an invasion of Grenada. While refusing, ostensibly with regret, to allow foreign journalists to go to Grenada, Austin asserted that Coard was playing no part in the government of the country, that he, Austin, had no idea of his whereabouts and that Coard could have left Grenada. The following day, Sunday, two days before the invasion, I was able to speak to Gehagen by telephone using the number on which I had on the two previous days spoken to Austin.

News gathering by telephone was not always so rewarding. Grenadians, with Wednesday's killings uppermost in their minds, were clearly intimidated and reluctant to speak their minds, especially to those telephoning from outside whom they did not know intimately. A call I put to one of the managers of Barclays Bank was parried by an unequivocal 'no comment'.

The RMC, unsuccessful at keeping control of flows of unfavourable news out of the island, was equally unsuccessful at getting its own version of events accepted by the outside world. Austin's statement on the killings, issued late on the Wednesday, was monitored in full from Radio Free Grenada but by now the propaganda initiative was moving firmly into the control of his enemies in the US and the Caribbean.

As Adams and Seaga consulted on Friday afternoon with Gillespie and the leader of the OECS governments the newspapers of the region went into attack, calling openly, indeed stridently, for an invasion of Grenada and the toppling of Austin.

The leader in the *Nation* of Friday 21 October ended:

The next hours and days will decide the future of the Spice Isle whose innocent people are now beating their breasts.

The likely intervention of the United States is very real, but their great concern must be for the nearly 1,000 Americans on the island.

The meeting of the Caribbean heads this weekend will provide the consensus from which any decision to rescue the people of Grenada will be made.

The task of our leaders is an unenviable one, but we are confident that they will respond to the exigencies of the hour.

The *Sunday Sun* two days later carried a stanza of verse on its front page which ended;

. . . 'tis time to act,
Act! Act! Not talk nor futile plan,
But swords unsheath, and war flames fan.

Inside its editorial read:

. . . the only possible solution will be the use of force. It should not be impossible for the defence forces of the region to institute a blockade of Grenada – and of Grenada's air space if we can obtain assistance from our international friends.

Such action, we believe, is justified by our regional interests.

The *Trinidad Express* in Port of Spain on Saturday was even more explicit:

It becomes, therefore, increasingly clear that the gangsters now in charge of Grenada by the gun are not only unapologetic about their execution of Prime Minister Maurice Bishop but are persisting in the bloodbath which they have unleashed against the people of Grenada. And it therefore also makes it urgent that the Caribbean heads of government not only meet quickly as they plan to do but take a firm decision to mount a security force to enter Grenada and free the people from this terror.

Under that editorial which was printed at the top of its front page was an item entitled 'more executions' which quoted unconfirmed reports that Hughes, his wife Cynthia, George Louison and Kendrick Radix had been 'among several new victims of executions now being carried out by the new military rulers in Grenada.'

The anxiety of the RMC to temporise and compromise when they sensed the revulsion that their murder of Bishop had caused was receiving no attention in the regional press.

While members of the RMC, Austin and Gehagan, continued to bar entry to Grenada to journalists, their opponents, ironically, started that weekend the process aimed at cutting off the flow of news from Grenada about the invasion which was about to begin. For a day or so there was the spectacle of journalists fighting both sides in an effort to secure information.

The decision taken by the leaders of Caricom at the meeting held in Port of Spain on 22/23 October to suspend Grenada

200

from membership of their organization and to back up the measures to cut sea and air links decided the previous day by the OECS governments at their meeting in Barbados were at least in part designed to allow any invasion of the island to go ahead free of observation by the press. With sea and air links cut off there would be no way in which foreign observers could see the deed being done, the RMC having already expelled foreign journalists caught in St George's the previous week and having imprisoned Hughes.

Catching Adams at Grantley Adams airport on Monday morning a group of journalists, of whom I was one, asked him directly to lift the ban on flights to Grenada for foreign correspondents.

His reply was, 'I hear you', a British legal phrase, but nothing was done.

The seven of us then set out on a twenty-four hour trip which was to land us in the Carenage the following midday and make three of us, Claude Urraca, of the French photo agency Sygma, Bernard Diederich of *Time* and I, the eye witnesses of the fall of St George's and the fighting that accompanied it.

Deciding that the island nearest to Grenadian territory, Union Island belonging to the newly independent St Vincent and the Grenadines, would be the most convenient stepping off point for St George's we chartered a light aircraft to take us there. Vincentian customs and immigration checks were passed without formality at the end of the 55-minute flight. We were on edge lest the Vincentian police, as they were later to do, tried to stop anyone leaving for the Grenadian island of Carriacou which lay clearly visible ten miles across the straits to the south. In less than two hours a boatman was found with an open twelve foot fishing vessel powered by an outboard motor. Within an hour of leaving the yacht-filled harbour of Union Island we landed at the broken down pier at Hillsborough on Carriacou. Grenadian passport and customs checks were passed without incident and we were legally admitted to the second largest island of the Grenadian archipelago, a place of 10,000 inhabitants less than 16 miles long by 5 miles wide. The reception from Edwin Stiell, the young administrator of Carriacou, and Milton Coy, the political education officer, was cordial and, after a lobster dinner at the battered Silver Beach Hotel, conversation about the crisis lasted well into the night.

The following morning before six the island was awakened by Radio Free Grenada announcing the invasion and calling on militia and medical personnel to report to their allotted places. Carriacou's only telecommunications link with the outside world was by radio telephone to Grenada which was not capable of dealing with international traffic so we had no opportunity of reporting back to our newspapers.

It took a further five-hour journey in an open boat for us to cover the thirty-four nautical miles to St George's. In the choppy waters which separate Carriacou from Grenada we had our first experience of the propaganda drive which backed up the invasion. Radio Free Grenada was silenced a little more than an hour after it had first issued its agonised call to arms.

The man and the woman announcers one moment were on the air telling key Grenadians what to do in the emergency. Interspersed with directions were declarations of adamantine defiance towards the invaders.

'We shall fight them on the beaches,' they declaimed, 'We shall bury them in the sea.'

They were soon silenced.

Shortly after we pulled out of Hillsborough at 7.25 a.m. in the 15 foot long *Odin C*, under the command of Captain Alfred and his mate we heard the first of a set of well prepared radio messages, beamed out by the US on 'Radio 1580'.

The justification for the US action was explained by the invitation from the OECS states and the message included a long denunciation of the Bishop government and the policies followed since 13 March 1979. In Spanish there came calls to the Cubans not to fight and to surrender.

Accompanying the message was a relay of the statements being made in Washington by President Reagan and Eugenia Charles. Tuning in late to the broadcasts the seven of us at first jumped to the conclusion that the US President had flown down to the Caribbean. It was only after the relay was repeated that it became clear to us that the Dominican Prime Minister had travelled up to the US capital.

As we came abreast of the northern tip of Grenada we saw the first military operations takng place as helicopters moved over the horizon. As I forecast to my colleagues it was not long before we ourselves were the object of examination by the invasion force. Two jets appeared from the south and described an arc round the *Odin C*. We waved with as much friendliness as we could muster and willed the pilots to understand that we were not some Grenadian force coming from Carriacou to bolster the defence of the main island. North of Victoria we saw a large plume of smoke which we took to be the result of some engagement. As we chugged on, soaked by the spray sweeping over us, and accompanied by sharks and flying fish, we were examined once more by the task force. Two helicopters circled us as the jets had done half an hour before and again we attempted as best we could be demonstrate our identity as journalists. We debated whether to raise a white flag, in the form of someone's shirt but decided that a white flag would indicate surrender when, in fact, we had never been part of the battle.

By now the phantom US radio transmitter had announced that the power station, the airfields and other points on the island had been taken by the US troops and that the quay in St George's had also fallen.

These pieces of information we used to persuade the increasingly restive Alfred to continue his course for St George's. He and, it must be said, we were alarmed by the sound of explosions and firing which drifted across the water from the capital and the distant sight of military aircraft swooping over Point Salines on the far southern horizon. The ships of the task force were visible on the horizon to the southwest.

We bickered with the unhappy Alfred about when we were going to hand over the fare for our trip and how much it was going to be. He wanted it paid before we landed, we were determined not to hand over a dollar before we were on dry land. But he was eventually persuaded to nose gingerly into the mouth of the harbour under the guns of Fort Rupert.

From the seaward side we had noticed the gaping hole in the green roof of the citadel inside Fort Rupert but, as the radio had not reported that the place had fallen to the US troops, we presumed, nervously, that it was still in Grenadian hands.

Though none of us realised it at the time we had narrowly missed death. Ten weeks after the event I learnt that a soldier of the PRA had the *Odin C* in the sights of his rocket launcher and, as we glided closer to the Carenage, was ready to fire a missile fully capable of sinking the boat and killing all its occupants. He decided not to fire only after a colleague identified Alfred, our skipper, as a loyal Grenadian.

We eventually put alongside the quiet Carenage. As we jumped ashore however US jets made a terrifying low pass over the city and provoked anti-aircraft fire from a group of Grenadian defenders at the eastern end of the quayside. Those of us on the quayside either dashed into the fire station or threw ourselves prone on the ground.

Seconds later four PRA appeared in a jeep and asked us our business. I reported that we had legally entered the state the previous day at Hillsborough but the soldiers ordered us to stay for the moment in the fire station across the road where the port immigration officer had his office. Our passports checked, we sat out the afternoon and the bombardment.

That evening the island's telephone and telex connections with the outside world were not in use and were to remain out of use for anything except the shortest life or death messages for more than a week thereafter.

The following day four of us accepted an invitation to be helicoptered to the *Guam* from Colonel Smith's tactical headquarters at Queen's Park. The four, Don Bohning of the *Miami Herald*, Ed Cody of the *Washington Post*, Greg Chamberlain of the *Guardian* and Morris Thomson of the Long Island newspaper *Newsday*, were not allowed access to telecommunications from the *Guam* and returned to Queen's Park by helicopter twenty-four hours later having learned little and having missed the US occupation of St George's.

The seven of us were able to transmit our accounts to our newspapers only late on Thursday evening after having waited for a helicopter to fly us to Point Salines – where we were told by Commander Tony Hilton, public affairs officer of the US Second Fleet to keep strictly to an area of the apron where little activity was visible – and from there by Hercules to Barbados.

A few other journalists sneaked into other parts of the island that day but the US forces took what for them were unprecedented measures to prevent eyewitness coverage of the invasion. The measures had been ordered by Caspar Weinberger, the Defense Secretary. His spokesmen attempted to justify them and the misinformation published by the administration before the invasion by arguing that secrecy was necessary for surprise and that the military could not be held responsible for the safety of journalists. Such arguments overlooked the fact that the RMC was aware days before it took place that an invasion was being mounted and that traditionally the US press had not held the military responsible for their safety in time of war.

The halting of the majority of reporters wanting to make their way to the island involved some unprecedented operations. A radio and TV crew from the US ABC network were intercepted at sea in a vessel they had chartered in Barbados to take them to Grenada. A US jet dropped a buoy in front of them with the message that they should turn back. After the jet made mock strafing passes over their boat with its bomb doors open the journalists made discretion the better part of valour and retired back to Barbados. Another group of journalists who managed to land at Pearls airport were ordered to return to Barbados.

When the first journalists, US citizens, all fifteen of them, were allowed to go to Grenada they went under heavily armed guard late on Thursday. Twenty-four followed on Friday but none was allowed to move out of the vicinity of Point Salines. Despite the fact that US aircraft were maintaining a virtual shuttle service between Barbados and Grenada no space was allocated to non-US journalists until the fighting was over. Even after the fighting was finished the US forces sought to control the flow of information from Grenada.

205

On 30 October, the Saturday after the invasion, Metcalf warned a group of reporters against acting independently.

'Any of you guys coming in on press boats? Well, I know how to stop those press boats. We've been shooting at them. We haven't sunk any yet, but who are we to know who's on them?'

It was clear that those who ordered the attempt to black out the news had in mind the fact that the war in Vietnam had been a public relations failure for Washington and was eventually lost in great part because the activities of journalists and TV reporters brought the horrors of the campaign into the homes of millions of US citizens. The US authorities, too, had before them the example of the British government, always much more secretive than US administrations, which virtually did away with any embarrassing reporting of the Falklands war by its strict control of reporting from the British task force and from the scene of battle in the Falklands.

The first reporters who were ferried in from Barbados were shown the large stocks of weapons and ammunition found by the invaders. The US forces banned the use by British journalists of an RAF Hercules which took Montgomery and other British diplomatic staff to Grenada during the weekend following the invasion. This ban produced more moments of Anglo-US friction.

A week after the attack, however, virtually any journalist who wanted to visit Grenada was able to board one of the three daily flights which linked the island with Barbados and space was found for reporters bitterly opposed to the US strategies. The change was due to pressure from Congress which came in the wake of furious lobbying of Reagan and of legislators by the executives of those media which did not have their own men on the spot.

One lesson to be learned from the coverage of the invasion, or lack of it, was that journalists for the printed media and for radio, unencumbered with the heavy paraphernalia of television cameras, still had a competitive edge over their TV colleagues.

The absence of the media from the invasion gave the US government full opportunity to manage the news to its own best advantage. It allowed it to distort in specific areas: the impression was conveyed to the world that the bulk of the fighting had been done by Cuban troops and that Grenadian resistance had been minimal. As the invasion proceeded the US authorities inflated the number of Cubans on the island to 1,600. This was reduced after the Cuban government, on Saturday 29 October, published a list specifying the job descriptions of all the 784 Cuban personnel on the island and the US, thereafter, admitted that the Cuban tally was correct.

It played down the strength of the men and equipment ultimately needed to reduce resistance on the island. At the beginning of the invasion official US sources said that no more than 3,000 marines and soldiers were involved. Late on Friday, however, Admiral Wesley McDonald, Commander of the US Second Fleet, said that the number had risen to 6,000. Overall, little prominence was given to the gigantic size, in comparison to the defenders' forces, of the battle fleet and troops deployed in the invasion.

The impression was given, which was especially important for Reagan vis-à-vis his domestic audience in the run up to the election campaign, that the invasion was carried out to save the lives of young US medical students who might otherwise have been in danger. The administration in Washington announced, in order to back up this assertion, that Pearls airport had been closed on the day prior to the invasion to prevent foreigners and others fleeing from the Austin régime. Only later did Larry Speakes, the White House spokesman, admit that four charter flights had indeed left Pearls airport on the Monday in question. The admission was made, however, after the emotional arrival aboard USAF aircraft of medical students from St George's University Medical School.

Obfuscation surrounded the US bombing of the Crazy House, in which, according to a hospital worker speaking on 2 November, eight days after the bombardment, thirty corpses had already been recovered and where digging was continuing. Despite the clear indication that more than thirty people died in the raid US spokesmen continued to claim that the death toll was no more than eighteen.

It allowed the impression to be bolstered that the construction of the airport at Point Salines by the Cubans was nothing more than an exercise in military strategy. No reference was made to the long gestation period of the Point Salines or to the very cogent economic arguments there were for its completion. To those who viewed the footage of the TV crews who were eventually allowed into Grenada Point Salines packed with soldiers and military aircraft simply *looked* like a military airport which was thankfully in US rather than Cuban or Soviet hands.

A statement from the British electronics company Plessey on 1 November listed eleven facilities that a military airbase would need: a parallel taxiway, arrangements for dispersed parking, radar, hardened aircraft shelters for protection against bomb blast, a secure set of underground fuel tanks, underground weapons storage, surface to air missile sites or other anti-aircraft defence, perimeter security, an 'operational readiness platform' with rapid access, aircraft engineering workshops and major stores and aircraft arrester gear.

None of these items existed at Point Salines, Plessey said. The facts were lost in the scramble to get over a White House point of view.

A direct part in the battle of information and disinformation was carried out by the US army itself.

Some of the least noticed but most important troops landed in Grenada were a handful of men from the Psychological Operations Battalion of the US Army, based, like the 82nd Airborne at Fort Bragg. The battalion was a unique unit of 150 men whose job it was to study and evolve techniques of propaganda which would be effective in the Caribbean, Latin America, Africa and Asia. Their own expertise on the various geographical areas was augmented by contacts with US academic and other experts on the various geographical areas the battalion targetted.

The psychological warfare unit had prepared, in consultation with the State Department, the tapes which were broadcast to the island by radio as the assault troops went in. These called on Grenadians in general to co-operate with the invading force which had come to put an end to what was termed the years of chaos of the Bishop administration. They called on members of the PRA to give themselves up and face their inevitable defeat. In Spanish a set of tapes promised that there would be no battle with the Cubans if they did not attack the invasion force and reminded the construction workers and others of their families back in Cuba. The US army said the 'Radio 1580' broadcasts were beamed from Barbados though other experts said that they came from the US armed forces transmitter in Antigua which is used by the Voice of America.

From the air and on the ground were distributed other examples of the battalion's work, green handbills for the Grenadians calling on them to join forces with the invaders, blue ones for the Cubans announcing that the US lead force had arrived 'to restore democracy'. There were safe conduct notices fashioned in the form of 5 peso Cuban banknotes bearing the legend in Spanish and English:

'To those who are resisting the Caribbean peace force. This pass will save your life if presented to any member of the Caribbean peace force. You will be taken to a safe place where your needs will be met. Food, clothing and medical treatment is (sic) available.'

A more gruesome poster carried a drawing of a bleeding corpse and a relieved group of soldiers surrendering with the caption '*Esto - o esto*' ("This - or this').

The six principles which guided the work of the battalion included an emphasis on the 'humanitarian' aspects of the invasion, the absence of any territorial ambitions by the US against Grenada, the re-establishment of law and order, the need for Grenadians to collaborate with the US, the re-establishment of democratic institutions 'amenable to US interests', and the acceptance of US action by Grenadians.

Major Douglas Frey, the military spokesman in Grenada, said in December that work had started on the preparation of the tapes and the printed material two days before the invasion and that the material used on the day of the invasion had been produced in the US. Though it is technically feasible it appears highly unlikely that so much matter could have been agreed between the army and the State Department, printed and delivered to the battlefield between the Sunday and the early hours of Tuesday. The existence of the tapes and printed material must be taken as strong evidence that the invasion was planned many days, perhaps weeks, before it was announced.

The battalion also provided lists of questions to those involved in interrogating detainees, culled from intelligence information available in Fort Bragg.

As soon as fighting permitted, the psychological detachment in Grenada which swelled to sixty men and which was commanded by the senior officer of the battalion, Colonel Ashworth, brought in its own printing press on which it ran off up to the minute material and posters offering the equivalent in local currency of US$500 reward for the information leading to the capture of a Cuban and smaller sums for guns in working order, explosives and ammunition.

No Cuban was ever turned in for reward by a Grenadian, according to Major Frey.

The detachment also provided material to be broadcast by loudspeaker from helicopter encouraging Cubans to give themselves up. The loudspeakers were used and the posters exhibited long after the last Cubans had returned to their island. The psychological unit, though it did not take responsibility for them, was probably responsible for various reports and rumours which circulated after the invasion. The two senior representatives on Carriacou, for instance, were said to have sold the island to the Cubans for US$36 million. On November two US soldiers were officially reported to have been wounded on Green Island off the north coast of Grenada near Sauteurs by two men who landed from a boat and who made off before they could be captured. No hard evidence was ever offered by the army for this incident but the rumours, the loudspeaker broadcasts from the air and the report of an otherwise unsubstantiated incident served to maintain a climate of anti-Cuban sentiment in Grenada and abroad, bolstered the misapprehension that Grenada and its revolutionary government was the political and military pawn of the administration in Havana and sought to increase the credibility of President Reagan's claim that Grenada had become a 'bastion' for Cuba and the USSR.

Among the first targets of the invaders were the transmitters of Radio Free Grenada at Beausejour which was built with powerful Soviet equipment during the revolution. It was knocked out within hours of the first landing by the US. The smaller transmitter at Morne Rouge was knocked out later that day when the adjacent studios were flattened by an attack from the air.

Their place was taken by a mobile transmitter brought ashore and operated by the US Navy which itself was superseded by 'Spice Island Radio' manned by Grenadians using US army equipment.

For its part, the Cuban government behaved with extraordinary and totally uncharacteristic rapidity in the propaganda field as the US attacked. As the troops went in on the Tuesday the leading news media in the US were told by Cuban representatives they could have visas for Cuba immediately and within hours a charter flight was organized in Miami.

In the early hours of Wednesday 26 October, a tired and drawn Castro was holding a press conference in Havana attended by a wide range of media from the *Washington Post* and the BBC to Radio Caracol of Colombia and *l'Humanité*, the French Communist daily newspaper.

Subsequently Ricardo Alarcón, the clever and very coherent Deputy Foreign Minister in charge of Western Hemisphere affairs and a member of the Central Committee of the Cuban Communist Party was to devote much of his time to giving briefings to the Western press. 'It was the first time we heard things in Cuba before they came out on the Voice of America', one journalist in Havana remarked.

Many newsmen stayed on to see the Cuban leadership led by Castro and his brother Raúl, Vice-President and Defence

Minister greet the wounded and the prisoners to martial music as they arrived at José Martin airport, Havana. Had it been more widely reported in the West the Cubans might have scored a more important propaganda coup over the question of the corpses. On 12 November a plane arrived at the Cuban provincial town of Holguín with thirty-seven corpses, only twenty-four of which, according to the Cubans, were Cuban. The US action in exporting thirteen Grenadian corpses is difficult to understand. Jonathan Steel of the *Guardian* reporting at the time from Grenada suggested that it was a move by the US to minimize the number of Grenadians reported dead in the fighting, and therefore their part in the resistance to the US invasion, while inflating the Cubans' role.

Some direct statements by, for instance, Admiral Metcalf, remain puzzling. On the morning of Thursday 27 October he offered the four reporters who had been helicoptered out from Queen's Park the opportunity of witnessing a major assault on Richmond Hill Prison which was represented as one of the last points of resistance in the island. Throughout that same day it was said that a big operation was about to be mounted on Fort Frederick. It seems inconceivable that Admiral Metcalf could have been unaware that Richmond Hill had, since the previous day, been occupied only by prisoners whose guards had fled. The situation had been reported to Colonel Smith by Bernard Diederich and me on the Wednesday night after Hughes and others had left the prison. In any event Richmond Hill Prison was overlooked by the marines at Fort Frederick who had captured that position virtually without a shot early on Wednesday afternoon. It is difficult not to believe that Admiral Metcalf was being disingenuous to the journalists about the situation on the ground. One could imagine that the US forces' interests were best served by spreading the impression that resistance was continuing in a minor way. That way there would be justification for a continuing military presence in Grenada.

For his part Speakes from the White House on Friday 28 October put out the version, which was later retracted, that 'several hundred armed Cubans' were believed to have taken to the hills where attempts to flush them out could encounter serious problems.

The same day it was announced that 200 of the 300 Caribbean auxiliaries had finally been deployed in St George's. In an engaging fit of frankness Admiral Metcalf commented:

'The Caribbean forces are doing what they were trained to do. They look good but they are not combat troops. They are, basically, policemen'.

The remark cannot have gone down well among the Sandhurst-trained officers of the Jamaican and Barbadian Forces. Admiral Metcalf's interventions went far to back up complaints by Henry Catto, a former Pentagon press officer, who had on 30 October complained that the US constraints on the press were unwise and who added,

'Unhappily, the average joint chiefs of staff member has all the public relations sense of Attila the Hun.'

In a country where the principle of open government and media access to decision making are respected to a far greater extent than in any other Western country – certainly far more than in Britain – the decision to bar journalists from the scene of operations created a storm of controversy and temporarily soured relations between the press corps and the White House.

Reporting from Washington nearly a month after the invasion Geoffrey Smith of *The Times* commented:

There is a burning sense of indignation, the strength of which takes even me as a journalist by surprise. It is clearly causing the Administration a good deal of anxiety . . . The outraged are . . . the most politically influential members of the news media of the country. If this colours their whole attitude to the Reagan Administration, it could be a serious matter for the President and his colleagues.

The US public did not necessarily share that outrage. Many felt that the President was entirely justified in excluding the media from an important and delicate operation. It must be added that the media sustained some self-inflicted wounds. Stewart Russell, the experienced and able correspondent of

Reuters, was ordered back from Barbados to his home base of Miami on Sunday 23 October, to his intense annoyance, as his editors decided that the story did not justify his further presence. Reuters thus missed the opportunity of travelling in the party of seven who reached Grenadian territory on the day before the invasion. Agence France-Presse, the French news agency actually had two staff members in the party of seven, Urraca and Chamberlain. Both men had, however, got to Grenada under their own steam without financial assistance from their employers.

A journalist from the Associated Press expressed bitterness to me that he had been 'bumped' from our charter flight to Union Island on 24 October which took the seven on the first leg of the journey to St George's. In reality he had not been on the spot at the right time. One European journalist who reached the Grand Anse area during the fighting frankly confessed that he was so frightened that he spent two days in hiding. Few who experienced the bombardment of the area would chide him for his decision.

The restriction on press access to Grenada during the invasion had an immediate impact not just on the interpretation given to the events but on the recounting of what in fact happened.

The issue of *Newsweek* dated 7 November, which made its appearance the week after the invasion, was a prime example of the effects of the news famine. Its Special Report on the invasion was entitled dramatically but accurately enough:

The Battle for Grenada
American troops take charge on the island but face surprisingly stiff opposition

The report contained the following vivid account of the fighting:

In order to minimize civilian casualties, the American commanders decided against a full-scale ground assault. Instead they deployed small units backed by heavy air power. Inside

St George's they fought a tough battle for Fort Rupert, where a week before troops loyal to the rebel junta had executed Grenadian Prime Minister Maurice Bishop. From behind the limestone walls of the French-built, 18th century fortress, Cuban and Grenadian defenders showered small-arms fire on the US attack squads. Grenadian soldiers fired their AK-47s straight up at dive-bombing US jets and helicopters. They managed to shoot down two Cobra gunships. Eventually the American air attack reduced Fort Rupert to a smouldering shell, with only one full wall left standing.

It is not clear how the editors of *Newsweek* were able to reconcile their account with the fact, recorded above, that Fort Rupert fell without a fight on the morning of 27 October, that no Cuban was observed fighting in St George's and that the fort still has its full complement of walls.

The Special Report continued:

Later the Marine reinforcements played a major role in the advance on the two last Cuban strongholds north of St George's Fort Frederick and Richmond Hill Prison. Near Fort Fredcrick, the Cubans fired at advancing American planes with heavy anti-aircraft fire. After more than a day of combat, the stronghold finally fell. Then the Rangers, paratroopers and Marines moved on to Richmond Hill.

The article went on:

The Americans . . . noted that the retreat to the hills was a classic guerrilla tactic – and that some hill fighters might hold out for weeks.

Referring to Grenada's island dependency from whence the only four Cubans had been evacuated four days before the invasion *Newsweek* reported:

The intervention forces also readied to storm Carriacou, a tiny island north of Grenada. Officers had delayed the action until they could get a better fix on the strength of the Grenadian and Cuban forces there. US intelligence had picked up radio signals from Carriacou, and also had evidence of sophisticated Cuban bunkers on the island.

A map of Grenada, purporting to illustrate the timing of the various stage of the invasion included the caption, 'US force moves on to fight Cubans and Grenadians at Richmond Hill Prison and Fort Frederick.'

The magazine's principal article about the US President's decision to invade Grenada said:

From the very first, Reagan was inclined to heed the call to go into Grenada: there were 1,000 American citizens there, none of whom had been allowed to leave since the coup in which the pro-Cuban Prime Minister and some of his Cabinet had been brutally murdered by an even more fervently pro-Cuban faction.

As was the case with other publications *Newsweek* accepted without question the US administration's contention that the Cubans on Grenada were a powerful force of soldiers which was likely to continue resistance in the interior of the island after the fall of Point Salines. In an article on 'The Cuban Connection', the magazine reported, ' . . . on the ground the US invaders quickly came up against a hardened professional corps of about 600 Cuban troops. Their arsenal bristled with AK-47 assault rifles, 82-mm mortars, anti-aircraft cannon BTR-60 armored personnel carriers and sophisticated communications gear.' Playing up the putative military role of the Point Salines airport, the article went on, 'Strategically the assault cost Castro a well-placed refuelling depot on the air route between Cuba and his troops in Africa. And it denied his Soviet sponsors a potentially valuable harbor convenient to Western oil lanes'.

The large number of major factual inaccuracies and the biased judgements combined to present to the magazine's readers a complete travesty of the circumstances surrounding the invasion and the events which took place during it. For a magazine which had not hesitated to embarrass the Reagan administration by the publication of a solidly researched exposé of the US-supported campaign by counter-revolutionaries operating from Honduras against the Sandinista government of Nicaragua its version of the Grenada affair was a sad lapse. Many of the same inaccuracies and biased judgements were repeated by the media in the US, and the rest of the Western world.

The day after the gruesome work had been carried out at Holguín of separating Cuban and Grenadian corpses Castro delivered the great funeral oration for the dead before a crowd of a million people in the Plaza de la Revolución in the Cuban capital. Tens of thousands of his listeners would have been sensing relief about the outcome in that the first dispatches from Grenada relayed to the Cuban public talked of 'the last six Cubans' dying at the hands of US troops as they embraced the Cuban flag. On Wednesday 26 October the general impression in Havana was that all 784 Cuban men and women had perished in Grenada, an impression which was not relieved by the fact that the radio and TV cancelled all comedy broadcasts and concentrated on solemn things.

As the invasion went ahead there were few dissenting voices to be heard in the media of the region. One notable exception was Rickey Singh, the combative Guyanese editor of *Caribbean Contact*, the Barbados-based monthly newspaper of the Caribbean Council of Churches which condemned the intervention. In a hard hitting article in the *Nation* Singh said:

> Today is a dark day in the history of the Commonwealth Caribbean. The invasion of Grenada, an independent nation and member of the Caribbean Community by the United States military, in collaboration with some Caricom govern ments, cannot be justified on any legal or moral ground. A dangerous precedent has been set that could have far reaching implications for the future peace and security of the entire Caribbean.

The CCC newspaper edited by Singh since 1974 had long been out of favour with the more conservative governments of the region and on Wednesday 2 November Singh was served with a deportation order signed by Adams. Though Singh's work permit still had 20 months to run and though he was married with six children, five of whom were attending school in Barbados, the Barbadian Prime Minister exercised his right not to give any reason for the expulsion order. The action of Adams brought a protest from the leading Jamaican newspaper, the *Gleaner*. In vain. Singh quit after the CCC under great local and US pressure appeared to soften its line on the invasion.

In the Soviet bloc the media carefully echoed the condemnations of US actions delivered by the politicians. But even there there was a moment of high farce. The earliest editions of Soviet TV news progammes screened after the invasions showed a map of the location of Grenada. Horrified Soviet viewers were led to believe that the US troops had invaded Spain, dropped on Andalusia and captured the city of Granada.

CHAPTER 8

A Judgement

'All too frequent are the cases when the stronger, by use of military force, intervene in the affairs of the weaker, imposing their will in order to enforce their so-called vital interests and to strengthen their hand in bloc rivalry.'
Ignac Golob, Yugoslav delegate,
UN Security Council, 27 October 1983

Three conclusions can fairly be drawn about the invasion of Grenada in October 1983; it was illegal, it was unnecessary as far as the rule of law in Grenada was concerned and it set back the cause of political democracy and long-term economic development in the region.

The most considered argument for the legality of the invasion was given in Louisville, Kentucky, to a meeting of newspaper editors on 4 November by Kenneth Dam, the Deputy Secretary of State who received Bishop in Washington in June. Dam cited three legal grounds. The first was an appeal from Scoon 'to the OECS and other regional states to restore order on the island'.

'The invitation of lawful governmental authority constitutes a recognized basis under international law for foreign states to provide requested assistance,' he added. Mystery surrounds the form of this appeal and conflicting accounts of it have done nothing to clarify the mystery. A written appeal was said to have been made by Scoon to Adams but the text, if there was one, was never submitted for public inspection.

In a television broadcast on the day after the invasion Adams chose his words carefully as he referred to the appeal.

Now that Sir Paul Scoon is safe, I can reveal that by the kind offices of a friendly government (but not the USA) his views were sought well before the military operations commenced on the issuing of an invitation to friendly countries to enter Grenada and restore order. According to my information Sir Paul agreed to do so as soon as possible. He has now given his sanction and Brigadier Lewis [Brigadier Rudyard Lewis, commander of the Caribbean forces in Grenada] is in possession of his signed letter of invitation to the OECS and other participating governments.

It was not available for inspection before the invasion and Scoon himself at a press conference at Government House on 3 November was noticeably elusive about the document. The suspicion must be that the document was drawn up and signed some time after the invasion, perhaps when Scoon was taken by the US forces to the *Guam* on the Morning of 2 October. If that is the case – and in the absence of any public sight of the document before the invasion the onus must be on the invading forces to try and prove that it was not the case – then any such document must be valueless. In his press statement after the invasion, Dr Vaughan Lewis, Secretary-General of the OECS, made no mention of any invitation from Scoon.

The general lack of concern about the documentation of the operation was instanced by Adams' approach to the British Government for its assistance. According to his account Adams saw Bullard, the British High Commissioner, at 12.30 p.m. on Friday 21 October and told him that a military intervention in Grenada was being contemplated and that Britain would be invited to participate.

Two days later, according to Adams, 'I again saw the British High Commissioner and made a fully formal verbal request indicating that a document of invitation would follow. This document was eventually delivered on Monday morning.'

Such a version is not supported in London. No document

220

inviting Britain was ever received. On the day of the invasion a message was received from diplomats representing the invading forces saying that difficulties with a telex machine and a typist had delayed the transmission of the invitation. By then the invitation had nothing but academic interest as the British government had made it abundantly clear that it would have nothing to do with any invasion.

The second legal ground for the invasion, according to Dam, was the 1981 OECS Treaty. We have seen, above, however that the Treaty must have at least the acquiescence of Grenada in any decision of the Organisation, an acquiescence that was clearly missing.

The third legal ground adduced by Dam was that 'US action to secure and evacuate endangered US citizens on the island was undertaken in accordance with well-established principles of international law regarding the protection of one's nationals.' Seeing that both Modica and Bourne for the St George's University Medical School denied before the invasion that their students were in danger and seeing also that those students and others who did want to leave were being evacuated from Grenada despite the obstacles being put in the way of that operation by the government of Adams and other governments with shareholdings in LIAT, the regional carrier, such an argument seems flimsy in the extreme.

The two basic objectives of the invasion, Dam said, were to protect the lives of US citizens and to 'help Grenada re-establish order so that governmental institutions and human rights can be restored.'

Given the circumstances before and after the invasion it is clear that the time of maximum danger to the lives of the US medical students was when the US forces attacked near their dormitory area on the second day after the invasion. Before the invasion both the Cubans and the RMC were keen to do all they could to safeguard US citizens, if only to rob Reagan of the excuse for carrying out the invasion.

In the context of US support for governments which have very bad records for human rights violations and which must bear the reponsibility for the murders of US citizens it is

221

difficult to believe the Reagan administration has any but a selective and, therefore, very suspect attitude to human rights. While no US civilian was killed in Grenada before the invasion the murder of four US women in El Salvador under the régime of President José Napoleón Duarte, for instance, and the deaths at the hands of the Salvadorean military of tens of thousands of Salvadoreans, brought no move from the Reagan administration to topple the Salvadorean government.

The invasion may have been an urgent priority for a US President. Two days before the US troops landed in Grenada US troops suffered an awful blow in Beirut. The spectre of the Iranians holding hostage US personnel in Iran and what that had done to the standing of President Carter was haunting the Reagan administration. In his Louisville speech Dam said, 'I don't think that I need remind you that today is the fourth anniversary of the seizure of the US Embassy in Tehran.'

There is every reason to think that in the case of Grenada the RMC would have collapsed under the great weight of the opprobrium it was suffering within the island, combined if there had been a need with the outside pressures exerted on it by its neighbours. Austin had announced, as we have seen, that the RMC was about to name a broadly based civilian cabinet. Had he and Coard not given up their narrowly dictatorial aspirations it is difficult to see what force they could have relied on to maintain them against the popular anger at the massacre they were responsible for.

The militia was demoralised and virtually disarmed, the PRA's morale, as had been demonstrated at Fort Rupert on 19 October was unreliable and any blockade of supplies to the island would, as the emergency economic measures being planned by the RMC in the days after the murder of Bishop showed, would have caused chaos in Grenada.

Abroad the RMC could have expected no help. Cuba had condemned Bishop's murder and the condemnation had been so trenchant that it precluded the Soviets from coming to the aid of the RMC. It would have been only a matter of time before the Leninist aspirations of Coard and Austin were swept away by Grenadians themselves. By mounting the invasion the US robbed them of that opportunity.

Perhaps the most tragic event of the invasion was that fighting between the US forces and the Cubans appears to have been a blunder willed by neither side. Cuba's note to the US of 22 October calling for care in the handling of the Grenada situation taken with the US reply delivered, however tardily, on the morning of the invasion, with the diplomatic exchanges between Havana and Washington on the afternoon of the invasion and with the lull in the fighting on the ground, point conclusively to the fact that, whatever their public posturings, neither the Cuban nor the US government wanted an armed confrontation.

That the fighting resumed the day after the invasion between the Cubans and US troops was clearly the result of a blunder on the part of some diplomat or military officer on the ground. If it was a military blunder it might be excused because of the inherently hectic and confused conditions of any war. If it was a diplomatic blunder it must be listed as another of those inexcusable mistakes and misapprehensions which dogged the whole course of the invasion.

Taken together the killing of Bishop and the US invasion had an extremely negative effect on the region as a whole. The events of October showed that the Commonwealth Caribbean was being sucked into a super-power confrontation which it had, until then, successfully avoided. The costs that the countries of the region will have to pay for that development have yet to be assessed. It will certainly mean increased defence expenditures, a waste of human and financial resources that the tiny economies cannot afford. It will as well lead to an embitterment and increasing violence in the politics of the region which bodes ill for the future. In the past the islands' politics have been judged by many to be excessively parochial and inward looking. While that was certainly a failing it was clearly preferable to the present situation where societies are beginning to be riven into pro-US and pro-Leninist factions.

For such a situation the Cuban, Soviet and US governments must all be blamed.

The events of October have, too, dimmed the prospects for greater political and economic collaboration among the countries of the region. For two centuries or more the islands and mainland territories of the English-speaking West Indies were bound willy-nilly together by virtue of their forming of the British Empire.

The dissolution of the British Empire after the Second World War, accompanied as it was by the smooth progression of the larger territories to independence, hid from many West Indians the fact that they were members of very small communities which were alone and vulnerable in an often hostile world.

The beginnings of a Leninist state in Grenada awoke many Caribbean governments to the fact that their islands were being drawn into the ideological tensions which had for years affected Europe and their neighbours in Latin America and other parts of the developing world. The stirrings of Leninism in the Caribbean reminded many West Indians that they were no longer bound together in a colonial society the rules of which were drawn up in London.

That realisation gave added urgency to the search for unity and a regional identity. It resulted in the establishment of the Caribbean Community (Caricom) and to smaller groupings like the OECS. Now the divisions of opinion over the attitudes that should have been adopted by the region towards Grenada have meant a setback to the process of regional collaboration. Not only are the governments of the countries which provided auxiliaries for the US invasion at odds with the governments of Guyana, Belize, the Bahamas and Trinidad and Tobago which opposed it, Caricom as an organization is weakened and divided as are such specialised regional bodies as the Caribbean Council of Churches.

Grenada, in particular, and the West Indies as a whole were the victims of power politics played out in capitals far away. The emergence of a West Indian identity linked to the growth of some sort of federal or confederal state, which the most far sighted of Caribbean leaders have seen as the only strategy if the territories were ever to have any realistic hope of minimising their extreme dependence on the rest of the world, has been delayed.

The super-powers could not have carried out their design of using the West Indies as a minor arena for their paranoias – or at least would have found it more difficult to do so – if they had not found willing acolytes in the region. Tragically they did find men and women who were willing to sell themselves and their countries for the favour of one side or the other. In Grenada there were those who were happy to commit treachery and murder for narrow ideological motives and in the hope of installing a dictatorial system which would give them absolute sway over their countrymen.

In Grenada and its neighbouring islands sat their opponents, happy to abdicate the responsibility they claimed they had taken on to find a regional solution to the crisis caused by Bishop's murder. While they sat with their colleagues at the Port of Spain meeting, held to consider a West Indian response to a Grenadian crisis, and they apparently assented to joint action within the Caribbean, some heads of government were fully prepared to act. They abandoned the Caribbean solutions to which they were paying lip service and threw in their lot with an imperial power which wanted to consolidate its hegemony in the area. In the most shameful way they abandoned their task of safeguarding the interests and identity of their countries. At the time of writing it appears that the first group, the revolutionaries, will be accused and judged by representatives of the second group, governments acting like usurpers. The second group, it seems, will have to be tried at the bar of history.

Through the actions of both groups the development of a West Indian nation, which had been looked forward to by generations of West Indians of political persuasions as diverse as those of Marryshow and C.L.R. James has been postponed once again.

In the sphere of super-power relations the Grenada crisis illustrated how the paranoias of one side nourish those of the

other. The US was unwilling to condemn a thuggish government in Grenada which had close and friendly relations with
Washington's prótége, the dictator of Chile, because both Gairy
and Pinochet were seen to be 'pro-West'. Washington's tacit
support for Gairy in its turn encouraged the Cuban and Soviet
governments to win the NJM for the pro-Soviet camp. Grenadian acceptance of Soviet criticisms of the US redoubled
Washington's hostility towards the Bishop government. Washington's hostility towards the NJM made Cuba all the more
eager to help Bishop. Bishop's acceptance of Cuban aid to
build a long planned and badly needed airport inflamed US
fears of some new strategic threat from the Soviets. US hostility
to Cuban assistance made the Bishop government all the more
committed to retaining Cuban help as it stockpiled arms from
the Soviet bloc.

The vicious circle was neverending and increasingly futile.

The principal lessons of the Grenadian tragedy are not, however, to be found in international politics. Since the US grew
to a regional and, thereafter, a world power it has, as we have
seen, sought hegemony over its immediate neighbours. (In the
nineteenth century Russia did the same in Asia and since the
late 1930s has done the same in Eastern and Central Europe.)
The invasion of Grenada, therefore, was no more than the
most recent of a long series of attempts to assert by force that
hegemony.

The principal lessons are rather to be found when we come
to consider the praxis of many features of Leninism in general
and of 'vanguardism' in particular.

The lengths to which the NJM took the theory of a vanguard
party, the party's application of the theory of democratic centralism and its rejection of any genuine popular accountability
were largely responsible for the rupture of the revolution in
the week's preceding Bishop's murder. A group of a few hundred
applicant, candidate and full members of the NJM, led by a
Central Committee of sixteen, which was itself run by a Political Bureau of no more than eight, sought to take on the
running of every aspect of a small but complex and extremely

vulnerable society. Such a degree of vanguardism was a manifest failure.

So was the democratic centralism practised by the NJM. The appointed members of the Central Committee were, after all, doing no more than trying to put into practice the theories of democratic centralism and the primacy of the Party over the State when they took the dire step of stripping Bishop of his functions and arresting him the week before his death.

The trouble was that the Central Committee had lost touch with the reality of what the Grenadian people wanted and what they would tolerate. The Grenadians wanted Bishop and they would not tolerate his murder. Part of the reason that the Central Committee had lost touch with what the people wanted was that they never sought to renew that informal mandate the revolutionary leaders had when in 1979 they overthrew Gairy. For this, at least at the beginning, Bishop himself was as responsible as anyone else in Grenada. He rejected the advice and entreaties of well-wishers who wanted the party to formalise, through a referendum or poll, the informal mandate it enjoyed. In practice the Grenadian leadership was accountable to no one and behaved increasingly in the manner of some autocratic nineteenth-century pope.

The fact that Bishop was apparently reconsidering this position and had put in hand work on a new constitution which was due to include some provisions for democratic accountability was of little help when the crisis of September and October arose. The constitution was not yet available and there had grown up in the party a penchant for autocracy and, fatally, a faction whose members were committed to increased autocracy. This faction was the one which was pressing for firmer Leninism, was seeking more democratic centralism and which was most alarmed when Bishop decided to appeal over the heads of the members of the Central Committee to the Grenadian people at large.

Vanguardism and democratic centralism, combined with a doctrinaire unwillingness of the majority of the Central Committee to submit itself to democratic accountability led to disaster. At the end the Central Committe and the RMC, which superseded it, were as bereft of legitimacy as, say, the Czech and the Polish Communist Parties are today.

Nor did events give the Central Committee or the RMC time to develop that carapace of nationalism which Leninist parties in the Soviet Union and elsewhere develop and which they hope will give them some part of the legitimacy which they are unwilling to seek by direct consultation with the people.

But Coard and Austin did not have time to build up any such appeal to nationalism. And even if they had it is difficult to see how they could have done it. Even they themselves realised and admitted how central Bishop was to the nascent sense of nationalism on a small Caribbean island which had been independent for less than a decade. But having killed him they could scarcely have to recourse to Bishop's memory to build up a Grenadian nationalism. And there were few enough alternative figures upon which to build such a nationalism.

It would be good if these lessons were not lost on other parties in the developing world as they cast about for models of political development.

If any hopes have been generated by the Grenadian experience they are that the débâcle of October 1983 will inspire West Indians eventually to seek out for themselves a fairer and more humane form of society than that which has been offered to them in the past by British colonialists, US imperialists or the small gang of ideological zealots for Leninism who killed their leader in Fort Rupert one afternoon in October.

Appendix 1

Text of Fidel Castro's Speech of 14 November 1983

On 15 October 1976, a little over seven years ago, we gathered here, in this same place, to deliver a funeral address for the fifty-seven Cubans who were vilely murdered in the Barbados plane sabotage, carried out by men who had been trained by the US Central Intelligence Agency. Today we have come once again to bid farewell – this time to twenty-four Cubans who died in Grenada, another island not very far from Barbados, as a result of US military actions.

Grenada was one of the smallest independent states in the world, both in territory and population. Even though Cuba is a small, underdeveloped country it was able to help Grenada considerably, because our efforts – which were modest in quantity though high in quality – meant a lot for a county less than 400 square kilometers in size, with a population of just over 100,000.

For instance, the value of our contribution to Grenada in the form of materials, designs and labour in building the new airport came to $60 million at international prices – over $500 per inhabitant. It is as if Cuba – with a population of almost 10 million – received a project worth $5000 million as a donation. In addition, there was the cooperation of our doctors, teachers and technicians in diverse specialties, plus an annual contribution of Cuban products worth about $3 million. This meant an additional annual contribution of $40 per inhabitant. It is impossible for Cuba to render material assistance on that scale to countries with significantly large populations and territories, but we were able to offer great assistance to a country like tiny Grenada.

Many other small Caribbean nations, used to the gross economic and strategic interests of colonialism and imperialism, were amazed by Cuba's generous assistance to that fraternal people. They may have thought that Cuba's selfless action was extraordinary; in the midst of the US government's dirty propaganda, some may even have found it difficult to understand.

Our people felt such deep friendship for Bishop and Grenada, and our respect for that country and its sovereignty was so irreproachable, that we never dared to express any opinions about what was being done there or how it was being done. In Grenada, we followed the same principle we apply to all revolutionary nations and movements: full respect for their policies, criteria and decisions; expressing our views on any matter only when asked to do so. Imperialism is incapable of understanding that the secret of our excellent relations with revolutionary countries and movements in the world lies precisely in this respect.

The US government looked down on Grenada and hated Bishop. It wanted to destroy Grenada's process and obliterate its example. It had even prepared military plans for invading the island – as Bishop had charged nearly two years ago – but it lacked a pretext.

Socioeconomically, Grenada was actually advancing satisfactorily. The people had received many benefits in spite of the hostile policy of the United States, and Grenada's Gross National Product was growing at a good rate in the midst of the world crisis. Bishop was not an extremist; rather, he was a true revolutionary – conscientious and honest. Far from disagreeing with his intelligent and realistic policy, we fully sympathized with it, since it was rigorously adapted to his country's specific conditions and possibilities. Grenada had become a true symbol of independence and progress in the Caribbean.

No one could have foreseen the tragedy that was drawing near. Attention was focused on other parts of the wold. Unfortunately, the Grenadian revolutionaries themselves unleashed the events that opened the door to imperialist aggression.

Hyenas emerged from the revolutionary ranks. Today no one can yet say whether those who used the dagger of division and internal confrontation did so *motu proprio* or were inspired and egged on by imperialism. It is something that could have been done by the CIA – and, if somebody else was responsible, the CIA could not have done it any better. The fact is that allegedly revolutionary arguments were used, invoking the purest principles of Marxism-Leninism and charging Bishop with practicing a personality cult and drawing away from the Leninist norms and methods of leadership.

In our view, nothing could be more absurd than to attribute such tendencies to Bishop. It was impossible to imagine anyone more noble, modest and unselfish. He could never have been guilty of being authoritarian; if he had any defect, it was his excessive tolerance and trust.

Were those who conspired against him within the Grenadian Party, army and security, by any chance, a group of extremists drunk on political theory? Were they simply a group of ambitious, opportunistic individuals, or were they enemy agents who wanted to destroy the Grenadian Revolution? History alone will have the last word, but it would not be the first time that such things occurred in a revolutionary process.

In our view, Coard's group objectively destroyed the Revolution and opened the door to imperialist aggression. Whatever their intentions, the brutal assassination of Bishop and his most loyal, closest comrades is a fact that can never be justified in that or any other revolution. As the 20 October statement by the Cuban Party and government put it, 'No crime can be committed in the name of revolution and liberty.'

In spite of his very close and affectionate links with our Party's leadership, Bishop never said anything about the internal dissensions that were developing. To the contrary, in his last conversation with us he was self-critical about his work regarding attention to the armed forces and the mass organizations. Nearly all of our Party and state leaders spent many friendly, fraternal hours with him on the evening of 7 October before his return trip to Grenada.

Coard's group never had such relations nor such intimacy and trust with us. Actually, we did not even know that group existed. It is to our Revolution's credit that, in spite of our profound indignation over Bishop's removal from office and arrest, we fully refrained from interfering in Grenada's internal affairs, even though our construction workers and all our other cooperation personnel in Grenada – who did not hesitate to confront the Yankee soldiers with the weapons Bishop himself had given them for their defence in case of an attack from abroad – could have been a decisive factor in those internal events. Those weapons were never meant to be used in an internal conflict in Grenada and we would never have allowed them to be so used; we would never have been willing to use them to shed a single drop of Grenadian blood.

On 12 October Bishop was removed from office by the Central Committee on which the conspirators had attained a majority. On the 13th, he was placed under house arrest. On the 19th, the people took to the streets and freed Bishop. On the same day, Coard's group

231

ordered the army to fire on the people and Bishop, Whiteman, Jacqueline Creft and other excellent revolutionary leaders were murdered.

As soon as the internal dissensions which came to light on 12 October were manifest the Yankee imperialists decided to invade.

The message sent by the leadership of the Cuban Party to Coard's group on 15 October has been made public; in it, we expressed our deep concern over both the internal and the external consequences of the split and appealed to the common sense, serenity, wisdom and generosity of revolutionaries. This reference to generosity was an appeal not to use violence against Bishop and his followers.

This group of Coard's that seized power in Grenada expressed serious reservations regarding Cuba from the very beginning because of our well-known and unquestionable friendship with Bishop.

The national and international press have published our strong denunciation of the events of 19 October, the day Bishop was murdered. Our relations with Austin's short-lived government, in which Coard was really in charge, were actually cold and tense, so that, at the time of the criminal Yankee aggression, there was no coordination whatsoever between the Grenadian army and the Cuban construction workers and other cooperation personnel. The basic points of the messages sent to our embassy in Grenada on 12 October through 25, the day on which the invasion took place, have been made public. Those documents stand in history as irrefutable proof of our clean principled position regarding Grenada.

Imperialism, however, presented the events as the coming to power of a group of hard-line Communists, loyal allies of Cuba. Were they really Communists? Were they really hard-liners? Could they really be loyal allies of Cuba? Or were they rather conscious or unconscious tools of Yankee imperialism?

Look at the history of the revolutionary movement, and you will find more than one connection between imperialism and those who take positions that appear to be on the extreme left.

Aren't Pol Pot and Ieng Sary – the ones responsible for the genocide in Kampuchea – the most loyal allies Yankee imperialism has in Southeast Asia at present? In Cuba, ever since the Grenadian crisis began we have called Coard's group – to give it a name – the 'Pol Pot group.'

Our relations with the new leaders of Grenada were to be subjected to profound analysis, as was set forth in the 20 October statement by the Party and government of Cuba. In it, we also stated that, due to our basic regard for the Grenadian people, we would not rush to 'take any steps regarding technical and economic cooperation which may jeopardize the basic services and vital economic interest of the people of Grenada.' We could not accept the idea of leaving the Grenadians without doctors or leaving the airport, which was vital to the nation's economy, unfinished. Most certainly, our construction workers were to leave Grenada when the project was completed, and the weapons that Bishop had given them were to be returned to the government. It was even possible that our very bad relations with the new government would make it necessary for us to leave much earlier.

The thing that placed Cuba in a morally complex, difficult situation was the announcement that Yankee naval forces were en route to Grenada. Under those circumstances, we couldn't possibly leave the country. If the imperialists really intended to attack Grenada, it was our duty to stay there. To withdraw at the time would have been dishonorable and could even have triggered aggression in that country then and in Cuba later on. In addition, events unfolded with such incredible speed that if the evacuation had been planned for, there would not have been time to carry it out.

In Grenada, however, the government was morally indefensible, and, since the Party, the government and the army had divorced themselves from the people, it was also impossible to defend the nation militarily, because a revolutionary war is only feasible and justifiable when united with the people. We could only fight, therefore, if we were directly attacked. There was no alternative.

It should nevertheless be noted that, despite these adverse circumstances, a number of Grenadian soldiers died in heroic combat against the invaders.

The internal events, however, in no way justified Yankee intervention. Since when has the government of the United States become the arbiter of internal conflicts between revolutionaries in any given country? What right did Reagan have to rend his mantle over the death of Bishop, whom he so hated and opposed? What reasons could there be for its brutal violation of the sovereignty of Grenada – a small independent nation that was a respected and acknowledged member of the international community? It would be the same as if another country believed it had the right to intervene in the United States because of the repulsive assassination of Martin Luther King

233

or so many other outrages, such as those that have been committed against the black and Hispanic minorities in the United States, or to intervene because John Kennedy was murdered.

The same may be said of the argument that the lives of 1000 Americans were in danger. There are many times more US citizens in dozens of other countries in the world. Does this, perchance, imply the right to intervene when internal conflicts arise in those countries? There are tens of thousands of Grenadians in the United States, England and Trinidad. Could tiny Grenada intervene if domestic policy problems arose that pose some threat to its compatriots in any of those countries? Putting aside the fallacy and falseness of such pretexts for invading Grenada, is this really an international norm that can be sustained?

A thousand lessons in Marxism could not teach us any better the dirty, perfidious and aggressive nature of imperialism than the attack unleashed against Grenada at dawn on 25 October and its later development.

In order to justify its invasion of Grenada and its subsequent actions, the US government and its spokesmen told 19 lies; Reagan personally told the first 13.

1. Cuba had to do with the coup d'état and the death of Bishop.
2. The American students were in danger of being taken hostage.
3. The main purpose of the invasion was to protect the lives of American citizens.
4. The invasion was a multinational operation undertaken at the request of Mr Scoon and the Eastern Caribbean nations.
5. Cuba was planning to invade and occupy Grenada.
6. Grenada was being turned into an important Soviet-Cuban military base.
7. The airport under construction was not civilian but military.
8. The weapons in Grenada would be used to export subversion and terrorism.
9. The Cubans fired first.
10. There were over 1000 Cubans in Grenada.
11. Most of the Cubans were not construction workers but professional soldiers.
12. The invading forces took care not to destroy civilian property or inflict civilian casualties.
13. The US troops would remain in Grenada for a week.
14. Missile silos were being built in Grenada.

15. The vessel *Viet Nam Heroico* was transporting special weapons.
16. Cuba was warned of the invasion.
17. Five hundred Cubans are fighting in the mountains of Grenada.
18. Cuba has issued instructions for reprisals to be taken against US citizens.
19. The journalists were excluded for their own protection.

None of these assertions were proved, none are true and all have been refuted by the facts. This cynical way of lying in order to justify invading a tiny country reminds us of the methods Adolf Hitler used during the years leading up to the Second World War.

The US students and officials of the medical school located there acknowledged that they were given full guarantees for US citizens and the necessary facilities for those who wanted to leave the country. Moreover, Cuba had informed the US Government on 22 October that no foreign citizens, including Cubans, had been disturbed, and it offered to cooperate in solving any difficulty that might arise, so that problems could be settled without violence or intervention in that country.

No US citizen had been disturbed at all prior to the invasion, and if anything endangered them, it was the war unleashed by the United States. Cuba's instructions to its personnel not to interfere with any actions to evacuate US citizens in the area of the runway under construction near the university contributed to protecting the US citizens residing in that country. Reagan's reference to the possibility that Grenada might turn into another Iran – a reference calculated to appeal to the US feelings wounded in that episode – is a demagogic, politicking, dishonest argument.

The assertion that the new airport was a military one – an old lie that the Reagan administration had dwelt on a lot – was categorically refuted by the English capitalist firm that supplied and installed the electrical and technical equipment for that airport. The British technicians of the Plessey company, which has made a name for itself internationally as a specialist in this field, worked alongside the Cuban construction workers, to whose civilian worker status they attest. Several countries of the European Community that are members of the Atlantic alliance cooperated in one way or another with the airport. How can anyone imagine them helping Cuba to build a military airport in Grenada?

235

However, the idea that Grenada was being turned into a Soviet-Cuban base is refuted by the proved fact that there wasn't even one Soviet military adviser on the island.

The supposedly secret documents that fell into the hands of the United States and were published by the Yankee administration a few days after the invasion refer to the agreement between the governments of Cuba and Grenada by virtue of which our country was to send Grenada 27 military advisers, which could later be increased to 40 – figures that coincide with the ones Cuba published on the number of advisers, which was 22 on the day of the attack, to which were added a similar number of translators and service personnel from the mission. Nowhere in those documents that they have been crowing over is there something that has anything to do with the idea of military bases in Grenada. What they do show is that the weapons that the Soviet Union supplied to the government of Grenada for the army and the militia were subject to an article that prohibited their export to third countries, which refutes the idea that Grenada had been turned into an arsenal for supplying weapons to subversive, terrorist organizations, as the present administration likes to call all the revolutionary and national liberation movements. No weapons ever left Grenada for any other country, and, therefore, Reagan can never prove that any did.

The assertion that Cuba was about to invade and occupy Grenada is so unrealistic, absurd, crazy and alien to our principles and international policy that it cannot even be taken seriously. What has been proved is the absolutely scrupulous way in which we refrained from meddling in the internal affairs of that country, in spite of our deep affection for Bishop and our total rejection of Coard and his group's conspiracy and coup, which could serve only the interests of imperialism and its plans for destroying the Grenadian Revolution. The messages containing precise, categorical instructions to our embassy in Grenada, which have been widely publicized by the government of Cuba, constitute irrefutable proof of the clear position of principles maintained by the leadership of our Party and state with regard to the internal events in Grenada.

The civilian status of the vast majority of the Cuban cooperation personnel in Grenada has been shown to the whole world by the hundreds of foreign journalists who saw them arriving in our country and who were able to interview each and every one of them. Nearly 50 per cent of them were over 40 years old. Who could question

236

their status as civilian cooperation personnel and workers with long years of experience on their jobs?

When the US government spokesman asserted that there were from 1000 to 1500 Cubans in Grenada at the time of the invasion and that hundreds of them were still fighting in the mountains, Cuba published the exact number of Cuban citizens who were in Grenada on the day of the invasion: 784, including diplomatic personnel with their children and other relatives. The agencies that sent them and the kind of work they did were also reported, as well as the instructions given them to fight in their work areas and camps if attacked, and the fact that it was impossible – according to the information we had – for hundreds to remain in the mountains. Later, the names and jobs of all co-operation workers were published, as well as the known or probable situation of each one. The facts have shown that the information provided by Cuba was absolutely true. There isn't a single fact in all that information that could be proven false.

The assertion that the Cubans initiated the acts of hostility is equally false and cynical. The irrefutable truth is that the Cubans were sleeping and their weapons were stored at the time of the air drop on the runway and around the camps. They had not been distributed. There weren't enough to go around, and they weren't distributed until the landing was already under way, and that is when the Cuban personnel went to the places assigned to them for that emergency. Even so, our personnel, now organized and armed, had time to see the US paratroopers regrouping on the runway and the first planes landing. That was the invaders' weakest moment. If the Cubans had fired first, they would have killed or wounded dozens – perhaps hundreds – of US soldiers in those early hours. What is strictly historical and strictly true is that the fighting began when the US troops advanced towards the Cubans in a belligerent way. It is also true that when a group of unarmed co-operation personnel was captured, they were used as hostages and forced to lead the way in front of the US soldiers.

The invasion of Grenada was a treacherous surprise attack, with no previous warning at all – just like Pearl Harbor, just like the Nazis. The note from the government of the United States to the government of Cuba on Tuesday, 25 October, in an attempted response to our note of Saturday, 22 October, was delivered at 8.30 in the morning, three hours after the landing had taken place and an hour and a half after the US troops began attacking our com-

237

patriots in Grenada. Actually, on the afternoon of the 25th, the US government sent the government of Cuba a deceitful note that led us to believe that the fighting would cease in a reasonable and honorable manner, thus avoiding greater bloodshed. Although we immediately responded to that note, accepting that possibility, what the US government did was to land the 82nd Airborne Division at dawn on the 26th and attack with all its forces the Cuban position that was still resisting. Is this the way a serious government behaves? Is this the way to warn of an attack? Was this the way to avoid greater bloodshed?

Mr Scoon blatantly declared that he approved of the invasion but that he had not previously asked anyone to invade Grenada. A few days after the landing, Mr Scoon – lodged in the *Guam* helicopter-carrier – signed a letter officially requesting the intervention. Reagan could not prove any of his false assertions.

When, as a pretext for keeping the *Viet Nam Heroico* – which was in the port of St George's on the day of the invasion – from being used as a means of transportation for evacuating the Cuban hostages from Grenada, it was alleged that it carried special weapons, its captain was immediately asked if by an chance he carried weapons on board, and the only thing that was determined was that it had just one fearful weapon – its name: Vietnam.

The slanderous charge that Cuba had given instructions to carry out actions against US citizens in other countries was given a worthy, official and public reply based on reality, proven by the history of the Revolution, that Cuba has always been opposed to acts of reprisal against innocent people.

The government of the United States has not condescended to offer the number of people arrested nor the figure of Grenadian losses, including civilian losses. A hospital for the mentally ill was bombed, killing dozens of patients.

And where is Mr Reagan's promise that US troops would withdraw in a week? President Reagan himself in his first address to the US people at 8.30 a.m. on the day of the invasion, in a speech prepared before the landing, stated that the situation was under control. That same day, his own spokesmen described the resistance the invading forces were facing. The military ride the Pentagon had planned would take four hours did not take into account the tenacious and heroic resistance of the Cuban cooperation personnel and of the Grenadian soldiers.

Who, then, has told the truth, and who has cynically lied about

238

the events in Grenada? No foreign journalists – not even those from the United States – were allowed to see and report on the events on the spot. The pretext that this prohibition was a security measure for the journalists is both superficial and ridiculous. What they obviously wanted was to monopolize and manipulate the information so they could lie without any let or hindrance to world public opinion, including the people of the United States. This was the only way they could spread deliberate lies and falsehoods of all kinds – which would be difficult to clear up and refute after their initial impact and effect on the people of the United States. Even in this, the method used by the US administration was fascist.

What is left now, objectively, of those 19 assertions? Where are the silos for strategic missiles that were being built in Grenada? But all those lies that the world did not believe, told by the US President and his spokesmen, made a tremendous impact on US public opinion.

Moreover, the invasion of Grenada was presented to the US people as a great victory for Reagan's foreign policy against the socialist camp and the revolutionary movement. It was linked to the tragic death of 240 US soldiers in Beirut, to the memory of the hostages in Iran, to the humiliating defeat in Vietnam and to the resurgence of the United States as an influential power on the world scene. A dirty, dishonest appeal was made to US patriotism, to national pride, to the grandeur and glory of the nation. This was how they got a majority of the US people – it is said that it was 65 per cent at first and then 71 per cent – to support the monstrous crime of invading a soverign country without any justification, the reprehensible method of launching a surprise attack, the press censorship and all the other similar procedures the US government used for invading and justifying its invasion of Grenada. Hitler acted the same way when he occupied Austria in 1938 and annexed Sudetenland, in Czechoslo vakia, in the name of German pride, German grandeur and glory and the happiness and security of German subjects. If a poll had been taken in Hitler Germany at that time, in the midst of the chauvinistic wave unleashed by the Nazis, around 80 or 90 per cent of the people would have approved of those aggressions.

The deplorable, truly dangerous fact – not only for the people of the Caribbean, Central America and Latin America, but for all the peoples of the world – is that, when world opinion unanimously denounced the warmongering, aggressive, unjustifiable action that violated a people's sovereignty and all international norms and prin-

239

ciples, most of the people of the United States – manipulated, disinformed and deceived – supported the monstrous crime committed by their government.

There is something even more disturbing: when this about-face was effected in US public opinion, many US politicians who initially had opposed these events ended up by condoning Reagan's actions, and the press – censured, humiliated and kept at a distance from the events – ended up moderating its complaints and criticisms.

Are these, perchance, the virtues of a society where the opinion and the political and informational institutions can be grossly manipulated by its rulers, as they were in German society in the time of fascism? Where is the glory, the grandeur and the victory in invading and defeating one of the tiniest countries in the world, of no economic or strategic significance? Where is the heroism in fighting a handful of workers and other civilian cooperation personnel whose heroic resistance – in spite of the surprise element; the shortage of ammunition; and their disadvantages in terms of terrain, arms and numbers – against the air, sea and land forces of the most powerful imperialist country in the world forced it to bring in the 82nd Airborne Division, when the last stronghold was being defended at dawn on 26 October by barely 50 fighters? The United States did not achieve any victory at all – not political or military or moral. If anything, it was a Pyrrhic military victory and a profound moral defeat, as we pointed out on another occasion.

The imperialist government of the United States wanted to kill the symbol of the Grenadian Revolution, but the symbol was already dead. The Grenadian revolutionaries themselves destroyed it with their split and their colossal errors. We believe that, after the death of Bishop and his closest comrades, after the army fired on the people and after the Party and the government divorced themselves from the masses and isolated themselves from the world, the Grenadian revolutionary process could not survive.

In its efforts to destroy a symbol, the United States killed a corpse and brought the symbol back to life at the same time. Was it for this that it challenged international law and won the repudiation and condemnation of the world?

Does it feel such contempt for the rest of mankind? Is that contempt really so great that Mr Reagan's appetite for breakfast on 3 November was not at all affected, as he declared before the press?

If unfortunately all this were true – and it seems to be – the

240

invasion of Grenada should lead us to an awareness of the realities and dangers that threaten the world.

Mr O'Neill, speaker of the House of Representatives, said that it was sinful that a man who was totally uninformed and ignorant about international problems and who doesn't even read the documents was President of the United States. If we consider that the United States has powerful sophisticated means of conventional and nuclear warfare and that the president of that country can declare war without consulting anyone, it is not only sinful but truly dramatic and tragic for all mankind.

An air of triumph reigns in the Reagan administration. The echoes of the last shots in Grenada have barely died away and already there is talk of intervening in El Salvador, Nicaragua and even Cuba.

In the Middle East and southern Africa imperialism's acts of interference and military aggression against progressive countries and national liberation movements continue unabated.

In Europe, the first of the 572 Pershing and Cruise missiles are already being deployed, surrounding the USSR and other socialist countries with a deadly ring of nuclear weapons that can reach their territories in a matter of minutes.

Not just the small countries, but all mankind is threatened. The bells tolling today for Grenada may toll tomorrow for the whole world.

The most prestigious and experienced scientists and doctors assure us that man could not survive a global nuclear conflict. The destructive power of these stockpiled weapons is a million times greater than that of the unsophisticated bombs that wiped out the cities of Hiroshima and Nagasaki in just a few seconds. This is what the Reagan administration's aggressive, warmongering policy can lead to.

Meanwhile, the arms race is already a reality in the midst of the worst economic crisis the world has witnessed since the '30s. And, with the problems of development of the vast majority of the peoples in the world still to be solved, who can feel confidence in a government that acts as precipitately, rashly and cynically as the US Government did in Grenada? Reagan did not even bother to listen to the advice of a government as closely linked to him politically, ideologically and militarily as the British Government. It is not strange that, in a poll taken just a few days ago, more then 90 per cent of the British were categorically opposed to the United States having the unilateral prerogative of using the Cruise missiles that are being deployed there.

In our hemisphere, just a year and a half ago, a NATO power used sophisticated war means to shed Argentine blood in the Malvinas. The Reagan administration supported that action. It did not even consider the Organization of American States or the so-called security pacts and agreements, but scornfully pushed them aside. Now, basing itself on the alleged Caribbean blood and Cuban blood. Nicaragua paid a price of over forty thousand lives for freedom, and nearly a thousand more sons of that noble people have been killed in the attacks made by mercenary bands organized, trained and equipped by the US Government. In El Salvador, over 50,000 people have been murdered by a genocidal regime whose army is equipped, trained and directed by the United States. In Guatemala, more than 100,000 have died at the hands of the repressive system installed by the CIA in 1954, when it overthrew the progressive Arbenz Government. How many have died in Chile since imperialism staged the overthrow and assassination of Salvador Allende? How many have died in Argentina, Uruguay, Paraguay, Brazil and Bolivia in the last 15 years?

What a high price our peoples have paid in blood, sacrifice, poverty and mourning for imperialist domination and the unjust social systems it has imposed on our nations!

Imperialism is bent on destroying symbols, because it knows the value of symbols, of examples and of ideas. It wanted to destroy them in Grenada and it wants to destroy them in El Salvador, Nicaragua and Cuba; but symbols, examples and ideas cannot be destroyed. When their enemies think they have destroyed them, what they have actually done is made them multiply. In trying to wipe out the first Christians, the Roman emperors spread Christianity throughout the world. Likewise, all attempts to destroy our ideas will only multiply them.

Grenada has already multiplied the Salvadorean, Nicaraguan and Cuban revolutionaries' patriotic conviction and fighting spirit. It has been proved that the best US troops can be fought and that they are not feared. The imperialists must not ignore the fact that they will encounter fierce resistance wherever they attack a revolutionary people. Let us hope that their Pyrrhic victory in Grenada and their air of triumph don't go to their heads, leading them to commit serious, irreversible errors.

They will not find in El Salvador, Nicaragua and Cuba the par-

242

ticular circumstances of revolutionaries divided among themselves and divorced from the people that they found in tiny Grenada.

In more than three years of heroic struggle, the Salvadorean revolutionaries have become experienced, fearsome and invincible fighters. There are thousands of them who know the land inch by inch, veterans of dozens of victorious combats who are accustomed to fighting and winning when the odds are one to ten against élite troops, trained, armed and advised by the United States. Their unity is more solid and indestructible than ever.

In Nicaragua, the imperialists would have to confront a deeply patriotic and revolutionary people that is united, organized, armed and ready to fight and that can never be subjugated.

With regard to Cuba, if in Grenada, the imperialists had to bring in an élite division to fight against a handful of isolated men struggling in a small stronghold, lacking fortifications, a thousand miles from their homeland, how many divisions would they need against millions of combatants fighting on their own soil alongside their own people?

Our country – as we have already said on other occasions – might be wiped off the face of the earth, but it will never be conquered and subjugated.

In the present conditions of our continent, a US war against a Latin American people would raise the morale of all the peoples of Latin America and turn their feelings against the aggressors. A bottomless abyss would be opened between peoples that, because they are in the same hemisphere, are called upon to live in peace, friendship and mutual respect, and cooperate with one another.

The experiences of Grenada will be examined in detail to extract the utmost benefit from them for use in case of another attack against a country where there are Cuban cooperation personnel or on our own homeland.

The Cubans who were captured and virtually turned into hostages had an unforgettable experience of what a country occupied by Yankee invading troops is like. The physical and psychological treatment given the cooperation personnel who were taken prisoner was insulting and a cause for indignation, and promises of all kinds were made to each of them to try to get them to go to the United States. But they were not able to break their steel-like staunchness. Not a single one deserted his homeland.

There was no manipulation of the news, nothing was hidden from the people, in our country. All reports concerning the invasion that were received directly from Grenada were transmitted to our population just as they arrived, even though the ones on October 26 turned out to be exaggerated. As a matter of principle, at no time were efforts made to play down the seriousness of the situation or to minimize the magnitude of the dangers facing our compatriots.

We are deeply grateful to the International Committee of the Red Cross for its interest, dedication and efficient efforts to identify and evacuate the wounded, sick and other prisoners and the dead as quickly as possible. We are also grateful to the Government of Spain and Colombia for the immediate efforts they made in this regard.

In bidding farewell to our beloved brothers who died heroically in combat, fulfilling with honour their patriotic and internationalist duties, and in expressing our deepest solidarity to their loved ones, we do not forget that there are Grenadian mothers and US mothers who are crying for their sons who died in Grenada. We send our condolences to the mothers and other relatives of the Grenadians who were killed and also to the mothers and other relatives of the US soldiers who died – because they, who also suffer from the loss of close relatives, are not to blame for their government's warmongering, aggressive, irresponsible actions; they, too, are its victims.

Every day, every hour, every minute – at work, at our study and combat positions – we will remember our comrades who died in Grenada.

The men whom we will bury this afternoon fought for us and for the world. They may seem to be corpses. Reagan wants to make corpses of all our people, men, women, the elderly and the children; he wants to make a corpse out of all mankind. But the peoples shall struggle to preserve their independence and their lives; they will struggle to prevent the world from becoming a huge cemetery; they will struggle and pay the price necessary for mankind to survive.

However, they are not corpses; they are symbols. They did not even die in the land where they were born. There, far away from Cuba, where they were contributing with the noble sweat of their internationalist work in a country poorer and smaller than ours, they were also capable of shedding their blood and offering their lives. But in that trench, they knew they were also defending their own people and their own homeland.

It is impossible to express the generosity of human beings and their willingness to make sacrifices in a more pure way. Their example will be multiplied, their ideas will be multiplied and they themselves will be multiplied in us. No power, no weapons, no forces can ever prevail over the patriotism, internationalism, feelings of human brotherhood and communist consciousness which they embody.

We shall be like them, in work and in combat!

Patria o Muerte!

Venceremos!

Appendix 2

Text of Kenneth Dam's Speech on Legal Bases for US Action, 4 November 1983

This is the eleventh day since the combined US-Caribbean peace force landed in Grenada to protect lives and restore order. That may not be enough time to make definitive historical judgments, but it is not too early to begin to reflect on the meaning of what happened.

So I would like today to talk both about the collective action itself and about its larger significance for US foreign policy.

Two basic objective motivated the President's decision last week to act jointly with Barbados and Jamaica in response to the urgent and formal agreement from the Organisation of Eastern Caribbean States (OECS). These objectives were:

To protect the lives of US citizens; and
to help Grenada re-establish order so that Governmental Institutions and Human Rights can be restored, thereby contributing also to the maintenance of regional peace and stability.

Prime Minister Charles of Dominica recently described the countries of the Eastern Caribbean as 'kith and kin.' Reuben Harris, the Education Minister of Antigua and Barbuda, was more specific last week at a UNESCO conference in Paris. He noted that these nations 'enjoy an economic community, a common currency, joint diplomatic representation and responsibility for . . . common defence and security.'

This unique institutional setting helps explain why ten days, days of brutality and instability ultimately brought about collective action to restore peace in Grenada.

Order began to disintegrate in Grenada the evening of 12 October with an attempt by Deputy Prime Minister Bernard Coard to force out Prime Minister Maurice Bishop. According to minutes of the

246

Party Central Committee, although Bishop had established close relations with Cuba and the Soviet Union, the Coard faction considered him a 'bourgeois deviationist' for moving too slowly to consolidate a 'Leninist' restructuring of Grenadian society.

Bishop was put under house arrest in the middle of the night 14 October, then freed by his supporters on 19 October. Troops opened fire on the crowd. Bishop and several Cabinet Ministers and union leaders were taken away, then executed. Education Minister Jacqueline Creft was apparently beaten to death.

In the wake of these murders, the People's Revolutionary Army announced the government was dissolved and a 24-hour curfew imposed: anyone found outside would be shot on sight. Army General Hudson Austin was head of a 16-member Revolutionary Military Council (RMC). But it was never clear that Austin or any coherent group was in fact in charge. No one knew when – or how – a new government would be formed.

The murders and breakdown of government order shocked repelled and alarmed leaders throughout the Caribbean. Without exception, the leaders of the Eastern Caribbean condemned the murders and expressed their sympathy for the people of Grenada.

Other Caribbean leaders were equally outraged. Prime Minister Tom Adams of Barbados said Bishop and his fellow Ministers had been killed by 'Disgusting murderers who had committed the most vicious act to disfigure the West Indies since the days of slavery.'

Prime Minister Edward Seaga of Jamaica expressed revulsion at 'the intensity of the barbarity' and broke diplomatic relations with Grenada. Even the Jamaica opposition party (People's National Party, the PNP), headed by former Prime Minister Michael Manley, severed all relations with the New Jewel Movement, recommended its expulsion from the Socialist International, and declared that the RMC had no right to speak for the Grenadian people.

Sometimes action is necessary to keep a bad situation from getting worse. This was such a time.

The disintegration of political authority in Grenada had created a dynamic that spread uncertainty and fear and that made further violence likely. The actions of Bishop's murderers made clear that they would have either driven the Island into further chaos or turned it into an armed fortress. In either event, the threat to US citizens and to the peace of the Eastern Caribbean would have increased. Inaction would have made a hostage situation more likely, and increased the costs in lives of any subsequent rescue operation.

247

The OECS decided to help its member states of Grenada and to ask Barbados, Jamaica, and the United States for assistance. In its formal request for US assistance, the OECS cited:

The current anarchic conditions, the serious violations of human rights and bloodshed that have occurred and the consequent unprecedented threat to the peace and security of the region created by the vacuum of authority in Grenada.

The OECS request also noted:

That military forces and supplies are likely to be shortly introduced to consolidate the position of the régime and that the country can be used as a staging post for acts of aggression against its members; and that the capability of the Grenada armed forces is already at a level of sophistication and size far beyond the internal needs of the country.

We had of course also been following events with increasing concern. As is well known, Grenada's ties to Cuba and the Soviet Union and its abandonment of democracy and poor human rights record had led the United States to have serious disagreements with the Bishop régime. Nonetheless, Bishop's visit to the United States in June, 1983 (when Judge Clark and I met with him in my office) had led us to hope that Grenada might adopt a more moderate course.

What became our overriding concern as events unfolded, however, was not Grenada's political system. Rather, it was the safety of US citizens in the midst of a growing anarchy which the countries of the Caribbean also saw as a direct threat.

Some 1,000 US citizens, mainly students, retirees and missionaries, made up the largest community of foreigners on Grenada. Our concern for their welfare was heightened by the murders, the shoot-on-sight curfew, and the difficulty of getting accurate information. And in the absence of a functioning government, there could be no credible assurances of their well-being and future prospects. I don't think that I need remind you that today is the fourth anniversary of the seizure of the US Embassy in Tehran.

After carefully considering these developments, and reviewing all aspects of the OECS request, President Reagan concluded that to wait passively would entail great and increasing risks. Before acting, however, the President sent a special emissary, Ambassador Frank

248

McNeil, to consult with OECS representatives and with Prime Minister Adams of Barbados and Prime Minister Seaga of Jamaica.

Ambassador McNeil found these leaders unanimous in their conviction that the deteriorating conditions of Grenada were a threat to the entire region and that the situation required immediate action.

US actions have been based on three legal grounds:

First, as these events were taking place, we were informed, on 24 October, by Prime Minister Adams of Barbados that Governor-General Sir Paul Scoon had used a confidential channel to transmit an appeal to the OECS and other regional states to restore order on the island. The Governor-General has since confirmed this appeal. We were unable to make this request public until the Governor-General's safety had been assured, but it was an important element – legally as well as politically – in our respective decisions to help Grenada. The legal authorities of the Governor-General were the sole remaining source of governmental legitimacy on the island in the wake of the tragic events I have described. We and the OECS countries accorded his appeal exceptional moral and legal weight. The invitation of lawful governmental authority constitutes a recognized basis under international law for foreign states to provide requested assistance.

Second, the OECS determined to take action under the 1981 treaty establishing that organization. That treaty contains a number of provisions, in Articles 3, 4 and 8, which deal with local as well as external threats to peace and security. Both the OAS charter, in Articles 22 and 28, and the UN charter, in Article 52, recognize the competence of regional security bodies in ensuring regional peace and stability. Article 22 of the OAS charter in particular makes clear that action pursuant to a special security treaty in force does not constitute intervention or use of force otherwise prohibited by Articles 18 or 20 of that charter. In taking lawful collective action, the OECS countries were entitled to call upon friendly states for appropriate assistance, and it was lawful for the United States, Jamaica and Barbados to respond to this request.

Third, US action to secure and evacuate endangered US citizens on the island was undertaken in accordance with well-established principles of international law regarding the protection of one's nationals. That the circumstances warranted this action has been amply documented by the returning students themselves. There is absolutely no requirement of international law that compelled the United States to await further deterioration of the situation that would have

249

jeopardized a successful operation. Nor was the United States required to await actual violence against US citizens before rescuing them from the anarchic and threatening conditions the students themselves have described.

Some are asking how this US action can be distinguished from acts of intervention by the Soviet Union. Let me say that the distinctions are clear. The United States participated in a genuine collective effort – the record makes clear the initiative of the Caribbean countries in proposing and defending this action. This action was based on an existing regional treaty and at the express invitation of the Governor-General of Grenada. Our concern for the safety of our citizens was genuine. The factual circumstances on Grenada were exceptional, and unprecedented in the Caribbean region – a collapse of law, order and governmental institutions. Our objectives are precise and limited – to evacuate foreign nationals and to cooperate in the restoration of order. Our objectives do not involve the imposition on the Grenadians of any particular form of Government. Grenadians are free to determine their institutions for themselves. Finally our troops have already begun to leave; we will complete our withdrawal as soon as local forces are ready to take over from us.

Those who do not see – or do not choose to see – these clearcut distinctions have failed to analyze the facts. We have not made, and do not seek to make, any broad new precedent for international action. Our actions themselves are well within accepted concepts of international law.

To minimize the potential loss of lives and maximize the chances of success, both the preparations for the multinational peace force and our final decision to participate had to be protected by keeping them secret.

When our forces arrived in Grenada they immediately came under fire. And the main resistance came from Cubans, not Grenadians. The Cubans were very well armed. They were deployed at the airport, at the medical school where a large number of US citizens were studying, at the Governor-General's house, and at a Cuban military encampment at Calivigny, and at several other forts and strategic points.

Despite the Cuban-led resistance, hostilities have now ended. US forces are withdrawing. The Rangers left Sunday, the Marines yesterday.

The Governor-General has thanked us for our assistance as a 'positive and decisive step forward in the restoration not only of peace and order but also of full sovereignty.'

The OECS is assisting the Governor-General and prominent Grenadians to establish a provisional government capable of restoring functioning institutions and permitting early elections.

Seventeen flights have safely evacuated, at their request, 599 Americans and 121 foreigners. Their accounts of conditions in Grenada and praise for their rescuers speak for themselves. The respected Grenadian journalist Alister Hughes evidently spoke for the vast majority of people in Grenada, Grenadians and foreigners alike, when he said of the Caribbean Peace Force: 'Thank God they came. If someone had not come in and done something, I hesitate to say what the situation in Grenada would be now.'

While we are still assembling and evaluating the evidence, what we have found suggests that Grenada would have become a fortified Soviet military outpost.

I mentioned earlier that we had been concerned well before the events which brought about our collective action – that Grenada be used as a staging area for subversion of nearby countries, for interdiction of shipping lanes, and for transit of troops and supplies from Cuba to Africa and from Eastern Europe and Libya to Central America.

What we found in Grenada may be summed up as the military underpinnings for just such uses. We found five secret treaties – three with the Soviet Union, one with North Korea, and one with Cuba – under which these Communist countries were to donate military equipment in amounts without precedent for a population of 110,000. We found artillery, anti-aircraft weapons, armored personnel carriers, and rocket launchers. We found thousands of rifles, thousands of fuses, tons of TNT, and millions of rounds of ammunition. We found communications gear and cryptographic devices. We found agreement authorizing the secret presence of Cuba military advisors, some of them on a 'permanent' basis.

All of the agreements stipulated that arms would be delivered to Grenada only by Cuban ships through Cuban ports. And although the Soviet Union was providing the arms and training free of charge, the Soviet Union required the Grenadians to keep all military arrangements secret, and delayed the opening of a Soviet embassy in Grenada until 18 months after entering into them.

Perhaps the first and the most basic lesson of events on Grenada

251

is that Cuban activities are not as benign as Fidel Castro would have us believe.

We have been regularly accused of exaggerating the dangers of Cuban/Soviet activities in countries like Grenada. However, what we found in Grenada suggests that, if anything, we were guilty of understating the dangers.

We now know that we had underestimated Soviet use of Cuba as a surrogate for the projection of military power in the Caribbean. Examine again what we found. Well-armed Cubans called construction workers. Fortifications, stockpiled weapons, secret military treaties, personnel from Eastern Europe, Africa and East Asia, all innocently enjoying a tourist paradise.

Think again about the facilities that all this would have secured. The Point Salines airport, which would have enabled a Mig 23 carrying four 1,000-pound bombs to strike and return from Puerto Rico in the north to Venezuela in the South. The Calivigny military training area. A 75,000-watt radio transmitter capable of blanketing the entire Caribbean basin. The potential for a deep-water harbour.

In light of this evidence, many Americans – and not a few Europeans – might productively reassess their estimate of the security concerns of the American Government and of the non-Communist countries of the Caribbean basin.

A second, related point worth thinking about is what happened to Maurice Bishop. His experience graphically shows what could happen to those who put their faith in military assistance and advisors from Cuba and the Soviet Union, then try to remain nonaligned. The threat to their freedom and survival may well come from the very system their friends have helped them put in place.

In the wake of Bishop's murder, Suriname expelled the Cuba Ambassador and a hundred Cuban 'technicians.' The nine *comandantes* of Nicaragua might also wish to ponder their relationship with their Soviet and Cuban mentors.

A third lesson, and again one of particular importance for the Sandinistas is that in the absence of democratic institutions and legal sageguards, policy differences tend to degenerate into violence. The way to end such violence is to fulfil their original promises of democracy and free elections.

A final lesson of the events in Grenada is that neighbours' actions should be consistent with each other's legitimate security concerns. In Nicaragua, for example, Sandinista willingness to negotiate seriously, to reduce reliance on military power, and most importantly, to stop belligerent behaviour towards their neighbours would represent the high road to peace in Central America.

Taken as a whole, what these lessons imply for Central America is that we must focus our resources on finding more creative ways to foster democratic development and regional cohesion. It is for this reason that we are firmly committed to a comprehensive approach to that region's conflicts.

As President Reagan told a special joint session of Congress on 27 April, our policy in Central America is based on four interlocking elements – democracy, development, dialogue and defence:

– Our policy is to actively support democracy, reform and human freedom in Central America – as much for El Salvador and Guatemala as for Nicaragua.
– The United States supports economic development, and is devoting three times the funds to such development as to military assistance. The Caribbean Basin Initiative, I should note, is as open to Nicaragua as to Costa Rica and Honduras.
– We support dialogue and negotiations – the internal dialogue of democracy in each country, and the multilateral negotiations of nations honestly trying to live peacefully with each other.
– And we have and will continue to provide what the President has called a security shield against those who oppose democratization, economic development and diplomacy.

In the interests of settling the conflicts in Central America before they reach a crisis stage, the United States is quietly but firmly supporting the regional Contadora process. It is no coincidence that the consensus of the nine countries involved about what is required for peace in Central America is parallel to our own. We support – as do Nicaragua's neighbours, especially the 'core four' countries of Costa Rica, El Salvador, Guatemala and Honduras an end to terrorism, destabilization, and guerrilla warfare; a reduction of military forces and armaments; political reconciliation through free elections and respect for human rights; the removal of foreign troops and military advisers; and the commitment of resources more for economic development and reform than for military build-up and destruction.

What this all adds up to is that the United States is pursuing a responsive and responsible role in this entire region. I believe that we have the confidence to do so, even in the face of violence and uncertainty, because we had already learned what may be the underlying lession of the collective response to the Grenada crisis: the best source of knowledge about an area is the people of that area – those most directly concerned with what is happening in their own neighbourhood.

What Prime Minister Charles and the others told us while the Grenada crisis was building proved to be accurate. The Caribbean leaders faithfully reflected the feelings, the concerns and hopes of the Grenadian people – and, may I add, of the US citizens there as well. We listened to Grenada's neighbours, and we are doing the same thing in Central America. Our policy is responsive to Central American opinion polls, the statements of respected democratic leaders, and the Contadora 'document of objectives'. And we are responding in the Caribbean basin initiative: we listened when Latin and Caribbean economies told us that they wanted 'trade not aid.'

Leadership means listening and acting intelligently on what is heard. That is what we did in Grenada. That is what we are doing in Central America. And I believe the American people are coming to understand what their government is doing – and why.

Bibliography

Fitzroy Ambursley and Robin Cohen (Editors), *Crisis in the Caribbean*, Heinemann

Cole Blasier, *The Hovering Giant*, University of Pittsburgh Press

William J. Brisk, *The Dilemma of a Ministate: Anguilla*, University of South Carolina

Stephen Clissold (Editor), *Soviet Relations with Latin America 1918–68*, Oxford University Press

Commonwealth Caribbean Regional Secretariat, *From Carifta to the Caribbean Community*

Herbert Corkran Jr, *Patterns of International Cooperation in the Caribbean 1942–1969*, Southern Methodist University Press

D. Sinclair DaBreo, *Of Men and Politics, The Agony of St Lucia*, Commonwealth Publishers International

Emanuel de Kadt (Editor), *Patterns of Foreign Influence in the Caribbean*, Oxford University Press

William G. Demas, *The Economics of Development in Small Countries*, McGill University Press

Epica Task Force, *Grenada, the Peaceful Revolution*

Fedon Publishers, *In the Mainstream of the Revolution*
'is Freedom we Making'
In the Spirit of Butler
'to construct from morning'
Grenada is not alone

Foreign Affairs Committee of the House of Commons, *Caribbean and Central America*, Her Majesty's Stationery Office

Lewis Hanke (Editor), *History of Latin American Civilization*, Methuen

Irene Hawkins, *The Changing Face of the Caribbean*, Cedar Press

R.A. Humphreys, *Latin America and the Second World War*, Athlone Press

C.L.R. James, *The Future in the Present*, Allison and Busby *Notes on Dialectics*, Allison and Busby

255

Frances Kay, *This – is Grenada*, Carenage Press
Gordon K. Lewis, *The Growth of the Modern West Indies*, MacGibbon and Kee
Jorge Luna, *Granada, la Nueva Joya del Caribe*, Editorial de Ciencias Sociales
Sir Harold Mitchell, Bt, *Caribbean Patterns*, Chambers
Rex Nettleford, *Manley and the New Jamaica*, Longman
Rollie Poppino, *International Communism in Latin America*, Free Press of Glencoe
Jenny Pearce, *Under the Eagle*, Latin America Bureau
Colin Rickards, *Caribbean Power*, Dennis Dobson
Chris Searle, *Grenada, The Struggle against Destablization*, Writers and Readers
David Shub, *Lenin*, Penguin
Eric Williams, *Capitalism and Slavery*, André Deutsch
World Bank, *Economic Survey of the Eastern Caribbean Common Market Countries*
    Economic Memorandum on Grenada 1980, 1981, 1982

Index

258

259

Montgomery, David, 152, 153, 160, 166, 206
Montserrat, 8, 39, 97, 170
Movement for Assemblies of the People (MAP), 46, 47, 52
Muravyev, D., 190, 191

Nelson, Second Lieutenant Raeburn, 137
New Jewel Movement (NJM), 3, 33, 47, 49, 51, 52, 66, 67, 70, 71, 72, 73, 74, 76, 81, 82, 83, 84, 85, 93, 95, 100, 101, 103, 104, 105, 106, 107, 108, 110, 111, 116, 118, 122, 124, 127, 130, 131, 142, 148, 185, 226
Nixon, President Richard, 59
Noel, Lloyd, 25, 110, 193
Noel, Vincent, 109, 138
North Korea, 10, 61, 106

Ogilvey, First Lieutenant Rudolph, 140
Oqueli, Héctor, 107
Organisation for Education and Liberation (OREL), 71, 72, 74, 82, 104, 127, 161
Organisation of American States, 70, 113
Organisation of Eastern Caribbean States (OECS), 8, 147, 156, 157, 158, 159, 160, 161, 162, 163, 165, 166, 169, 170, 199, 202, 219, 220
Ortiz, Frank, 78, 81
Osbourne, John, 157, 163, 170

Pearls airport, 22, 49, 69, 88, 122, 166, 197, 205, 207
People's Revolutionary Army (PRA), 1, 10, 11, 12, 13, 22, 23, 105, 121, 123, 124, 133, 134, 136, 137, 144, 161, 183, 204, 209, 222
People's Revolutionary Government (PRG), 80, 182
Petit Martinique, 91, 171
Pindling, Sir Lynden, 163, 165
Plessey (company), 145, 208
Point Salines, 21, 22, 26, 29, 88, 89, 96, 145, 183, 194, 195, 203, 208
Presentation College, 42, 71, 132
Price, George, 163 165
Puerto Rico, 55, 56, 64, 154, 197

Radio Antilles, 132
Radio Free Grenada (RFG), 12, 26, 126, 128, 131, 140, 147, 169, 181, 199, 202, 211
Radix, Kendrick, 45, 46, 49, 110, 185, 197, 200
Radix, Dr. Roger, 136, 137
Ramphal, Sonny, 148, 184
Rastafarians, 101
Reagan, President Ronald, 2, 4, 13, 24, 113, 114, 155, 156, 159, 163, 167, 168, 170, 171, 172, 173, 174, 175, 176, 179, 202, 206, 213
Redhead, Captain Lester, 141
Regan, Donald, 159
Revolutionary Military Council, 141, 142, 143, 144, 145, 146, 147, 150, 151, 152, 153, 157, 160, 161, 162, 165, 171, 183, 187, 200, 221, 222
Roberts, Major Keith 'Chicken', 123, 129, 141
Romain, Captain Huey, 141
Roosevelt, President Franklin, 58

261